SUPER INVESTMENT TRENDS
Cashing in on the Dynamic '90s

SUPER INVESTMENT TRENDS
Cashing in on the Dynamic '90s

James B. Powell

with the assistance of
Will Thomas

BUSINESS ONE IRWIN
Homewood, IL 60430

This publication is designed to provide accurate and
authoritative information in regard to the subject matter
covered. It is sold with the understanding that neither the
author nor the publisher is engaged in rendering legal, accounting,
or other professional service. If legal advice or other expert
assistance is required, the services of a competent
professional person should be sought.

*From a Declaration of Principles jointly adopted by a Committee
of the American Bar Association and a Committee of Publishers.*

Sponsoring editor: Amy Hollands
Project editor: Gladys True
Production manager: Diane Palmer
Designer: Larry J. Cope
Jacket Designer: Michael Finkelman
Compositor: The Wheetley Company
Typeface: 11/13 Times Roman
Printer: The Book Press, Inc.

Library of Congress Cataloging-in-Publication Data

Powell, James B.
    Super investment trends: cashing in on the dynamic '90s / James
B. Powell with the assistance of Will Thomas.
        p.   cm.
    1. ISBN 1-55623-500-3
    1. Investments.   I. Thomas, Will.   II. Title.
HG4528.P68   1992
332.6'78—dc20   91-30573

Printed in the United States of America
1 2 3 4 5 6 7 8 9 0 BP 8 7 6 5 4 3 2 1

Never expect the key that unlocked yesterday's market to open the door to tomorrow's.

Gerald M. Loeb

To the memory of Lt. John B. Moore, U.S.M.C., who gave his life for his country. He is greatly missed.

INTRODUCTION

There are many ways to make money on Wall Street. Because most of them are logical and are often sophisticated, each of them has a wide following. However, almost all the popular investment strategies have a costly flaw: they require active portfolio management. Unfortunately, each buy and sell order costs money, which detracts from profits and magnifies losses. Each turnover also increases an investor's exposure to losing positions, and usually terminates winners long before they reach their full potential. Finally, high taxes on capital gains make it difficult to compound multiple trades into a significant amount of money.

A BETTER INVESTMENT STRATEGY FOR THE 1990s

Fortunately, there is a much better way to make investment profits that minimizes the pitfalls common to other techniques. The strategy also delivers profits that most investors can only dream about. It does so because it makes use of the driving force that lies behind most of the huge gains that have become Wall Street legends.

The investment strategy that I urge investors to adopt for the 1990s is as simple as it is profitable—buy key stocks that have their fortunes linked to the development of powerful long-range trends. Because such trends outlive recessions and bear markets, the investments they support commonly deliver gains of several hundred percent. Returns of well over 1000 percent also occur, a claim that I will substantiate shortly.

Investing in trends offers other advantages as well. Because positions are held long term, the strategy requires less work than is true of alternative techniques. Trend investing also involves much less anxiety than Wall Street commonly offers. Economic downturns and market shocks are of little concern to long-term investors whose fortunes are tied to unstoppable trends. In fact, downturns permit such investors to

TABLE 1
Industry Scoreboard

Industry	Percent Price Change in 10 Years
Retailing	976
Consumer nondurables	850
Food, drink, tobacco	670
Entertainment & information	603
Health	519
Business services	506
Dow Industrials	214

Source: Eric Hardy, "Who's Where In The Stock Market," *Forbes,* January 8, 1990. Reprinted by permission of FORBES magazine © Forbes Inc., 1990.

increase their positions at bargain prices. All in all, investing in long-range trends is a strategy that makes the most sense for the 1990s.

THE POWERFUL CASE FOR TREND INVESTING

History proves conclusively that taking long-term positions in major trends is the best way for individuals to make investment profits. The strategy is behind nearly every great fortune that has been made in this century. In every case the big winners took positions in the dominant trends of their time and played them for all they were worth. For example, McDonalds, Coca-Cola, Disney, and dozens of other stocks have delivered over thirty years of compounded profits to long-term investors who saw the potential for such major trends as fast foods, the youth market, and mass entertainment.

For solid evidence that long-term trend investing continues to work very well, just look at Table 1. It is the industry scoreboard for the 1980s. As may be seen, several entire industries went up over 600, 800, and 900 percent during the decade in spite of a severe recession, stiff foreign competition, a devastating stock crash, and many other problems.

Each industry that did well was propelled through the 1980s by a strong trend that bulldozed its way through every problem it encountered. For example, retailing and consumer durables were firmly tied to the maturing baby boomers who were starting careers and families of their own. Those millions of people didn't put their lives on hold because of the recession. They didn't stop buying baby clothes and washing machines because jobs were tight, inflation was high, and the stock market crashed. They pressed on, and in doing so created enormous profits for the industries that provided the needed goods and services.

It gets better. Within the top industries dozens of individual stocks went up over 1,000, 3,000, 5,000, and even 10,000 percent and made fortunes for astute investors. Look at the abbreviated column of big winners in Table 2, and remember that the list could easily run several pages.

The biggest investment profits of the 1980s went to people who understood the trends, purchased key stocks, and held on for the gains which the maturation of those trends created. The winners of the last decade—as in every other period in history—took a long-range, big gains approach to making investment profits. The same will be true in the 1990s.

It is important to point out that the big winners in investing are not usually early birds who attempt to spot trends before they actually begin. Investment research proves conclusively that waiting until a trend is underway before taking a position is the surest road to profits. As Ned Davis, one of Wall Street's most respected observers, often asks, "Do you want to be right? Or do you want to make money?"[1]

MARKING TRENDS: GOOD FOR BUSINESS TOO

If you are a business person as well as an investor, it can also pay handsomely to look carefully at developing trends. Just look how careful trend analysis transformed Presidential Life Corporation from an insurance wallflower to the top performing stock company of the 1980s.

In the late 1970s Presidential Life's president Herbert Kurz noticed two strong trends that he thought were related. He reasoned that if he could create a product that fit both trends he might win a bigger share of the insurance market. Kurz noticed that affluent baby boomers liked the security of life insurance. He also noticed that the boomers were attracted to the growth potential of mutual funds, but hated the

---

1. Frederick E. Rowe, Jr., "Rich? Or Right?" *Forbes,* August 5, 1991.

TABLE 2
Big Stock Winners of the 1980s

Company Name	Percent Price Change in 10 Years
Presidential Life	10,771
Circuit City Stores	8,108
Mark IV Industries	7,387
Mylan Labs	6,721
The Limited	6,177
International Dairy Queen	4,880
Wal–Mart	3,975
Dillard Dept. Stores	3,728
The Gap	3,556
Dreyfus	3,299
MCI Communications	2,817
And dozens more....	

Source: Karen Slater, "The '80s: The Decade Investors Cashed in Despite the Crash and Other Traumas," *The Wall Street Journal*, December 15, 1989. "Reprinted by permission of *The Wall Street Journal*, © 1989 Dow Jones & Company, Inc. All Rights Reserved Worldwide."

fact that the returns were not guaranteed. Kurz mulled over his obser-vations for a few weeks, then decided to combine guaranteed invest-ments with insurance, and test market the concept.

Before the test was over Kurz knew that he had a winning idea. Presidential's single premium policies—actually annuities—have been a runaway success for over ten years with no letup in sight. During the 1980s Presidential's earnings went through the roof. The company's stock price soared from $0.18 per share to over $19.25 per share.

HOW TO USE THIS BOOK

In this book I will identify the best of the major trends at work today. Unlike related books that lack an investment focus, I will also show you the best ways to cash in on each trend as it develops over the next several years.

To make the book easier to use, I will begin each chapter with an overview of an individual trend and highlight its essential features. I will then identify the specific investment areas which the trend should favor. Within those areas I will discuss specific investments that I believe have the greatest promise to appreciate as the trend matures.

Whenever possible, I will present several investments in each area for your consideration. Often they will range from conservative to more speculative. If you intend to make purchases for the long term—which is the very best way to profit from major trends—I would urge you to stick with the conservative investments.

As you read through the book you will see that some stocks appear in more than one chapter. Such multiple listings are not an oversight. Instead, they strengthen the case for acquiring such issues. After all, a company with products and services firmly tied to many powerful trends is a company with a particularly bright future.

Although trend investing is a long-range strategy that irons out the inevitable setbacks which occur with all stocks, there is no advantage to buying an issue when it is overvalued. A much better plan is to make your purchases during periods when prices are attractive. Not only will that maximize your profits, but it will also make it easier—both financially and psychologically—to hold onto an attractive position until it matures.

Before you buy *any* stock you should investigate it thoroughly. Fortunes can change quickly on Wall Street which could affect the outlook for any of the issues mentioned in this book. To maximize your chances for top profits I would urge you to do a final update on your selections before adding them to your portfolio. You will find each featured stock and mutual fund in the Appendix along with its ticker symbol, exchange, and telephone number.

MY FIRST PREDICTION

I have no doubt that by the turn of the century—which is only a few years away—many of today's thoughtful trend investors will be millionaires, as were countless people who put relatively modest amounts of money in the top stocks of the 1980s. If you make good use of the ideas and strategies in the following chapters, one of these millionaires could be you!

James B. Powell

ACKNOWLEDGMENTS

No book of this scope could be created by one person. My team consisted of Will Thomas, Associate Writer, who took my research and notes on many topics and helped turn them into finished chapters. The book was enriched by his contributions, which included many valuable insights and observations. Donald G. DuBeau, Ph.D., used his considerable abilities as a mathematical researcher to work up much of the data used in this book. Robert W. Jensen was of considerable help with many of the demographic projections which were critical to several chapters. Finally, I benefitted enormously from dozens of business leaders and Wall Street professionals who provided valuable information and guidance for this book. Of the group, Robert H. Meier deserves special mention, not only for his help, but also for his considerable patience in dealing with my many requests.

CONTENTS

CHAPTER 1

WELCOME TO THE 1990s

The U.S. economy of the 1990s promises to provide investors with many profitable opportunities. However, many of those opportunities will be significantly different from those of the 1980s. Investors will need to shift their focus considerably if they expect to continue doing well. Looked at in the broadest terms, here is what I expect to occur for at least the first few years of the decade.

A switch from consumption to production will mark the United States business environment of the 1990s. This move is being facilitated by increased savings by our maturing population which will create a large cash pool for capital spending. An ample supply of cash will also lower interest rates which will make capital spending even more attractive.

The shift to production is also being stimulated by a growing world economy that is hungry for modern goods. Millions of people are now free to buy from anyone they choose and they are acquiring the money to do so. The global market is exploding due to the fall of communism, the formation of the European Community (EC), the dynamic growth of the Pacific Rim nations, and the increasing vitality of many Third World countries. Although many setbacks can be expected on our way to a global economy, the overall movement will be toward increased trade between nations.

For investors, the broad shift toward production must be clearly reflected in one's portfolio. Over the next few years capital spending companies, manufacturers, exporters, carriers, and others should be weighted more heavily than retail chains, shopping centers, and the other consumer sectors that were the big winners of the 1980s.

A healthier economy will emerge as the United States begins to produce more of what it consumes. However, there is a good chance that our economic activity will not be particularly robust, at least for the first few years of the decade. That is because we started the 1990s with high debts left over from the 1980s and a long overdue recession. When we emerge from the downturn we will almost certainly have an extended period during which we will continue to pay for the excesses of the previous ten years.

I expect our national resolve to settle debts and live within our means will result in a weak recovery instead of the usual roaring rebound that was common in the past. If so, the early 1990s will be a time to take positions for long range gains as opposed to making frothy profits from short-term trading. Highly selective stock pickers rather than indexers should see the greatest rewards during the decade, a sharp reversal from the 1980s.

Inflation should remain moderate—less than 5 percent—through at least the first few years of the 1990s. The cleansing effect of the recession followed by a period of national debt paying should put a damper on price increases. The increased availability of cash from higher savings rates should also help keep inflation in check. Last, as the world becomes more of a global economy our trading partners will provide stern discipline against the erosion of profits which occurs when inflation is allowed to rise.

THE TOP INVESTMENT TRENDS OF THE 1990s

Of course, no one can invest in the economy, we must purchase individual stocks. As I stressed in the Introduction the best stocks are linked to powerful trends that plow through economic cycles and deliver top long-term profits. This section is a quick overview of the most powerful of those trends which will yield high rewards over the next few years.

A Decade of World Trade Gets Underway

After suffering through 45 years of communist stagnation, Eastern Europe will finally have its post-World War II recovery. At the same time, Western Europe is forming economic alliances that will put it on an equal footing with the United States and Japan. Southeast Asian countries are rapidly transforming themselves into modern industrial and high tech centers. Many other less developed countries (LDCs) throughout the world are rapidly becoming newly emerging countries (NECs) with strong economies. Profiting from it all are a handful of U.S. firms that are becoming global powerhouses. Altogether, it is an exciting time to be alive and an even more exciting time to be an investor.

The European Community will finally get underway next year after years of bickering and many false starts.   The event is of such enormous importance that the EC is often referred to as the United States of Europe. Whatever analysts choose to call it, the EC will potentially rival the United States as an economic power. The removal of archaic trade barriers, nationalistic commercial practices, and widely differing product standards will allow European firms to unite, expand, and become multinational forces. By the middle of the decade many European companies will be world leaders in their respective industries.

Eastern Europe's recent liberation and its move toward a market economy will double the power of continental Europe by the end of the decade.   The emergence of Eastern Europe is particularly exciting because it will give investors a second shot at the explosive post-World War II boom which transformed Western Europe nearly a half-century ago. Now that a market economy is emerging, Eastern Europe will experience tremendous growth in supply and demand. The biggest profits from this event will go to investors who take strategic positions early and then hold them until they fully develop.

Newly industrialized countries (NICs) of the Pacific Rim will also have a major effect on the world economy in the 1990s and will one day rival the power of Japan.   Countries emerging with new strength include South Korea, Taiwan and the Crown Colony of Hong Kong. Together with Japan the region will soon surpass the economic power of every other part of the world including the United States. As that evolution occurs the NICs will generate returns that have not been seen by investors since the 1970s and 1980s when Japan was in its prime.

Many less developed countries (LDCs) will make their growing strength felt during the 1990s.   For investors, strategic positions in Thailand, Singapore, Indonesia, Malaysia, the Philippines, India, and Mexico will be particularly rewarding. These countries have already emerged from their agricultural-based economies and are becoming modern nations. The newly emerging countries will enter the steepest part of their growth curves early in this decade. As was the case with the recovery of Japan 30 years ago, only the most unbiased and observant investors will cash in on the opportunities this event presents.

Global lifestyles will create global markets in the 1990s which will favor selected multinational stocks. During the decade lifestyles, tastes, and aspirations throughout the world will become much more uniform. Television coverage of mass events from places as far away as Beijing, Moscow, Bombay, and Manila already show that people are rapidly adopting the same dress everywhere—from their baseball hats to their running shoes.

The rapidly developing trend toward market uniformity very clearly favors megacompanies. Only the largest and strongest of the world's multinational firms have the necessary marketing, distribution, and production capabilities to first create and then meet the demands of an entire planet. Investors who take long-range positions in the bluest of the world's blue chip stocks should expect to be rewarded in the 1990s. Because of world demand for established American products, I believe those issues, which many analysts now dismiss as being "fully mature," will turn out to be the growth stocks of this decade.

Demographic Changes Create Opportunities

In the 1990s our population will undergo many changes which will create new investment opportunities in real estate, consumer goods, entertainment, transportation, and many other industries. Because population changes in a country the size of the United States are major events, the potential for profits is huge.

America will grow older and healthier in the 1990s. The over 50 population is already our most affluent consumer group. During the 1990s it will also become our largest market. Investors will find that taking a position in this trend will require careful thought. Older Americans are different from other consumers in many ways. In particular, they are no longer making major acquisitions. Instead, they are scaling back on property and are spending more heavily on recreation, travel, health and vitality, and medical concerns.

Fortunately, many companies are moving into position to serve this affluent market. I expect those companies to make the biggest gains in the new decade. Best of all, the growing "senior industry" will perform smoothly without the frightening volatility common to most highfliers.

Baby boomers and busters will have a big—and profitable— influence on the 1990s. As the baby boomers grow older they are becoming more conservative, conventional citizens. To their great surprise millions of them report that they are already starting to sound remarkably like their parents in terms of values and lifestyles. Mindless consumption is on the way out. Having children is once again becoming important. Career advancement is becoming secondary to family needs. Spiritual pursuits are replacing BMWs for satisfaction. The list goes on and on.

In the 1990s companies which supply children's clothing, quality family recreation, secure retirement programs, and so forth will prosper. In addition, since both parents normally have jobs new "paraparental services" such as child care and preschools will do very well. So will house cleaning, yard care, and delivery services of every type. All in all, serving the needs of today's boomers and busters will return billions of dollars to knowledgeable investors over the next several years.

Life will become more difficult for millions of Americans in the 1990s. Global competition began pushing down blue collar wages during the last decade. Now the squeeze is starting to affect white collar workers as well. Adding to our burdens are sharply rising taxes that are becoming more difficult for average people to avoid. Enormous social and structural problems in our society, including growing ranks of the disadvantaged, decaying roads, poor schools, and a deteriorating environment promise to boost taxes even more. Meanwhile, costs for medical care, housing, and other necessities continue to climb.

As the crunch continues, the troubling gap between the haves and the have-nots will widen further. Those who have exactly the right skills will prosper as never before. Those who do not will fall even further behind. The split will trigger serious social and economic problems which will affect every aspect of life in America.

Manufacturers and retailers are already beginning to adjust by shifting focus from the shrinking center of the middle class to its growing extremes. In the 1990s luxury automobiles and imported bicycles should both sell very well. The same applies to upscale housing developments and mobile homes. Many people will pay for top-notch security services. These changes are of enormous importance to companies and investors.

New and Rebounding Industries for the 1990s

In every period of history there are certain industries that do much better than others because they meet the most pressing needs of the age. That will also be true in the 1990s. Some of those industries have fallen on hard times and are in the process of recovering. Others are emerging for the first time.

Many oversold real estate investments will be star performers in the 1990s. The tax reform act of 1986 devastated the real estate partnership industry. Before that date prices were at peak levels due to the promise of double, triple, and even quadruple tax write-offs. When those advantages evaporated so did the lofty multiples for many properties.

Because of tax reform and the recession of 1990–91 there was also a mass exodus from real estate stocks by early 1991 and many solid issues with good histories were selling for as little as 30 cents on the dollar.

Meanwhile, our population continues to expand which is creating additional demand for housing and, in the long run, commercial developments. Investors who can put some of their money away for a few years will find that carefully selected real estate issues will outperform anything else Wall Street has to offer.

We will rebuild much of America's infrastructure in the 1990s. It is no secret that our once worldclass freeway system is now over 20 years old and in terrible shape. Moreover, it needs to be expanded by about one third. State and local roads and nearly all bridges are in equally poor condition—as are sewer systems and electric power grids. All were neglected during the 1980s but can be neglected no longer.

The deteriorating condition of our infrastructure is now having such a depressing effect on the economy that it simply must be fixed. Rebuilding and expanding will take billions of dollars over the next ten years and will create huge profits for people who invest in the leading companies.

America will turn to private education in the new decade.   The job of educating American workers will increasingly become the responsibility of employers. The public school system clearly is in need of costly reform, which national, state, and local budgets cannot cover. In response, our biggest firms now do much of their own training, including the teaching of basic skills. To get the job done employers use the services of specialized training companies that will see their fortunes soar in the 1990s as this trend becomes more common.

Parents and students are also turning from public schools to private schools which offer specific skills and guaranteed jobs. Such schools will be represented among the top growth stocks of the 1990s. Overall, the private education sector appears to be very attractive.

We will see some form of government-supplied medical insurance in the 1990s—possibly quite early in the decade.   The result will be a boom for the extremes of medical care. The lowest cost providers of services and equipment will prosper as every public-plan organization will be forced to do business with them. At the other extreme will be private clinics that will serve the affluent and will find it possible to remain outside the system—and outside the limits on profits. Signs of unusual stock activity in the health care industry are already occurring as smart money gets positioned to ride this trend for all it's worth.

The environment will become an even greater concern in the 1990s than it was in the 1970s and 1980s.   Although we now have a start in solving our environmental problems, over 90 percent of the actual work is yet to be done. In the 1990s the focus will shift from environmental consulting and evaluation to environmental engineering, capital spending, and other problem-solving actions. Of course, that shift will also be reflected in the leadership of the environmental industry.

Environmental problem solving will become one of America's biggest exports in the 1990s.   Environmental issues are relatively well managed in comparison to much of Western Europe and nearly all of Eastern Europe and the Soviet Union. The socialist countries in particular must clean up to avoid massive public health emergencies. Now that the citizens of those countries have a voice in their national affairs, environmental issues will be a priority. Indeed, it is already happening in Moscow, Berlin, and Prague. All in all, unusually high returns can be made by investors who understand that environmental concerns are becoming global and will become stronger than ever in the 1990s.

New Technology Lives Up To Its Promise

Several formerly "disappointing technologies" of the 1980s will mature over the next few years and finally generate large profits for their investors. The events will mark the conclusion of a familiar scenario that has been seen several times on Wall Street; i.e., a promising technology is invented—the press touts it to the moon—investors flock to tiny companies with no profits—and stock prices soar. Then when the profits don't come as expected, the bubble bursts and everybody loses. After that, the technology is blacklisted by the media and ignored by investors.

Several years later, while nobody is watching, the out-of-favor technology slowly matures and begins to make money. Gradually, the profit trickle becomes a flood. Rock-bottom stock prices begin to move up. At some point investors rediscover the opportunities—but are too late to cash in on the biggest gains. In the 1990s that pattern will be repeated in several areas.

Alternative and nuclear energy will fulfill their promises in the 1990s. The rebirth will occur primarily because the technologies to produce and use them both safely and economically have greatly improved. Photovoltaic cells are much more efficient than was thought a few years ago and are less expensive to make. The same applies to methanol and ethanol engines which are already being tested by mainstream consumers.

Even nuclear energy is receiving a second look by informed citizens and scientists. Due to global warming we now know that nuclear power is potentially less harmful to the environment than burning fossil fuels. That will be even more true when nuclear waste facilities are completed. All in all, people are rethinking their positions on nuclear power. Smart investors should do the same.

Biotechnology looks very good for the 1990s. Despite several surprising spurts, the biotech industry has generally been a big disappointment. Biotech, however, will come of age over the next few years and will make knowledgeable investors very attractive profits. A handful of companies promise to become investment classics. Most of these companies specialize in human disease, but others focus on agricultural and veterinary products. Other players supply the leading biotech firms with equipment and chemicals. The suppliers are particularly attractive because they share in the growth of the biotech industry without sharing its risks.

Industrial automation will re-emerge in the next few years and finally live up to its promise. The expensive robots and automated machine tools of the 1980s were sidelined by skilled workers in less developed countries who were happy to do the jobs for much less money. However, sharply higher labor costs overseas, lower capital costs at home, and an increased emphasis on U.S. productivity will revitalize the industrial automation movement. We will see a tremendous boom in capital spending for state-of-the-art production equipment.

A second computer revolution is also in the works. Twenty years ago, when computerized electronics became a reality, visionaries predicted the machines would transform the way we work, learn, and play. Paper files would be obsolete. We were promised systems that would combine video, graphics, text, sound, and telecommunications in ways that would permit almost limitless uses. Later, when cellular telephones, fax machines, and laser copiers came on the scene, the high tech industry promised to integrate them as well.

The next step in the electronics revolution is underway. It will bring us integrated computer and telecommunication systems plus long-awaited paperless filing. I predict that this event will trigger the second office electronics buying spree of our age and will generate billions of dollars in profits for selected companies and their investors. Best of all, since most people don't know that this is coming, it is still possible to take "early bird" positions in the industry leaders.

REMAIN OPEN TO NEW OPPORTUNITIES

Of course, there will undoubtedly be some unexpected opportunities that develop over the next few years. They crop up every decade. For example, in 1937 the U.S. Department of the Interior sponsored a report that identified trends for the coming ten years. The report proved to be remarkably accurate in many respects. However, the authors of the study missed atomic energy, computers, radar, antibiotics, and World War II.[1]

The lesson from the 1937 study is clear—it is important to remain sufficiently well informed and openminded so that you will be able to recognize new opportunities as they present themselves. Fortunately, you can use the strategies discussed in this book to put those opportunities to profitable use.

NOTES

1. Gregory Benford, *Timescape* (Pocket Books, 1980).

SECTION 1

A DECADE OF WORLD TRADE GETS UNDERWAY

CHAPTER 2

WESTERN EUROPE UNITES

One of the most powerful trends of the 1990s will be the unification of individual European countries into a single economic entity. The European Community (EC)—which will become a reality in 1992—will be a much larger market than the United States. By the year 2000 the EC will grow to 350 million people—about 80 million more than in the United States.

The new "United States of Europe" will also be a larger economic power. Europe's gross domestic product of $4,263 billion is already just $200 billion less than America's, and it is growing rapidly.[1] All in all, the coming decade may be the greatest era of economic growth in Europe in this century.

Cor van der Klugt, president of Philips' Gloeilampenfabrieken of the Netherlands, the largest consumer electronics firm in Europe, commented on the EC in February 1988 when he said, "The drive for economic unity is the most important thing that will happen here in the next 50 years."[2] The event should present today's investors with some of the most promising opportunities of our age.

MORE LAWS MEAN MORE TRADE

Since the Age of Enlightenment, the trend in European trade between countries has been, in a word, restrictive. Facing a variety of often conflicting manufacturing preferences, engineering standards, and safety requirements, it has not been possible for a firm to build a single product for all its markets. Instead, several variations of nearly everything needed to be produced.

Because European markets are small and fragmented, the benefits of large-scale production have never been fully realized in the region. High import tariffs have made matters worse by increasing operating expenses. Not surprisingly, many products never got beyond the borders of their countries of origin. Those products that were exported have been slower to get to market, and priced higher than the competing domestic products.

Now, all that is changing. In 1985 the EC's planners established the goal of providing a true Common Market to its member countries. It will be in place by the end of 1992. To accomplish the task, the EC is turning a series of about 300 free-trade directives into the law of the Community.

ABUNDANCE OF FORMS AND STANDARDS

To measure the full potential of the EC, it is important to understand how important its reforms will be for European businesses and the European economy. This is particularly true for American investors who have never experienced the crippling regulations and high costs of doing business that have held back European firms for generations.

For example, European truckers have endured a plethora of shipping vouchers, import permits, transportation forms and tax reports at each border—usually about 35 pages worth. Border delays frequently took hours while customs agents checked every form. In 1988 it was estimated that the bureaucratic delays cost European businesses about $6 billion.[3]

A year ago that red tape was replaced by one new EC customs and shipping form—consisting of two pages. Even that form will disappear by 1992, as will all border checks throughout the EC. The change represents the general trend throughout Europe in the reduction of paperwork, delays, and costs that have been required to satisfy regulations in each country.

Equally damaging to trade has been a maze of conflicting product standards from country to country. Even an "ordinary" loaf of pumpernickel bread could not be exported to a neighboring country unless it met that country's local standards. In a bold stroke to cut through hundreds of such conflicting standards, the EC issued a proclamation: If a food or beverage is licensed in one country it may be sold in any other EC country. In cases where standards have been retained they have been simplified and now apply to the whole of the EC.

A STRONG ECONOMY CREATES STRONG MARKETS

The European economy is already responding to the impending EC boom. Economic growth during the 1980s hovered around a lackluster 2 percent per year. By 1988 the rate had increased to a very healthy 3.7 percent.[4] EC economists forecast a solid continuation of this trend through the 1990s.

The EC is also creating 1.5 million new jobs each year, putting an end to historically high unemployment figures. In Great Britain alone, the unemployment rate fell from 12 percent in 1987 to 7.2 percent by early 1990. At the same time, wages rose 3.8 percent from about half that in 1984.[5] Although some problems remain with inflation and high interest rates, analysts anticipate generally improving economic statistics through the 1990s.

Of course, the combination of more jobs and higher wages will have enormous effects on Europe's consumer markets. Declining product costs resulting from streamlined regulations and large-scale production will continue to grow. These trends will produce boom times for every consumer company that can supply the EC's expanding needs.

WHO'S WHO IN EUROPE

There are 12 nations in the European Economic Community, which is becoming known more simply as the European Community or EC. These countries are Belgium, Great Britain, Denmark, France, Greece, Ireland, Italy, Luxembourg, the Netherlands, Portugal, Spain, and Germany. Three other countries are presently EC associates: Cyprus, Malta, and Turkey. Six more European nations are in another economic community that is similar to the EC; the European Free Trade Association (EFTA). They are Austria, Finland, Iceland, Norway, Sweden, and Switzerland.

Although the EFTA may be the result of a different trade agreement in practice, there is little that separates the group from the EC. Members will share the same broad economic growth of Western Europe. Every country in the European theater will benefit from the healthier free trade economy and its growing international business.

Eastern Europe—consisting of Bulgaria, Czechoslovakia, Hungary, Poland, and Romania—is presently outside both the EC or the EFTA. Later in the decade, it may be possible that all of those countries plus the Soviet Union form alliances with their western neighbors. Those agreements will include some trade barriers to protect developing industries in the former Comecon nations from being overwhelmed by outside conglomerates. At the same time Eastern Europe will be allowed free access to Western markets. Although these developments will take many years, investment opportunities do exist, and will be discussed in Chapter 3.

AMERICAN FIRMS JOIN THE EC PARTY

American corporate giants are also involved in European markets. They have been doing business there on a large scale since before World War II. As "Europhoria" spread, in the late 1980s their activities increased dramatically.

For example in the last four years of the 1980s, Ford Motor Company bought Great Britain's famed Jaguar for $2.5 billion; General Motors purchased half of Sweden's Saab–Scania car operations for $600 million; AT&T bought a 20 percent interest in Italy's Italtel for $135 million; and Businessland acquired Bowe Systemvertrieb, a West German personal computer dealer for an undisclosed amount.[6] The list could go on for many pages. The total amount invested in Europe by U.S. firms in 1989 alone was $24 billion. Commented Salomon Brothers Managing Director, Ronald M. Freeman, in March 1990, "...American companies are realizing that 1992 gets closer every day, and that it will have consequences for their business."[7]

Nevertheless, I recommend that investors focus on European firms, or the mutual funds that invest in them, rather than those U.S. companies that do business in Europe. That is because the EC will have the greatest effect upon European companies that are already well established in the region.

Of course, many large American companies are also well positioned in the European market and are well accepted by its consumers. However, these big firms are involved around the globe, not in just the EC. Consequently, any fair discussion of them requires a global viewpoint, which is the focus of Chapter 5.

THE TIMING IS RIGHT FOR EUROPEAN INVESTMENTS

As planning for the EC gathered momentum during the late 1980s, European stock markets reacted with a dizzying rally that pushed prices well above any reasonable values. After a few months, however, the euphoric buying ended and sent prices tumbling. It was a classic pattern that has been seen dozens of times when a major new fad hits the investment community.

Unfortunately, many investors don't know how the boom and bust pattern usually ends. After the fad collapses and investors turn to other opportunities, the real move generally begins. Because the secondary move happens gradually over a long period of time, most investors fail to take notice. Eventually, prices surpass their old highs and return top profits to investors who took positions when no one else was interested.

I feel very strongly that European stocks will continue to follow this trend to its rewarding conclusion. Since we are just now entering the strongest and longest-lasting part of the European growth curve, the time to make purchases is now.

HOW TO INVEST IN THE EUROPEAN COMMUNITY

There are four basic ways to invest in foreign markets, each with its own advantages and disadvantages.

1. Invest directly in a European stock on a European exchange through an American broker with foreign affiliates or an American branch of a foreign brokerage firm. This approach offers an investor the full selection of European stocks from which to choose.

However, problems with investing directly in Europe include high fees, information delays, different accounting practices, the lack of an SEC watchdog, occasional illiquidity problems, currency conversion costs, and foreign tax declarations. For example, dividend income from a German investment is subject to that country's withholding tax of 25 percent. American investors are entitled to a refund of such taxes in excess of 15 percent—provided they fill out the paperwork. American investors may also be able to take these taxes as a deduction on their tax returns, which requires additional paperwork.

2. Invest in European stocks that are traded on U.S. exchanges usually by means of American Depository Receipts (ADRs). ADRs are certificates that trade in lieu of shares of stock. A major U.S. financial institution buys the stocks then issues the certificates to establish ownership.

The major advantage to buying an ADR instead of the stock itself is that the issuing institution handles the delivery of dividend checks, forwards financial reports, and deals with taxes. ADRs are also much less expensive to trade than foreign stocks which are purchased on overseas exchanges. In practice, buying an ADR is just like buying an American stock. There are more than 750 ADRs available in the United States. Hundreds of them are for promising European firms featured in this chapter. For the average investor who wishes to buy individual issues, buying ADRs is the path to take.

3. Buy a U.S. mutual fund that invests in the stocks of firms within a single European country. Almost all single country funds are closed-end funds, which means that they issue a fixed number of shares that are traded on an exchange. Of course, the shares can rise and fall with the changing expectations of investors. When investors are optimistic about the future of a particular country, the fund can trade for more than the total worth (net asset value or NAV) of its portfolio. For example, an investor that put $10,000 into the Germany Fund in February 1989 would have been able to collect $31,695 in 1990.[8]

Naturally, the big price swings of single country funds can also go the other way. A year ago the Spain Fund traded at a 165 percent premium. Later, it fell 50 percent during a period when the Spanish market was down less than 15 percent. Consequently, single country funds are best suited to investors who have done their homework and are confident that their conclusions are correct.

The growth potential for Europe is so good that in June 1990 Jon Woronoff, publisher of "International Fund Monitor," suggested that nearly every country fund, including the unrestricted market specials, often deserved to sell for a premium of at least 5 percent. "They're really a blessing to small investors," he said, "It's the only way you can buy a balanced portfolio at reasonable trading costs with good research."[9]

I recommend buying a single country fund when the long-term fundamentals for a nation are good but the fund is still out of favor. Do not buy until the NAV is greater than both the fund's current price and greater than the NAV of similar funds—conditions which can easily be determined by looking through the fund tables in *The Wall Street Journal* and *Barron's*. When premiums and profits soar, investors should sell.

4. Buy a regional fund that invests broadly throughout Europe. Regional funds hold stocks from many countries within a given area. Because they are diversified to a greater extent than single country funds, they offer greater safety. Moreover, regional funds can sometimes perform better overall, since their managers have a broader range of companies from which to choose. When one country begins to have trouble, assets can be shifted to another within the region than looks better. Of course, regional funds cannot reap the full potential of sudden growth within one country. As John Dessauer, editor of *Dessauer's Journal,* observed in March 1990, "The more precise you can be, the more money you'll make."[10]

A few regional funds are closed-end funds. However, most of them are open-end funds which means their shares are not traded on an exchange. Investors take positions by dealing directly with the funds that issue shares as they are needed and withdraw them when they are redeemed. Because there is no bid and ask systems at work, their prices remain fixed to their net asset values. As the fund's NAV rises and falls, so does the value of whatever shares an investor may hold.

However a person takes positions overseas, profits will be determined not only by the investment's performance but also by the foreign exchange value of the U.S. dollar. A rising dollar will lower profits while a falling dollar will boost them. For example, assume an investor buys a German stock that costs $100 per share. If the dollar falls by 10 percent against the German mark, the stock price will rise to $110 thanks to exchange rate profits. However, if the dollar rises by 10 percent against the German mark, the stock will drop to $90, resulting in an exchange rate loss.

TAKE ADVANTAGE OF THIS OPPORTUNITY

The European Community offers the safest, most stable of all overseas investment opportunities. They are far more of a sure thing than most Asian stocks, especially if an investor sticks with those issues that are already considered blue chips in the EC. As Rosalind Altmann, chief international strategist for N.M. Rothschild International Asset Management Ltd. in London said in January 1991, "On every level you compare, Europe comes out with much better value or as a safer place to invest."[11]

The biggest mistake that investors can make about international investing, is not doing it—just "...sitting there with 100 percent of your assets in the U.S.," said "International Fund Monitor's" Jon Woronoff in March 1990, "The U.S. stock market has been one of the top five major performing markets only once in the past 10 years."[12]

INVESTMENTS TO WATCH

There are many attractive European stocks, European country funds, and regional funds which are available to U.S. investors. Of the group, about 20 look particularly attractive. Investors will notice that the individual stocks which are featured are all quite large. That is because the biggest companies are in the best position to capture the greatly expanded markets created by a united Europe. Although some smaller firms will rise to the opportunity most of them will be swallowed up instead. Of course, that can create attractive short-term profits. However, the largest gains will go to investors who take long-term positions with the big companies that are on their way to becoming the corporate giants of Europe. All in all, I believe investors should stick to the leading European firms or the mutual funds which favor them.

Great Britain Leads the Way

The single largest stimulus behind the European Community is the decline of socialism as a viable economic system. The trend began in Great Britain by former Minister Margaret Thatcher during the 1970s. She demonstrated to both Europe and the rest of the world that giving up the reins of tight economic control could create very positive results in a country's economy. Even the staunch socialists in Italy and France could not ignore the evidence of a revitalized Great Britain.

Because Great Britain was the first of the socialized welfare states to begin turning around, it is well ahead of its competition. The country has the trauma of its transition period largely behind it and is now positioned to grow strongly as EC markets develop. New privately held firms have adjusted to open market conditions, British workers expect to earn their keep, and the government is pro-business.

Equally important is Great Britain's decision to become a full member of the EC. That may not sound like a momentus decision to many Americans, but it represents a major shift in outlook by an island people who have historically enjoyed their isolation and independence. Although many British are nervous about accepting the controls which go with EC membership the long-term benefits to the country should be very positive.

Those benefits will come primarily from a revitalization of Great Britain's historic role as a trading nation. Already, some top British companies are resuming their roles as "merchants to the world." Thanks to the immediate stimulus of the EC—and to growing world prosperity—British firms are once again heading for top profits.

One of the major developments in England's decision to embrace the European Community is the modern engineering miracle which is taking place below the English Channel. The "Chunnel," a 17-mile tunnel which has already been drilled to France, is expected to be fully operational in 1992. The new undersea transportation link will open up many markets for both the United Kingdom and continental countries, because it will handle more volume faster and cheaper than current water transportation systems allow.

For several years British companies have had all the right ingredients for success but they have not been able to make full use of them. Now with the nation's revitalized business climate, expanding EC markets, the Chunnel, and a new spirit of merchantilism the barriers are down.

United Kingdom Fund was formed in 1987 when it became apparent that Great Britain's turnaround would be further enhanced by the formation of the European Community. The policy of the closed-end fund is to keep at least 65 percent of its assets in British companies. In 1990, that rate was 90 percent in anticipation of the 1992 opening of the EC.

At the beginning of the 1990s the fund was keeping an impressive 24 percent of its assets in British industrials and about 14 percent in its electrical industries. These two traditionally strong segments of the United Kingdom's economy should provide a way to tap the growth of both the EC as well as that of Great Britain. The fund also focuses on commercial firms which market every type of product throughout Europe and the world. The investment manager for the fund is Warburg Investment Management International Ltd. Its U.S. administrator is Bear Stearns Funds Management, Inc.

Grand Metropolitan is one of the top five marketers of multinational brands in the world. About 45 percent of the firm's profits come from American investments; 36 percent from United Kingdom companies; and 18 percent from the rest of its worldwide operations. In March 1991 this British stock was listed on the New York Stock Exchange which will give it greater exposure and a much more active market.

Grand Met's assets are strategically placed in popular drink, food, and retailing businesses. That gives the company a broad exposure to rapidly growing consumer markets, not only in Europe and the United States, but increasingly throughout the world. The company's food sector alone accounts for one-eighth of all packaged food sales in the world. Notable company brands include Pillsbury, Green Giant, J&B, Bailey's, Smirnoff, Haagen-Daz, Lancers, Christian Brothers, Almaden Vineyards, Burger King, Cinzano, Heublein, Cointreau, Ski Yogurt, and Alpo pet foods. Grand Met is becoming so large and globally oriented that it may represent a broader diversification than some mutual funds. The company's size and its number of well-known brands, combined with growing markets, should lead to top profits in the 1990s.

Reuters Holdings is the world's leading supplier of general news and specialized financial data as readers who watch the popular television program "The Nightly Business Report" undoubtedly know. The company relys heavily on high-tech communication systems to distribute its information services to the far corners of the earth.

Reuters is particularly timely because its heavy business and financial orientation positions it solidly for growth as world trade increases the need for such information. In addition, the company will reap the rewards of worldwide electronic securities trading, an important trend that is just now emerging. Reuters' business can be cyclical because many of its services are linked to economic events. However, the long-term outlook for the company appears to be excellent.

Germany: Europe's Economic Powerhouse

When it became apparent that the EC was going to become a reality many Europeans were immediately nervous about the influence of Germany. Nobody seriously expected a return to German nationalism, but worries about the economic power of the nation were well founded.

As the decade progresses Germany's economy will increase dramatically. No other country will match its involvement in expanding European markets or profit more. Not only are German industries among the most competent and competitive in the world, but financially its banks are among Europe's strongest. As a French industrialist told me recently, "What they don't build they will finance. Sometimes they will do both. Always they will make money."

As you may have expected, as the EC's debut grew closer, international investors pushed German stocks through the roof. Then the Berlin wall came down. When that happened many investors backed away from Germany because they knew that reunification would place a staggering economic burden on the country. Of course, German stock prices dropped sharply. However, as the richest and most heavily industrialized country in the EC, Germany has nowhere to go but up—despite the reunification costs. As David C. Roche, a fund manager for Morgan Stanley & Co. in London said in May 1991, "If you take the longer view, Frankfurt is the most undervalued market in Europe."[13] I agree. Of all the countries in Europe, I believe that Germany is the most important for investors in this decade. If you can invest in only one country other than the United States, I would recommend Germany.

Germany Fund was formed in 1986 to give American investors a way to participate in the growth of German equities. The closed-end fund emphasizes Germany's "blue chips" including Siemens, Volkswagen, Linotype, Daimler–Benz, Wella, and Bayerische Hypotheken-und Wechsel-Bank, to name only a few. Current income from debt securities may be consideration of the fund but it is not a major objective.

The fund's portfolio includes a broad selection of German securities from the automotive, banking, chemical, insurance, manufacturing, electrical, retail, and other sectors. The fund will not put more than 25 percent of its assets in any one industry. This fund, which is managed by Deutsche Bank Capital Corp. (see the next entry), offers investors an attractive and reasonably safe way to play the growth of Germany and the EC. It should do very well during the 1990s.

Deutsche Bank is one of Germany's major banks. The firm is assuming an important role providing funds to German companies that are expanding to make use of EC opportunities. In addition, the bank will finance several development projects throughout Europe. Deutsche Bank is particularly noteworthy for its position as a key lending institution for the reunification of East and West Germany. The bank's focus is directed toward lending funds to private companies within what was once East Germany, and other former Soviet bloc countries, rather than lending to their governments.

Deutsche Bank's business more than doubled from 1980 to 1990, with a corresponding increase in profits. The company has been active in mergers and acquisitions throughout Europe; specifically in Spain, Portugal, Switzerland, England, France, Hungary, Czechoslovakia, and Poland. In addition, the bank's management is stressing greater customer services in a region of the world that has traditionally not seen consumer-oriented banking. Deutsche Bank appears to be well positioned to profit substantially from both banking and European growth trends of the 1990s.

Siemens is one of the best-known and most successful German electrical and electronics companies. The firm has over 375,000 employees—140,000 of whom work outside Germany. Operations exist in almost every country in the world, although the main focus of development is in Europe and North America.

Siemens is involved in several basic industries which are essential for modern countries including power generation, power transmission and distribution, building systems, industrial automation, data and information systems, private communication systems, public communication networks, defense electronics, transportation, automotive systems, medical engineering, semiconductors, and a host of others. It is safe to say that virtually every major development project in Europe will be a candidate for Siemens' products and services.

Siemens already has enormous market share in Western Europe with very strong expansion programs underway. At the beginning of the 1990s orders for Siemens' products in Western Europe rose by 30 percent. Germany's orders increased 45 percent for the year. Those increases bode well for the future of this company.

France Becomes a Major Player

France was among the last countries to get on the EC bandwagon. However, the country has been working hard to catch up by building its industries to meet the demands of growing markets. By 1989 France had become the largest country pursuing these efforts, making one-third of all acquisitions in Europe.

France's turn toward decentralization was even more dramatic than the move taken by Great Britain. Prior to 1982 French industries were under layers of direct government regulation. Moreover, the economy was so vertically integrated (*pour efficacite*) that one industry barely knew another existed. Although the French have retained some government controls, the country's business community is now able to compete on favorable terms with other nations. Thanks to economic liberalization, many French firms have gained leading positions in steel, cement, tires, packaging, foods, and hotels. France is also becoming an important high tech center with products ranging from computers to biotechnology. The rapid growth is accompanied by some aches and pains. However, the problems of quick expansion will pass leaving the future for France very promising during the 1990s.

France currently enjoys moderate but healthy economic growth and one of the lowest inflation rates of the EC countries. Due largely to the Gulf Crisis, the Paris Bourse declined 25 percent during 1990. However, the end of the war, the opening of the EC, and the growing strength of French industry signals resumed growth in the coming years.

France Growth Fund is a closed-end investment company that offers Americans the opportunity to take broad positions in the French economy of the 1990s. At least 65 percent of the fund's assets will be invested in equity securities listed on the country's seven securities exchanges.

The fund owns a wide selection of the French stocks, including financial services, food and beverages, distribution services, consumer nondurables, electronics, and other growing industries. Investment advice and management is provided by Indosuez International Investment Services, a subsidiary of Banque Indosuez, a French financial institution with assets in excess of $50 billion at the beginning of the 1990s. The fund's U.S. administrator is Mitchell Hutchins Asset Management, Inc.

LVMH, the merged companies of Louis Vuiton and Moet-Hennessy, presents an extraordinary assemblage of high-end French products to the EC and the world. The company's well-known holdings include six champagnes and two cognacs plus several perfumes and cosmetic products. LVMH goods are highly prized throughout Europe. However, many of its products are highly taxed and uncompetitive. Now that such trade barriers are coming down, the company should see rapidly rising sales. Those sales should receive a further boost as growing prosperity throughout Europe makes high quality LVMH products affordable to millions of additional consumers.

Spain Becomes the "California of Europe"

Spain is rapidly becoming one of the brightest stars in Europe. This former wallflower is benefitting from the same sunbelt phenomenon that made Florida, Arizona, and California among the most prosperous places in America. The migration to Spain, and to some extent Portugal, is being fueled by EC regulations which allow European retirees to live and collect their pensions anywhere they wish. German and British pensioners are particularly eager to leave bad weather behind them and are flocking to the warm cities and beaches of the south.

The "California of Europe" is not just becoming a tourist and retirement center. Spain's industries are also moving forward in anticipation of the growing markets to be made available by the EC. That move is gaining additional strength from Spain's abundant labor force which is the least expensive in Europe. Spain's workforce is particularly valuable at this time since the labor pool is shrinking in northern European countries.

On the negative side, Spain is experiencing growing pains from being thrust rather quickly into the European fast track. In 1990 growing inflation and interest rates prompted the Bank of Spain to institute a tight money policy which put the brakes on the economy. The Gulf War also took its toll. Nevertheless, these events are unlikely to impact Spain's prosperous long-term outlook. Japanese investors are now moving strongly into Spain. They were largely responsible for driving the stock market up sharply in 1989. Fortunately for today's investors, stocks subsequently dropped back to reasonable levels. From that new base, I would expect them to begin their long-term rise.

The Spain Fund was formed in 1988 to provide an investment vehicle to the Spanish economy. During normal conditions, the closed-end fund keeps at least 65 percent of its assets in Spain's equity securities. In the fall of 1990 approximately 80 percent of assets were invested. The fund's broad portfolio includes financial services, consumer staples, utilities, capital goods, consumer services, consumer manufacturing, and energy. Construction and materials companies are also held and should do well in the 1990s. The fund is administered by Alliance Capital Management L.P.

Empresa Nacional de Electricidad is the largest electric utility in Spain. The company provides one-third of the country's power needs, as well as serving the Balearic and Canary islands. Approximately 59 percent of the utility's income comes from sales of electricity to other major utility companies. In addition, Empresa is a 50-percent owner of the transmission network through which its power is distributed. At the close of the 1980s Empresa was serving about 2.8 million customers, about two-thirds of which were commercial and industrial.

A potential source of trouble is the utility's 60 percent reliance on coal-fired furnaces which could lead to toxic emission problems. However, the excellent growth in the country's population and economy should provide the resources to solve whatever troubles may occur. Empresa's key position in Spain's development should ensure its success.

Telefonica Nacional de Espana is Spain's telephone company. In response to Spain's rapid growth, the company installed more than 2 million new lines in the last two years of the 1980s. As good as that looks, the number of lines per person in Spain, 32 per 100, is a lot less than the European average of 43. Clearly, there is a substantial amount of growth left for the company even without Spain's current boom.

In early 1991, analysts at Hoare Govett Investment Research Ltd. forecasted a net earnings growth for this company of 15 to 20 percent per year during the early 1990s. An added benefit is growth in mobile telephone use which is expected to top more than 400,000 units by 1993. Spain's telephone company has a monopoly on mobile networks through 1993 and will receive the benefit of all that business. As is the case with Empresa, it is difficult to see how this company could fail to profit as Spain continues to develop in the 1990s.

New Iberian Fund is a closed-end investment company with a portfolio containing stocks from both Spain and Portugal. The fund should be of interest to investors who are attracted to the sunbelt phenomenon of southern Europe but who do not wish to invest in just one country.

Of the two nations, Spain, by far, offers the better economy and the quickest prospects for growth. However, the opportunity presented by Portugal is considerable—simply because it has such a long way to go to catch up with other EC countries. Portugal will be a longer term investment than Spain, but it may ultimately surpass its neighbor's rate of growth.

Small Countries with Big Opportunities

Sweden, Switzerland, and the Netherlands are countries which appear to lack the potential for explosive internal growth that may be found in several other European nations. However, these three smaller countries have several companies that will benefit handsomely from increasing European trade and development. Three of them, Nestlé, ASEA AB, and AEGON N.V. look especially promising.

Swiss companies are of particular interest at this time because of improving attitudes toward outside investors. International stockholders were once snubbed but are now being accepted graciously. Normally tight-lipped Swiss firms have also made accounting changes which more accurately reveal their profit levels.

Nestlé, a famous Swiss company which is best-known in the United States for its chocolate bars, is also the world's leading food processing firm. At the close of the 1980s, about 46 percent of Nestlé's sales came from European markets, 26 percent from North America, 12 percent from Asia, and the rest from Latin America and other countries.

Nestlé has not been content to settle for its already considerable success. In anticipation of the 1992 debut of the EC the company acquired L'Oreal, a French producer of cosmetics and pharmaceuticals; Alcon, a U.S. ophthalmic care and pharmaceutical firm; Hills Brothers, the coffee producer; Carnation, foods and pet food; Buitoni, an Italian pasta and confectionery maker; Rowntree, an English confectionery group; and Curtiss Brands, makers of chocolate and confectionery. Investors should note that those acquisitions are in addition to Nestlé's large existing lineup of consumer products.

Nestlé is well positioned to make full use of the growing consumer markets that the EC will produce in the 1990s. The company should be of particular interest to investors who are seriously considering taking positions in Grand Metropolitan but who would prefer a more seasoned company with a longer track record.

ASEA AB is a Swedish company that gets nearly 90 percent of its income from its joint venture with Swiss-based Brown Boveri et Cie. The closely held composite firm, Asea Brown Boveri (ABB) whose headquarters are located in Zurich, is one of the world's largest manufacturers of power generation and transmission equipment, transportation systems, industrial machinery, and other capital goods.

Activities focus on infrastructure needs such as power plants, distribution networks, and heavy industry.

ABB, and therefore ASEA, holds a key position in Europe from which it will directly benefit from the increased development brought about by the EC. The company's wider, global interests also help ensure that it will have a profitable future. Because ASEA's prospects are also growing strongly in Eastern Europe, it will be discussed more in the next chapter. Note that Brown Boveri recently became available in the United States by means of its ADRs. However, the market for ASEA is considerably larger and more liquid. ASEA is clearly the way for U.S. investors to play the growth of the ABB joint venture.

AEGON N.V. is a large, diversified, Netherlands-based insurance company with a growing international business. The company offers a complete range of policies including life, property, accident, health, and general insurance. A recent acquisition in Florida expanded the company's U.S. presence.

Besides being attractive for its own strengths, AEGON will benefit substantially from the EC. After 1992 people in any part of the Community will be able to purchase insurance and financial services from anywhere else in the EC. In addition, insurance companies will not be required to buy large holdings of low-paying government bonds from their host countries. That means insurance companies will finally be able to offer market interest rates and compete effectively with other members of the financial service industry. The result should be a sharp and continuing increase in business for AEGON.

Regional Funds Offer Diversified Plays

Nearly every major mutual fund sponsor in America has one or more regional fund that focuses on Europe. The best of them have large holdings of infrastructure and financial service stocks, two industries that will benefit significantly from European growth in the 1990s. The top funds also hold leading consumer product and service firms from throughout the EC.

Closed-end Regional Funds
Investors who wish to use investor sentiment to their advantage should choose a closed-end regional fund. Two such funds which appear to have excellent potential are included here.

Europe Fund is a closed-end investment company whose goal is long-term capital appreciation from European equities. Under normal conditions the fund intends to keep at least 65 percent of its assets in European markets. Remaining funds will be invested in various debt securities, primarily in Europe.

Under normal circumstances the fund's assets are distributed broadly throughout Europe. However, when conditions warrant a tighter focus, the fund may concentrate on as few as three countries. At the end of 1990, approximately 70 percent of assets were invested— 25 percent in the United Kingdom, 11 percent in Switzerland, and the rest distributed among eight other nations.

Europe Fund is also noteworthy for its interest in Eastern Europe, an area that some funds neglect. Up to 20 percent of assets may be placed in emerging companies of Eastern Europe as they become available. The fund is managed by Mercury Asset Management PLC, one of Europe's largest management firms. The U.S. administrator is Princeton Administrators, Inc.

Scudder New Europe Fund is a closed-end investment company whose goal is also capital appreciation. This fund's focus is on smaller or emerging European companies that are expected to benefit from the EC and other trends in the region. As of October 1990, the fund's assets were fairly evenly distributed throughout the leading countries of the EC and the EFTA.

The New Europe Fund also includes privately held firms in its portfolio which gives it expanded opportunities for growth, particularly in Eastern Europe where few publically traded securities are yet available. Under current rules, no more than 20 percent of the fund's assets will be placed in Eastern European securities. The fund is both managed and administered by the U.S. firm, Scudder, Stevens & Clark.

Open-end, No-load Regional Funds

Investors who would rather own funds where values are solely dependent on the net asset values of their portfolios have a wide variety of open-end opportunities from which to chose. Three representative examples from well respected sponsors are examined here. Because more are being created almost monthly, investors should consult a current mutual fund directory for an up-to-date list before making a final selection. Two excellent sources of mutual fund information are published quarterly by *The Wall Street Journal* and *Barron's*.

For the convenience of investors, and only for that reason, I have chosen to use examples of open-end funds whose sponsors offer nearly identical funds that focus on other attractive regions. Having a "family" of related funds makes it easy to apportion assets between regions and switch them as conditions indicate. Consequently, the fund sponsors that are featured in this section will also be mentioned in Chapter 3, and featured again in Chapter 5.

Financial Strategic Portfolio: European Portfolio is a no-load, open-end fund that invests broadly throughout Europe. Under normal conditions, at least 80 percent of the fund's assets are invested in England, France, Germany, Belgium, Italy, the Netherlands, Switzerland, Denmark, Sweden, Norway, Finland, and Spain. Securities will be from the principal stock exchanges of these countries. Remaining funds will be in various debt instruments from Europe and the United States. Financial Strategic Portfolio also offers a Pacific Basin Fund that is managed similarly to the European Portfolio.

Vanguard International Equity Index Fund: European Portfolio is a unique no-load, open-end fund that seeks to track the movements of the Morgan Stanley International Europe Index. The index consists of more than 600 companies from 13 European countries. Approximately two-thirds of the European Portfolio consists of securities from three countries, the United Kingdom, Germany, and France—the current EC leaders. Vanguard also offers a Pacific (Index) Portfolio and a Combined Portfolio that tracks both regions.

T. Rowe Price European Stock Fund is a no-load, open-end fund that invests in both large and small European companies which appear to have strong growth potential. The fund also seeks to take advantage of the growth opportunities presented by Eastern Europe. The fund will normally have its assets in no less than five countries. Current income is a secondary objective of the fund. T. Rowe Price also offers a New Asia Fund which is managed similarly to its European Stock Fund.

NOTES

1. "Europe 1992" (Table), *The Wall Street Journal,* May 3, 1989.
2. Shawn Tully, "Europe Gets Ready for 1992," *Fortune,* February 1, 1988.
3. Ibid.
4. Shawn Tully, "The Coming Boom in Europe," *Fortune,* April 10, 1989.

5. Ibid.

6. Blanca Riemer, et al., "America's New Rush to Europe," *Business Week,* March 26, 1990.

7. Ibid.

8. Manuel Schiffres, "The Case For Closed-End Funds," *Changing Times,* April 1990.

9. Manuel Schiffres, "Chasing the Foreign Stock Jackpot," *Changing Times,* June 1990.

10. Earl C. Gottschalk, Jr., "How to Choose a Mutual Fund That Invests Overseas," *The Wall Street Journal,* March 2, 1990.

11. Michael R. Sesit, "Global Money Managers, Despite Losses Incurred Last Year, Are Back in European Stock Markets," *The Wall Street Journal,* January 4, 1991.

12. Gottschalk, "How to Choose a Mutual Fund."

13. Terrence Roth, "Bargain Hunters Rediscovering Berman Stocks," *The Wall Street Journal,* May 13, 1991.

CHAPTER 3

A DELAYED POSTWAR BOOM
FOR EASTERN EUROPE AND
THE SOVIET UNION

At the end of World War II the free nations of Western Europe began immediately to rebuild. Within a few years, not only were the worst scars of the war erased, but most of the region was firmly back in the global economic mainstream. By the mid-1950s a genuine boom had swept through the area. The same cannot be told about Eastern Europe. Under communism, that region began a 45 year period of stagnation. Not only was the Eastern bloc's economy put on standby but so was every aspect of life. It was as if the entire region had been placed in suspended animation.

Now the "Evil Empire" is fading away. In its place is a determination by millions of people in Eastern Europe to make up for the decades of progress they lost. Although many obstacles stand between those people and their goals, they are working hard to overcome them. As a result, Eastern Europe finally seems to be headed for the postwar boom that its neighbors enjoyed nearly half a century earlier. When it comes, it will be worth billions of dollars to investors who take strategic positions in the firms that are presently establishing themselves in the region.

THE PATH TO LONG-TERM DEVELOPMENT

Many investors might look at the rubble and chaos in Eastern Europe and the Soviet Union left by decades of communist mismanagement and dismiss the region as too troubled to be of interest. That would be a mistake. Behind the enormous problems that exist throughout the Eastern bloc are many developments which offer great promise. Although those developments are still in their very early stages, some attractive investments are already emerging. Many more will present themselves as the decade progresses.

First to appear on the economic scene after liberation were profit-minded entrepreneurs who capitalized on Eastern Europe's enormous demand for consumer goods of every type. Many such businesses started as enterprising people traveled to the West and returned with suitcases packed with products. The desire was so great for the goods that huge profits could be made. Although illegal, the trade was tolerated. "We have no money and no energy to go after them," said Hungarian Industry Minister Peter Bod in April 1991, "we're just happy that they exist."[1] Former suitcase entrepreneurs are now becoming legitimate importers who are prospering in the free-for-all climate that presently exists in the East. The most successful of the entrepreneurs are forming alliances with Western interests and consolidating among themselves for greater efficiency. Among this group are many firms that will someday become the commercial giants of the East.

Already a few leaders are emerging and they are attracting the attention of risk-tolerant investors. With a little help from outsiders, Witold Zaraska of Poland is planning to open an international business center near Warsaw. Zoltan Palmai and his son came back from the West to reopen the Victoria Hotel in Budapest. On a smaller scale, Andrea Gallai of Hungary is using money from an entrepreneur's fund to start a chain of framing galleries.[2] There are hundreds of such entrepreneurial opportunities available at this writing, and a few thousand more are expected during the 1990s. However, the risk level of this avenue is high because the attrition rate is likely to be excessive. In addition, investments in entrepreneurial firms will be illiquid; i.e., it will be very difficult to sell a position. Consequently, this is an investment area where the early birds will probably lose money. Being second, or even third, in line a few years down the road should pay much greater rewards.

A second development that holds great promise for Eastern Europe—and its investors—is the privatization of former state-owned businesses. A good example is the Czech engineering firm Skoda. This vertically integrated and very inefficient company made everything from steel to nuclear reactors. Now the Czech government is selling it off piece by piece into what they hope will be a series of smaller but more efficient firms. Privatization is of particular interest to investors because it usually involves selling shares of stock to the public. However, privatization presents several major problems that should be allowed to resolve themselves before investors take positions.

The biggest danger is that nobody really knows what the state-owned firms are worth. Prices are set by government agencies which simply put their heads together and think up a number. Since there are no business-oriented accounting or valuation standards in Eastern Europe, potential investors have no real way to judge whether or not the state's price is realistic. For example, the Hungarian telephone company is now privately owned with shares available on the new Hungarian Stock Exchange. What few shares have traded hands so far have done so for widely varying prices—usually each one lower than the last. The pattern is likely to continue for months, perhaps years, until the real value of the company is determined by the market.

Newly privatized firms can also be expected to have a high failure rate. Managers of Eastern bloc countries have no idea how to compete in a free market system. "The question is how to get them over the management-expertise hump" observed Jacek Rostiwski, a British economist advising the Polish government, in April 1991.[3]

To see how much trouble Eastern European managers face, look what happened in our own country when AT&T was broken up by Judge Harold H. Greene in 1984. After the company was stripped of its government-approved monopoly (similar to Eastern bloc state-owned firms), AT&T had a terrible time adjusting to a competitive environment. Presumably, AT&T's managers were more familiar with free market systems than are the new managers of the Eastern European firms. The message is clear—privatization is no guarantee of future profits.

Much more promising at this time are outside investments into Eastern Europe that are being made by large Western firms. Dozens of companies, ranging from General Electric to Sara Lee, are moving cautiously into the region. Usually they encounter enormous problems that they had not anticipated. However, these firms realize that they must take positions during the early years after liberation in order to capture market share and make the best commercial acquisitions.

Investing in Eastern Europe early in the 1990s can be a wise strategy—but only for corporate investors with deep pockets. At this juncture, individual investors who wish to take positions should do so indirectly by purchasing shares of the leading firms that are carving out solid long-term positions. Even safer, although somewhat less focused, is investing in mutual funds which include such companies in their portfolios.

WARNING SIGNS

Although Eastern Europe has great promise, it is important not to let optimism get in the way of good judgment. Eastern Europe's problems are enormous and will hold back the region's development, at least for the short term.

Particularly troublesome is the poor state of the Eastern bloc's infrastructure. Highways, railroads, utilities, and telecommunication systems are inadequate even for the depressed needs of socialist economies. They are completely incapable of meeting the needs of a modern country. Although some initial economic progress has been made since liberation, little more can occur without improving the region's infrastructure. That job will take a lot of time and money.

The Eastern bloc's industrial base is also in bad shape. The region's manufacturers often rely upon tooling that dates to the 1940s. Much of the equipment was worn out by the Soviets during World War II, and it was then shipped to their client states instead of being scrapped. The situation is so bad that many potential investors who visit Eastern Europe find that virtually nothing can be used as it is except the company's name and its real estate.

Sometimes not even the real estate is usable. Crushing environmental problems have left many areas unfit for human occupation. Unlike the situation in the West where environmental problems often revolve around aesthetics, the problems in Eastern Europe are killing people. Before the region can be turned around economically much of it must be rehabilitated. That will take much of the money that might otherwise go to development.

A crippling civil service mentality also prevails among Eastern Europe's workers. After nearly 50 years of guaranteed employment under state ownership, most Eastern bloc workers have become complacent. A visitor may often hear the humorous excuse "They pretend to pay us and we pretend to work." Unfortunately, the "joke" has become a way of life that must change if the region is to modernize.

Economic and legal uncertainty is also a major problem throughout Eastern Europe. Inflation is rampant in many areas. Economic development is further hampered by skyrocketing interest rates, high taxes, constantly changing regulations, and unconvertible currencies. Although these problems will resolve themselves in time they will take their toll in the short term.

Finally, in some Eastern bloc countries ethnic unrest has become a major problem. In Yugoslavia and Romania, social tensions threaten to split the countries apart. In other areas seething resentments that often go back centuries threaten to block any significant economic progress.

LOOKING AT THE EAST, COUNTRY BY COUNTRY

As checkered as the picture of Eastern Europe may be, the region offers increasingly attractive investment opportunities. This section will explore the trends to look for.

Hungary

The economic future of Hungary is among the most promising in Eastern Europe. Its government is considered the most stable in the region. Moreover, the country does not contain the potential for civil strife—ethnic, national, or religious—that is to be found in many other nations of the Eastern bloc and within the Soviet Union.

Perhaps the biggest advantage Hungary has is its strong history of successful private enterprise. Not only did the country have a market economy before World War II, but it was also allowed to have some private business during its long Communist occupation. As a result, when communism made its unceremonial exit in 1989, Hungary immediately started to turn around. It is doing so with the help of savvy foreign investors who poured almost $600 million into the country in 1990—more than half of all the money invested in Eastern Europe that year.[4]

However, the move to capitalism is not going as fast as it could. Privatization efforts are proceeding through wary government officials who do not want the country's new economy to wind up in the hands of former Communist Party leaders or under the total control of foreign investors. This caution could prove beneficial to American investors because it may create a slower growing and more stable economy than might exist in a free-for-all atmosphere.

Hungary has about 2,400 large companies for sale to private owners, and 400 were on the block in 1991. About 16,000 smaller operations were also up for auction in 1991.[5] Most of them will end up on the country's new stock exchange, and a few will be purchased outright by foreign interests. Hungary's stock market, which made its landmark debut in March 1990, was the first in Eastern Europe. However, its issues are still illiquid and are unsuitable for individual investors. In February 1990, Ilona Hardy, head of Hungarian Securities Trading Committee and former lawyer for the country's State Development Bank said, "There's vigorous issuance of new securities taking place. However, there's virtually an imperceptible secondary market."[6]

Even in dynamic Hungary the best investment plays are currently to be found outside the country.

Poland

Poland is the second most promising country in the former Eastern bloc. Economic progress is already occurring and will accelerate quickly. I believe by 1995 people will be amazed by Poland's progress. Poland has many advantages over its Eastern bloc neighbors. As in Hungary, the country has none of the deep ethnic unrest that is common to the region. Instead, the Polish people have rallied around former Solidarity leader Lech Walesa who is now the president of the country.

Walesa has been encouraging free market systems within Poland, and he has attracted a great deal of investment from abroad, especially from the United States. Much of that money is coming from America's large population of people of Polish descent, who are providing their relatives in Poland with the seed money to start new businesses.

Poland's history is also a big plus for the country. Before World War II, Poland was one of the most industrialized countries in Europe. It was also market oriented. Because the Polish people have not forgotten how to run businesses, the country opened shop almost immediately after the Soviets pulled out.

The new Polish government is also dealing swiftly to clear away former anticapitalistic regulations. In their place are new laws which promote free trade. Judging from the results so far, the new atmosphere is working. In 1990 alone, more than 500,000 new businesses were formed in Poland. The nation's exports to the West increased by 34 percent, amounting to more than $11 billion.[7]

Of particular importance to investors is Poland's decision to encourage foreign firms to start joint ventures in the country. A package of supporting laws were adopted by the Polish Parliament on January 1, 1990. By the following January, there were 215 joint U.S.–Polish ventures. Investments by U.S. interests in the country totaled $15 million in 1989 then rose to $36 million during 1990.[8] A new stock market opened in July 1991.

Jerzy Kapuscinski, the Polish Embassy's commercial counselor in New York, indicated in April 1991 that the pace of these investments continues to accelerate. Money coming in from *all* foreign countries is expected to reach as high as $750 million by the end of 1991.[9] "With thousands of good-sized companies to be privatized, the business opportunities blow your mind," said Mitchell Kobelinski, a former administrator of the U.S. Small Business Administration that began several enterprises in Poland in 1990.[10]

Czechoslovakia

Czechoslovakia began its return to a free market economy at the beginning of 1991. The previous year was spent by Finance Minister Vaclav Klaus in developing a foundation of agreement among its parliament for his trade emancipation plans. The backing he achieved was reluctantly bestowed and required a great deal of hard work. Klaus spent weeks running [President Vaclav] Havel through Economics 101, according to a top aide to the Czech Finance Ministry.

The source of the resistance to reform is mostly historical. After more than four decades of communism, the majority of Czech political leaders still harbor a basic suspicion of Western ideas. Even though communism has been shown to lead slowly to bankruptcy, the West's profit-oriented business system is still viewed by many Czechs as inherently parasitic.

Another lingering problem is that while some private enterprises in Poland and Hungary had been allowed under Communist rule, the Czechs nationalized everything from factories to corner bakery shops. Consequently, there is more to privatize and more to be undone before the economy will begin to show positive results. There are about 4,500 large companies on the Czech auction block with many more smaller concerns left to be listed.[11] A little more than one thousand were sold during the first half of 1991—a mere drop in the bucket.

A more stubborn pocket of resistance to economic reform appeared in the Republic of Slovakia. Workers in the region's troubled armament factories reacted strongly to fears of widescale unemployment by calling for a slower pace of change. However, Klaus' plan, which orders managers to form their own methods of going private or lose their jobs continued at full speed. Area experts also indicate that Slovakian foot-dragging is angering the rest of the population and could develop into civil unrest. However, at this point, the animosities appear to be manageable and are unlikely to disrupt economic development. In the early summer of 1991 both sides had agreed to settle their differences peacefully and work for their mutual advantage.

Also on the positive side, Czechoslovakia was the second most industrialized country in the "Combloc" after East Germany. Many experts believe it was also the most efficient. In addition, Czech workers are considered to be among the hardest working in the region. Czechoslovakia appears to be one of the top three Eastern European candidates for making a complete turnaround to a free market system. However, the country will undoubtedly take more years to do so than Poland and Hungary.

Former East Germany

Former East Germany is a special case. Because of its unification with West Germany, the latter country is taking responsibility for its recovery. Massive financial and management assistance is currently flowing from former West German to former East German firms. Although that assistance has yet to produce visible fruit, it will almost certainly begin to do so within a few years. Consequently, what was once East Germany must be counted among the region's promising opportunities.

The most important agents for change in the former East Germany are the former West German banks. In the spring of 1990 new East German leaders disassembled their state-run banking system and invited foreign banks to come in. By that summer Deutsche Bank AG assembled the first of 100 new branches in East Germany. Deutsche Bank, Germany's largest bank, also formed a joint venture with Kreditbank, which was assembled from the remnants of the East German bank.[12] Currently

Deutsche Bank appears to be the financial intermediary for about 20 percent of the country's Eastern bloc business.

West German industry moved across the border almost as quickly as did the banks. Volkswagen, Daimler–Benz, BASF, Mannesmann, Siemens, and a host of others are now on the scene with a variety of ventures. As the new operations come up to speed so will the German economy. I expect positive results to be evident by 1995.

Clearly, the best way for investors to participate in the German recovery is to take positions in former West German industrial companies and financial institutions. That's especially true since these firms will emerge from the process as the most experienced Eastern bloc investors in the world. The Germans are cutting their teeth on the economic problems in the Eastern part of their country. What they learn from their experiences they can be expected to apply to other countries. All in all, top German firms offer investors some of the best opportunities to be found in all of Europe.

The Soviet Union

During World War II, Winston Churchill defined Russia as "a riddle wrapped in a mystery inside an enigma." Decades later, the Soviet Union remains as much of a puzzle for investors as it has always been for diplomats. That is unfortunate, because the country is the single largest territory available to Western business interests in this century.

Despite the Soviet Union's murky future, the colossal size of the opportunity it represents is luring American business. For example, the Soviet Union has a fleet of 900,000 railroad tank cars, compared to 200,000 in the United States. Mark Hungerford, chairman of tank car parts maker Transciso Industries, said in November 1990, "It is by far the largest railroad in the world and we have to be there."[13] That sentiment is common among almost all Western firms who plan to do business in the Soviet Union.

Internal unrest and a deeply troubled economy highlight the problems in the Soviet Union. Examples of such troubles are legion. About half of the record agricultural harvest in 1990 was lost to waste and inefficiency. Immense reserves of standing timber go uncut while socialist planners build with scarce concrete blocks. The country is famous for its top-quality vodka but as many as half of the defective bottles break in transit. Soviet engineers are among the best trained in the world but few of their designs are ever translated into products. The list goes on and on.

Even worse, the problems affect the very structure of Soviet society. Nobody knows how to make any meaningful improvements because so many factors must be changed at once. As a Soviet biologist mentioned to me in early 1991, "It's as if we were redesigning an ecosystem and need to get everything right for it to work."

Another obstacle to reform are the Soviet politicians and policy makers who fervently believe that capitalism is evil. This group has already fabricated an "excess profits tax" for new free trade business owners. A new personal income tax is also designed to prevent anyone "... from getting too big." Undoubtedly the main reason behind the Soviets' reluctance to welcome a completely free market economy is that they never had one. Unlike many Eastern European people that once enjoyed freedom and open markets, most Soviets were serfs before the revolution. They don't know how to run the most basic business. As Donald Du-Beau, Ph.D. an applied mathematics consultant in Corvallis, Oregon, told me in December 1990, "My Soviet clients are bright enough but not one of them even had a lemonade stand or a paper route when they were kids. They don't know the first thing about business."

The Soviet workforce is another problem. As is true in other Combloc countries, Soviet workers are used to low-key job demands with little fear of termination. The threat of being made to compete, and perhaps lose their jobs, is causing considerable anger throughout the country. Ilva Konstantinov, a member of the Soviet Commission on Economic Reform, warned in November 1990, "Privatization is not as simple an issue as it seems. Right now, the workers in our country are in a completely explosive frame of mind. Anything could set them off. We simply can't come in and start selling off parts of the enterprises that they have traditionally thought of as their own—let alone selling those factories to foreigners.[14]

Although many experts urge caution regarding Soviet investments, some outside developments are already underway. PepsiCo has been in the country since 1971. In addition, McDonald's and Baskin-Robbins have outlets in Moscow. Federal Express and United Parcel Service are also present and are planning to expand.

On the positive side, the Soviet Union is enormous, with an abundant wealth of undeveloped resources, especially oil, gas, lumber, and minerals. When these vast raw materials can be delivered to an efficient production and distribution system, the country could become one of the most prosperous in the world. Another plus for the country is U.S. goodwill. America seems committed to help the Soviets succeed. Though it is costly, many Americans believe that the only real hope for developing a lasting peace between our two countries is to help the Soviet Union develop its economy. John Williamson of the Institute for International Economics spoke for many U.S. citizens in May 1991 when he said, "It seems to me it's the best chance we have of moving toward a far more peaceful, constructive world than I've ever lived in. That's the benefit."[15]

At the present time there aren't any direct investments in the Soviet Union that are suitable for individuals. The country has few privatized industries. Neither does it have a stock market—although two are slated to open in late 1991. There are no Soviet mutual funds. The best option is to take a position in a Western company that is positioning itself for future profits in the region.

Note: As we went to press there was an attempted coup in the Soviet Union. In the aftermath of the coup many republics decided to break away from the former U.S.S.R. and become autonomous states.

Unfortunately, independence will not solve many of the major problems that limited development in the republics when they were part of a strong U.S.S.R. For example, there is still a critical lack of business skills and an abundance of built-in inefficiencies that will make economic reform difficult. However, the end of communism and central control should allow obstacles to reform to be removed more quickly than was formerly the case. Consequently, profitable investments in the region should begin occurring within a few years instead of much later in the decade.

The situation with the newly independent Baltic states is more promising short term. Because Latvia, Estonia, and Lithuania have strong histories of pre-communist business experience, the countries can be expected to present investment opportunities very soon, just as we are seeing in Poland and Hungary. The same companies that are moving strongly into those two Eastern European countries are the most likely to make moves into the Baltics as well. I urge you to watch for news regarding such developments and take positions accordingly.

Yugoslavia, Romania, and Bulgaria

Investments in Yugoslavia, Romania, and Bulgaria are very risky propositions no matter how indirect a strategy an investor may use. Yugoslavia is particularly troubling. Its seven areas of separate ethnic heritage have been deeply divided for generations. When communism was removed, that unrest began boiling over into the streets. In June 1991, with an enormous margin, Slovenia and Croatia voted to break away as independent nations, a move the Serbs vowed to prevent. As this is being written fighting has erupted which could mark the beginning of the end for Yugoslavia.

Romania is in little better shape. The country suffered horribly under Ceausescu and will take years to recover. In addition, since the region was once part of the Ottoman Empire, its population is divided between people of European and Turkish extraction. Unfortunately, there is little love lost between the two groups whose cultures are very different. The tinderbox atmosphere has been aggravated by four decades of authoritarian control. The people seem ready to revolt against any government that can't solve their distress immediately.

Bulgaria's prospects for meaningful economic change also seem unlikely, at least for many years. The country, which almost became the Soviet Union's sixteenth republic, has been slow to take advantage of its newly acquired freedom to strike out in new directions. Although the Bulgarian people would like to see an end to the secret police and to many of the restrictions on civil liberties, they seem content with a state-dominated economy.

INVESTMENTS TO WATCH

Currently there are three ways to take positions in the growth in Eastern Europe.

1. Invest in an Eastern Europe mutual fund. This is a theoretical approach for Americans because these funds are not available in the United States. The best of them are registered in London. Although many London-based funds are respectable and are legal for Americans to own, I would not recommend doing so. As explained in the previous chapter, there are simply too many problems associated with making direct investments in foreign countries to make them worthwhile. In addition, Eastern Europe is still too unstable for individual investors. There are also too few private companies to provide a base for a diversified portfolio.

2. Investors can buy the stocks of top Western European and U.S. firms that are taking strategic, long-term positions in Eastern Europe.

These firms are loaning money, entering joint ventures, providing Western management advice, or actually fulfilling development contracts. Many such companies are available that are already showing promise. As will be seen, the best of them are European.

3. Invest in U.S. mutual funds that focus on Western Europe but include Eastern Europe in their portfolios. In my opinion these funds offer the greatest blend of low risk and high opportunity that is presently available. The funds which I recommend for this approach are German and are featured in this chapter.

Overall, the best approach to investing in Eastern Europe is to consider that region's potential as an added attraction to an opportunity that has already been judged worthwhile. That is, if an investment looks attractive for other reasons, then its stake in Eastern Europe could be a deciding factor in making a purchase.

U.S. Firms with Eastern European Opportunities

By 1991 Eastern Europe had received $1.8 billion in outside investments. PlanEcon, a Washington-based data service, estimated in early 1991 that the leading countries could receive as much as $3.5 billion per year in foreign money. That amount is in addition to the $13 billion slated for Eastern European development by the new European Bank for Reconstruction and Development.[16]

Several U.S. firms are adding to the total by establishing operations in Eastern European countries. But although those investments often have high dollar values, they usually represent a small percentage of a company's assets. In addition, the newly formed operations are likely to take a long time to develop. Consequently, it would be unrealistic for investors in those firms to expect to see the Eastern European activities contribute to profits anytime soon.

As mentioned in the previous chapter, the leading U.S. firms which are moving strongly into Europe—and Eastern Europe—are also doing a fine job globally. Since the global play is the larger play, I again refer investors to Chapter 5, which discusses this topic in depth.

European Firms That Will Profit from
Eastern European Developments

By far, European firms offer the most promising opportunities to U.S. investors who wish to share in the delayed postwar boom of Eastern

Europe and the Soviet Union. Not only are European firms already on the scene but they are also familiar with doing business in the East, a region with complex cultural and ethnic differences. In addition, European firms also have more patience than U.S. companies, and they are more likely to stick to their plans until they eventually pay off. Overall, European companies have the upper hand in this region.

VOLKSWAGEN AB of Germany is well ahead of the game in Eastern Europe having invested the largest of all outside automotive giants. Over $6.1 billion was recently placed in a venture with the Czechoslovakian automaker Skoda. Volkswagen expects to be selling half a million Czech-made autos to all of Europe by the end of the 1990s. It is important not to judge the investment potential of VW from its performance in the United States where sales have not been particularly good. The company is doing much better in Europe where it both manufactures and sells its vehicles.

ELECTROLUX AB is a large Swedish conglomerate with many consumer products. In early 1991 the company invested $83 million in Hungary's Lehel appliance plant. The move gives Electrolux an early position in a region that should develop into an excellent consumer market. Electrolux is also attractive because of its expansion into other areas of the world. The firm presently operates in about 50 countries where it manufactures and sells a wide variety of household appliances including vacuum cleaners, absorption refrigerators (no electricity needed), and sewing machines. The company also makes equipment for commercial firms in various industries. Prospects appear very good for Electrolux.

ASEA AB is a Swedish-based company with global operations in the electrotechnical, power generation, marine equipment, heavy machinery, and shipping industries. As mentioned in the previous chapter the firm has a 50 percent interest in ASEA Brown Boveri Ltd. (ABB), from which it derives about 90 percent of its income. The firm also owns a significant part of Electrolux AB.

About half of ASEA's sales have been for large infrastructure projects in Europe. The company is in an excellent position to benefit from the development of free trade in both Eastern Europe and the EC. "One of its biggest businesses is power generation, which should be in great demand over the next several years," said Guy Rigden, director of strategy at UBS Phillips & Drew in London, in 1990.

L.M. ERICSSON is an important Swedish supplier of telecommunications equipment. The company has particularly good capabilities with systems which are designed for emerging nations. Not only are Ericsson's products among the best in the world, but Ericsson is also adept at arranging "creative financing" for its customers. As a result, Ericsson's systems are found everywhere in the world—from remote villages to the most crowded cities. Some of them are in Eastern Europe. Within a few years many more will be installed.

DEUTSCHE BANK AB needs little additional discussion here as its activities have been mentioned in both chapters dealing with European opportunities. Suffice it to say that the bank is firmly involved in nearly every aspect of growth in the EC and in Eastern Europe. Apart from a good mutual fund, the company represents one of the broadest and most conservative plays in the region that may be found. In fact, Deutsche Bank manages two attractive funds that are available to U.S. investors.

European Country Funds with Eastern European Holdings

There are three closed-end country funds registered in the United States which offer attractive opportunities to American investors who wish to participate in the growth of Eastern Europe.

One of them, the **Germany Fund,** was discussed in the previous chapter. Although that fund does not specifically focus on Eastern Europe, its portfolio includes many of the leading German firms which will benefit directly from developments in the East.

The other two funds, which are listed here, devote a significant portion of their portfolios to Eastern European ventures. As that region begins to develop and more opportunities present themselves these funds will undoubtedly increase their holdings. Meanwhile, the fund's German investments should pay handsome rewards as the EC continues to boost prosperity in that country.

New Germany Fund was formed in 1990 to invest primarily in equity and equity-linked securities of German companies. A maximum of 20 percent of its assets will be put into non-German firms. An important part of this closed-end fund's selection criteria is the potential of a company to profit from developments which are taking place in what was formerly East Germany and other Eastern European countries. The fund seeks to keep at least 80 percent of its assets in German equities during normal times. A minimum of 65 percent of assets will be placed in stocks of small- and medium-sized companies. New Germany Fund is managed by Deutsche Bank Capital Corp. Its investment advisor is DB Capital Management International GmbH. Both organizations are subsidiaries of Deutsche Bank AB.

Future Germany Fund is similar to the New Germany Fund but with an even stronger focus on companies that are expected to benefit from developments in the former East Germany. Future Germany Fund is also managed by Deutsche Bank Capital Corp., and is advised by DB Capital Management International GmbH.

European Regional Funds with Eastern European Holdings

In addition to country funds with an Eastern European exposure, there are several regional funds that also devote portions of their portfolios to the region. Such funds are the broadest and the safest way to play the growth of Eastern Europe while enjoying the more immediate benefits brought about by the newly formed European Community.

Both the **Europe Fund** and the **Scudder New Europe Fund,** that were discussed in the previous chapter, devote portions of their portfolios to Eastern bloc investments. Of the two closed-end funds the Europe Fund appears to be the most conservative. Of course, the New Europe Fund may prove to be the top performer because of its focus on small- and medium-sized companies.

The three open-end European funds that were discussed in Chapter 2 are also attractive for their Eastern European potential. **Financial Strategic's European Portfolio, Vanguard's International European Index Fund,** and **T. Rowe Price's European Stock Fund** all hold companies that will benefit from developments in Eastern Europe. Of the three, the Vanguard offering appears to have the broadest portfolio due to its focus on the Morgan Stanley European Index. Relative to Eastern Europe, the two remaining funds appear to be very similar.

Investment Conclusions

Although much of Eastern Europe has serious social and economic problems to overcome, all the signs indicate that the strongest countries in the region will be able to develop despite these obstacles. When it happens, an enormous period of unprecedented growth will begin as the former communist countries move as rapidly as possible to catch up to the West.

The greatest growth in Eastern Europe will occur in the middle to the second half of the 1990s. However, patient investors should begin taking some small positions early in the decade in order to maximize profits from the delayed postwar boom which is surely coming to the region. The investment focus should be on Western European companies which are already on the scene—or on the mutual funds which invest in them.

NOTES

1. Gail E. Schares, et al., "Eastern Europe: A Market Economy Takes Root," *Business Week*, April 15, 1991.
2. Ibid.
3. Ibid.
4. Philip Revzin, "Ventures in Hungary Test Theory That West Can Uplift East Bloc," *The Wall Street Journal*, April 5, 1990.
5. Gail E. Schares, et al., "Hungary: A Giant Step Ahead," *Business Week*, April 15, 1991.
6. Thomas G. Donlan, "Hungary for Stocks," *Barron's*, February 5, 1990.
7. Gail E. Schares, et al., "Poland: The Pain and The Gain," *Business Week*, April 15, 1991.
8. Brent Bowers, "American Entrepreneurship in Poland Is Picking Up," *The Wall Street Journal*, April 8, 1991.
9. Ibid.
10. Ibid.
11. Gail E. Schares, et al., "Czechoslovakia: Reluctant Reform," *Business Week*, April 5, 1991.
12. Terence Roth, "Big West German Banks Jockey to Seize Positions of Strength Across East Border," *The Wall Street Journal*, May 8, 1990.
13. Paul Klebnikov, "Prospecting in the Wild East," *Forbes*, November 12, 1990.
14. Ibid.
15. Robert A. Rankin, "Self-Interest Moves West to Aid Soviets," *The Oregonian*, May 25, 1991.
16. Gail E. Schares, et al., "Eastward Ho! The Pioneers Plunge In," *Business Week*, April 15, 1991.

CHAPTER 4

EMERGING NATIONS DEVELOP DYNAMIC ECONOMIES

Around the globe a quiet revolution is occurring that is rapidly transforming many Third World countries into nations with fast growing economies. From Canton to Cancun, the determined efforts of millions of people to control birthrates, expand educational opportunities, and build industrial capabilities are beginning to pay off handsomely.

In dozens of countries, poverty is giving way to rapid expansion, increased trade, and growing prosperity. The Western Pacific and Mexico look especially promising. During the 1990s those regions will offer investors opportunities for gains that are unlikely to be found anywhere else in the world. Although such opportunities are not without risks they can be kept to a minimum by sticking with promising mutual funds and larger stocks in basic industries.

THE WESTERN PACIFIC HEADS THE LIST

Nowhere will the opportunities for investment profits be greater than in the emerging nations of Asia. The Nomura Research Institute predicts that the Western Pacific's economy will overtake the European Community's by the end of the 1990s.[1] Already, there is more trade crossing the Pacific Ocean than the Atlantic—and the gap is widening. United States–Pacific trade averaged a 9 percent growth rate during the 1980s, while United States–Atlantic trade turned in a 7 percent rate. By 1989 America's business in the Pacific was valued at $297 billion, again, nearly double its trade with Europe.[2]

The potential of the Western Pacific looks so good that economists expect that international business in the 1990s will be divided into three roughly equal trading blocs: North America, Europe, and Asia. Investors who plan to take full advantage of the major growth trends of the 1990s will take positions in all three areas.

AN INCREDIBLE TRANSFORMATION

Although it is not generally known in the United States, many Western Pacific countries have become modern in virtually every respect, prompting world economists to coin a new term for them: newly industrialized countries (NICs).

The emerging nations have flowing currencies, established infrastructures, self-sustaining domestic markets, and many resources they are now beginning to use to their advantage. Those resources include enormous pools of inexpensive, but often talented, labor that are propelling many formerly poor nations into world markets in nearly every industry. The NICs are also lowering trade barriers and aggressively developing international alliances for their mutual benefit.

It is important to understand that the emerging countries are not just pulling unskilled laborers out of rice paddies to produce trinkets for export markets. That was the situation some 20 years ago for what were then "ox-cart economies." Today, we are seeing the emergence of high-tech factories staffed by trained, competent employees who make products that are just as advanced as those which are obtained from any other part of the world.

It is also important to realize that the pace of development is far higher than one might expect. That is primarily because growth is being driven by economic rather than political forces. As Sanjoy Chowdhury, chief economist for Asia at Merrill Lynch, observed in November 1990, "Asian economic integration is largely driven by economic and business logic, not by governments as in the European common market."[3] This foundation of good business practices and market forces is giving the region more strength a great deal quicker than would otherwise be the case. Of course, it also means that investors who wish to take early bird positions in the region should act in the next year or two.

Another reason for the accelerated development in the Western Pacific is the ready availability of huge sums of money from Japan. During the last half of the 1980s Japan invested $11 billion in Malaysia, Thailand, and Indonesia alone.[4] Wherever the Japanese see opportunity—and wherever the host country is amenable to having Japanese partners—the monetary floodgates open. As a result, major changes that U.S. observers might expect to require 20 years can take as little time as 2 years. This is yet another reason for investors to move sooner rather than later in Pacific markets.

A MAJOR ECONOMY UNTO ITSELF

Until recently, the emerging nations of the Western Pacific exported more goods to the United States than to each other, but that is no longer the case. Development has progressed to the point where Pacific nations have sizable domestic markets for their own goods. That is a major consideration for investors because it means the region presents opportunities that are not dependent upon exports to the United States and Europe.

Western Pacific countries are developing a diversified intraregional trade following the billions of dollars that was spent on intraregional investment. According to the Nomura Research Institute, the percentage of trade in Southeast Asia that was intra-Asian grew from 34 percent in 1986 to 42 percent by 1989.[5] That trade should rise substantially by the end of the 1990s. Hirotaka Tsurusa, a manager in the Asian division of Toyota Motor Company, observed in November 1990, "Investment from Japan is encouraging the creation of a middle class in Southeast Asia. . . . This will help Toyota's overall market grow."[6] That sentiment is echoed throughout the boardrooms of the world's major corporations.

The Western Pacific economy is becoming so strong and self-sufficient that it can now run along on its own steam without major concern for the recession/growth cycles of the rest of the world. This means that the area offers investors an increasingly stable base for continued growth. It also means that the Western Pacific offers investors another opportunity to diversify their portfolios for safety. As one of my clients observed in early 1991, "I like the fact that at least one major region of the world may not dance to the same economic tune as the United States and Europe."

AVOID JAPAN

Since Japan is clearly the engine behind much of the growth in the Western Pacific, a case can be made for investing in that country instead of emerging nations. However, I feel that strategy would almost certainly be a mistake, at least for investors who look to the Pacific for dramatic growth.

Although Japan still has considerable potential, it now has a mature economy that can't possibly expand as strongly as it did in the past. In fact, my research indicates that the country's $3 trillion economy is dropping from its nearly 6 percent growth rate at the end of the 1980s to an expected level of about 3 percent through the early 1990s. Clearly, the steepest part of growth curve is over for Japan. That potential has shifted to the Pacific's smaller nations that are now where Japan was in the early 1960s. Investors who missed that move now have a second chance for top gains.

OPPORTUNITIES IN OUR HEMISPHERE ARE ALSO ATTRACTIVE

Much closer to home are other attractive opportunities that are being overlooked by many U.S. investors. Several countries in South and Central America are developing as quickly as those in the Western Pacific. Brazil, Argentina, Chile, and Mexico are especially noteworthy for their recent progress and for their potential for further growth.

Of the group, Mexico offers the most promise for U.S. investors. That country, which is rich in both labor and natural resources, is finally coming out of decades of economic slumber. In addition, Mexico will soon join the United States and Canada to form a "North American Community," a group that will rival every other economic alliance on earth. As the three nations move toward implementing that union, investors will be presented with many excellent opportunities for profits. The most attractive of those opportunities will be found "South of the border."

INVESTING IN EMERGING NATIONS

As is the case with European issues, U.S. investors can buy Third World stocks by means of ADRs that are traded on our exchanges. The leading public companies in almost every country have been registered in the United States and can be bought and sold with a phone call.

However, trading Third World stocks is an entirely different proposition from buying large European issues. Particularly troublesome is a lack of good—and timely—information. Even when data is available, it can't always be trusted. Overseas accounting standards are frequently different than those which are used in the United States and Europe. In many cases no standards exist at all. Even worse, overseas stock manipulators sometimes "cook the books" and engage in other fraudulent practices which are uncommon in this country.

That warning notwithstanding, American investors with very long time frames may still find it worthwhile to take positions in basic infrastructure stocks of promising small countries. In particular, telephone and electric companies are likely to be rewarding over the long term because they will mirror the growth of their nations. Large contractors, leading concrete plants, and major banks can also be good investments. With emerging nations the rule is to go big and go basic.

Single country funds can also be used to take positions in emerging nations as is the case when investing in Europe. Of course, investing in a fund that targets a small nation is riskier than investing in a fund that takes positions in a large, well developed country. In the former case, prices can change on a dime and can be dramatic, often as a result of overnight political changes. Although most country funds employ local experts who can limit such problems, they are not always successful.

One troublesome factor that affects both stocks and single country funds is changing currency valuations. Fluctuations can be hairraising with small countries that are undergoing great changes. Large price declines can sometimes come without warning as when the Mexican peso was devalued repeatedly in the 1970s. Again, a country fund's local contacts can offer some protection against sudden shocks but their abilities are limited. Holders of ADRs have no protection at all unless they diversify broadly between countries.

A more conservative way to invest in emerging nations is to use a regional fund that targets a selected group of countries. Because of their diversification, regional funds offer good protection against negative events in one country. In fact, conditions which hurt one small country can often help another. For example, an attempted coup in the Philippines that devastates local agricultural stocks can send equivalent issues soaring in nearby Malaysia.

INVESTMENTS TO WATCH

Around the globe there are many emerging countries—in Asia, South America, and Africa—that offer considerable promise for the future. However, a full presentation of the opportunities that are available would be overwhelming and counterproductive. Instead I will focus on those countries that appear to offer the very best prospects for U.S. investors who wish to take positions in the near future. Among them will be found what I believe might very well become some of the top performers of the 1990s as they benefit from a decade of expanding global trade.

Greater China Emerges

Taiwan, Hong Kong, and the People's Republic of China share a common geographical area. They also share a common future as they learn to work together for their mutual benefit. Judging from the results so far, the future for "Greater China" will be very prosperous.

A few years ago the expectation was that the antibusiness policies of Red China would dominate the surrounding region. However, the recent changes that swept through communist Europe had huge effects on China as well. Although China has yet to guarantee many personal freedoms, the country is clearly liberalizing its economic policies. Private ownership is growing—central control is on the wane. Shanghai even has a small stock exchange now.

Coastal Chinese provinces are particularly important to Greater China as they have been given permission to act quite independently of Beijing's official party line. Most of the coastal provinces have major commercial agreements with Hong Kong and unofficial alliances with organizations in Taiwan. Those ties to the industries and cheap labor of China are creating enormous prosperity for all the nations of the region.

The People's Republic of China Rediscovers Enterprise
Although a small stock market now exists in China, the country is as yet unsuited for direct investment by noncitizens even if it were legal. For the present, the best way to take positions in the awakening of "The Sleeping Giant" is to invest in Taiwan and Hong Kong.

Taiwan

Taiwan is already a successful nation that needs little introduction to Americans. For all its success, however, Taiwan's potential has yet to be realized. Unfortunately, Taiwan neglected many basic needs during its high growth years and now faces huge costs to catch up. The government plans to spend $300 billion in six years on a countrywide development program which is expected to raise the per capita wealth from $6,000 to $16,000 by the end of the decade.[7] That level is roughly equal to the wealthiest oil-producing nations. The plan's focus is on improving the nation's infrastructure and is generally designed to make Taiwan more competitive as well as making it a better place to live.

For the present, Taiwan's massive infrastructure costs will be a burden on the economy. The recession in the United States has also taken its toll. The combination of problems sent the nation's stock market into a tailspin in 1990. However, savvy investors should consider using the present slump to take long-term positions with this proven winner that will almost certainly have a profitable decade. Taiwan discourages direct foreign investments by foreign nationals. Consequently, investors who wish to participate in the country's future must do so by means of a country fund.

Taiwan Fund is a closed-end fund that looks for long-term capital appreciation by focusing on Taiwan equity securities. Common stocks in the portfolio include banks, chemicals, plastics, textiles, and, of course, the country's huge electronics industry. The fund's goal is to have at least 75 percent of its assets in equity securities during normal times.

Taiwan Fund receives investment advice from the China Securities Investment Trust Corporation which is 65-percent owned by the China Development Corporation. Merrill Lynch International, Inc., owns 15 percent of the advisor's stock. The fund's administrator is Fidelity International Ltd.

Hong Kong

On July 1, 1997, Hong Kong's long term lease with China will come to an end. Although the termination agreement calls for 50 years of minimal interference by China it isn't known with certainty whether Hong Kong's freewheeling economy will be reined in or allowed to continue.

I feel very strongly that Hong Kong's economy will not only be allowed to prosper but it will be encouraged to do so. I base that prediction on the fact that the colony is of enormous economic value to China. That is why the country has taken no steps to seriously interfere with Hong Kong even though it could have easily done so for nearly half a century. In addition, China has copied many of Hong Kong's liberal economic policies and has instituted them in its coastal provinces. If Beijing wasn't satisfied with Hong Kong, it seems unlikely that they would have used it as a model.

China has also been investing in Hong Kong, despite all the proclamations about being loyal to a communist way of life. Asia's tallest building is the Bank of China office in Hong Kong. China has also taken a significant position in Cathay Pacific Airways Ltd. All in all, the Chinese may be looking forward to taking over Hong Kong but they do not appear to be looking forward to shutting it down.

Significantly, most business leaders in Hong Kong are not following the 50,000 people who leave per year. The stay-at-homes are not waiting in fear of 1997, they are waiting in anticipation. They see the end of the border with China as a once-in-a-lifetime opportunity to expand their operations into the large, well-populated mainland. With over 1.1 billion people eager to be both workers and consumers, China could turn Hong Kong's industries into world leaders.

Hong Kong Telecommunications is a holding company for the organizations which supply telephone, mobile telephone, facsimile, data, PBX, and telex services to the Colony. The system is noteworthy for its high level of sophistication which makes use of the latest in telecommunications equipment. Under various agreements, the company has the right to supply some of its services on an exclusive basis until 2006. Of course, anything can happen after China takes over in 1997.

In my opinion the only effect 1997 will have on the company is to remove constraints on its ability to expand. Hong Kong Telecom is the logical choice to supply modern services into the coastal colonies and beyond once the borders come down. Although the company will undoubtedly need to compete with outside suppliers, it will bring obvious geographic and economic advantages to the bargaining table. Of course, there are no guarantees that Hong Kong Telecom will do as well as expected. However, of all the various ways to play the expanding role of the Colony and the People's Republic of China, this company appears to offer the greatest prospects.

Growth Triangle Lives up to Its Name

Another geographic and economic region which has considerable promise is composed of Singapore, Malaysia, and Indonesia. Together they constitute the Southeast Asian "Growth Triangle." Its driving force is Singapore.

Singapore, a city-state, has been highly successful. It is often called the "Berlin of Southeast Asia" because it is a center of prosperity, cleanliness, and order in an area that is often just the opposite. Singapore is surrounded on two sides by the poorer countries of Malaysia and Indonesia. Several years ago the city's leaders realized that their nation was becoming vulnerable to mass immigration by its poor neighbors—and perhaps even a takeover. In response, Singapore decided to defuse the situation by helping its neighbors develop. Millions of dollars and even more valuable professional help have been invested so far.

Singapore's efforts to jump start Malaysia and Indonesia are clearly working. The economies in both nations are now growing rapidly. By the middle of the decade the two nations will stand easily on their own without any further assistance. At that time the Growth Triangle will be a major economic center of the Pacific.

Singapore Prospers

Not only can Singapore afford to help its neighbors, it is also prospering from its efforts. The city-state's economy grew by 8.3 percent in 1990 versus 9.2 percent in 1989. Unemployment was only 1.7 percent. Inflation was a modest 3.4 percent and productivity grew by 3.4 percent as well.[8] Singapore's stellar performance has been possible due to its well-developed infrastructure and its educated workforce.

Singapore is rapidly becoming a major financial and business center. Many foreign companies have their regional headquarters in the city-state which offers special tax incentives and other local perks. Japanese business leaders have responded particularly well, locating the marketing, finance, research and development, design, and parts-procurement operations of many of their firms in Singapore. The huge investments of the 1980s signal additional growth in the 1990s.

Singapore Fund is a closed-end investment company that intends to seek capital appreciation by placing at least 65 percent of its assets in Singapore equity securities. Because the Singapore market is small, the balance of the fund includes the securities of several other countries in the region. Investments are primarily in common stocks. Additional purchases can include preferred stock, convertible securities, and warrants. The fund is managed by DBS Asset Management Prd. Ltd., which is a subsidiary of the Development Bank of Singapore, Ltd. The fund's administrator is Daiwa Securities Trust Co., a respected Japanese investment company.

Malaysia Is Rising Fast

Until recently, Malaysia was one of the most impoverished nations on earth. Now the country's economy could be among the fastest-growing in the Western Pacific. The country's GNP experienced a stunning 8 percent growth rate during the last three years of the 1980s thanks largely to investments by Singapore and Japanese business interests.

Malaysia's potential appears to be excellent for several reasons—besides its growing foreign investment. Most important, is the scrapping of nationalistic and often socialistic policies that kept the country in the doldrums for years. Under the new rules, many of the country's previously nationalized companies are going private. Examples include the national airline in 1985 and the country's international shipping corporation soon after. Railroads, container ports, and airports are likely to follow.

Malaysia is also abundant in natural resources that include petroleum, rubber, tin, and palm oil—products that are needed by nearly every industrial nation in the world. Malaysia is finding growing markets for its exports by opening up its own markets to its customers throughout the world.

Lastly, Britain left its former colony with a well-established infrastructure that rivals the facilities which are found in many industrialized nations. As a result, Malaysia will be able to take immediate advantage of opportunities as they occur.

Malaysia Fund was formed in 1987 to invest primarily in the country's equity securities. The closed-end fund plans to keep at least 80 percent of its investments in Malaysian companies listed on the Kuala Lumpur Stock Exchange. The rest of its investments will be in Malaysian debt securities, money-market instruments in Malaysia, and—for safety—U.S. debt securities. The fund currently benefits from a Malaysian tax exemption that will continue until November 1, 1995. The Malaysia Fund's investment advisor is Morgan Stanley Asset Management Inc. It is administrated by The Vanguard Group, Inc.

Indonesia Catches up to Its Neighbors

Indonesia is the least developed nation in the Southeast Asian Growth Triangle. Its history mirrors that of Malaysia, because nationalistic laws prevented the country's natural advantages to be developed significantly. Finally in 1988, after seeing what liberalization did for its neighbors, Indonesia's government took the plunge into the modern world. Trade restrictions were rolled back and so were tough barriers to foreign investment. Now the country is moving forward towards long-term economic growth.

Because Indonesia is a Third World nation, most U.S. investors assume that it is quite small. In fact, the population of the country is a little more than 180 million—the fifth-largest in the world. Of course, Indonesia's population represents a potentially rich consumer market. In addition, the country's huge labor pool is an enormous resource for growth. Since Indonesia lags its neighbors in economic development, its labor costs are among the least expensive in the region. That in turn is creating larger consumer markets and the need for more production. It is a classic formula for success.

Participatory capitalism is relatively new to Indonesia. The Djakarta (often spelled *Jakarta*) Stock Exchange did not even exist until the late 1970s. It was generally a poor performer through most of the 1980s. However, after the Indonesian government let up on economic sanctions, stocks jumped 500 percent within two years.

Nothing goes up in a straight line forever, and Indonesia offers no exception. The country is now reacting to its first spurt of explosive growth by taking an economic breathing spell. However, the fundamentals remain the same for this emerging nation, and the indication is that additional growth will certainly occur.

Jakarta Growth Fund is a closed-end investment company which has assets spread widely across the country's economy. The fund's portfolio includes equity securities of Indonesian companies, as well as those of non-Indonesian firms that have sizable investments in the country. Stocks include consumer goods, finance, manufacturing, cement, oil, gas, textiles (a major industry), agriculture, and various short-term Indonesian and U.S. debt securities.

Because some of its investments are outside the country, this fund may offer a little more safety than one that invests totally within Indonesia. Still, the number of companies available for investment plus the small market for them can be expected to cause prices to be volatile.

On the positive side is the considerable experience of the fund's manager and advisors who are subsidiaries of the Nomura Securities Company of Japan, a company that is very familiar with the region.

Indonesia Fund is a recently-organized, closed-end investment company that seeks capital appreciation by investing at least 65 percent of its assets in Indonesian equity and debt securities. A portion of the fund's assets are invested in Indonesian and U.S. debt securities. Because Indonesia is a newly emerging country with few stocks of its own, this fund also invests in nearby countries which share the region's growth, including Malaysia, Thailand, Singapore, and the Philippines. This diversified approach could prove to be wise because of the volatile nature of emerging nations in Southeast Asia. Indonesia Fund is advised by BEA Associates, a U.S. firm, that is assisted by James Capel Ltd, a company that provides Indonesian economic analysis. The administrator is Provident Financial Processing Corp.

Many Individual Nations Offer Promise

Although there are many advantages for small nations that cooperate with each other within a particular geographic region, many individual countries also offer considerable promise. South Korea, Thailand, and the Philippines are especially worthy of notice. Longer term, Vietnam may also offer attractive opportunities although they are unlikely to payoff until after the turn of the century.

South Korea Stumbles, Catches Its Breath

During the last two decades South Korea rose from a postwar economy to a global competitor. Then in the late 1980s, just as everything was finally going well, the nation stumbled. The trouble occurred largely because Korea's growing prosperity wasn't finding its way to the majority of workers. As the years wore on from the nation's 35-year-old civil war with the North, many Koreans became tired of making "heroic sacrifices" to help the country rebuild. Labor unrest, which was often violent, led to large wage hikes, which in turn led to increased costs and lowered productivity.

Now the Koreans appear to be in the process of adjusting to the new economic conditions. Better management has calmed the labor storm, although there remains a significant potential for civil unrest. Korea's huge family-owned businesses are importing American-trained managers who are modernizing the country's traditional top-down management systems. All in all, the country appears to be getting ready for the second phase of its growth curve.

Korea Fund, formed in 1984, invests at least 80 percent of its assets in securities that are listed on the Korean Stock Exchange. The fund's portfolio includes major firms in construction, automobiles, electronics, chemicals, banking, retailing, and metals. Stocks include up-and-coming companies such as Samsung Electronics Co., Korean Airlines, and Hyundai Motor Services—all of which are giving Japanese firms a run for their money in world markets. Until Korea stumbled in the late 1980s this closed-end fund performed very well. I would expect to see it perform well again during the 1990s as the country regains its economic footing. The Korea Fund is managed by Scudder, Stevens & Clark. The investment advisor is a subsidiary of Daewoo Securities Co., Ltd., the largest securities firm in Korea.

Philippine Potential Is Huge but Long Term

The Philippines share many characteristics with their rapidly emerging neighbors in the Western Pacific basin. The islands have large and industrious populations, rich resources, and enormous potential for development. However, the Philippines boil with internal problems. Double-digit inflation, political unrest, rampant corruption, poverty, illiteracy, and terrorism all retard the country's bid for prosperity. As of the spring of 1991 there have been seven attempts to overthrow the Aquino government. One coup in December 1989, held Manila's financial district hostage for nearly an entire week.

Nevertheless, Asian investors from several countries are making their move into the Philippines. For example, Japan and Korea are building a combined auto manufacturing plant. Mazda and KIA expect to be producing their line of passenger cars in 1993. Similar deals are in various stages of development throughout the country.

The Philippines have also produced some impressive economic statistics, including an annual growth rate of 5 to 6 percent a year from 1987 through 1989.[9] Some trade barriers have also been reduced which will almost certainly attract additional investment.

The good news notwithstanding, any significant improvement in the Philippine economy appears unlikely until the latter half of the decade. Consequently, I am afraid that the 1991 runup in Philippine stocks won't be sustained. However, Philippine investments could pay off handsomely over the long term, particularly if an opportunity to buy them inexpensively presents itself.

First Philippine Fund was the first closed-end investment company to make the Philippine stock market available to U.S. investors. The fund usually keeps 80 percent of its assets in equity securities, which derive at least 50 percent of their income from the Philippine economy. The fund may also invest in non-Philippine companies that have substantial assets within the country. The remaining 20 percent of the fund's assets can be found in stocks of both established and new companies including some that are not listed on an exchange. The fund's investment advisor is Clemente Capital, Inc., assisted by a subsidiary of the Philippine National Bank. The fund's administrator is Provident Financial Processing Corp.

Thailand Invests for the Future

Thailand is a nation whose considerable potential is just beginning to unfold. The country has the advantage of being one of the few in its region to escape the devastation of the Vietnam conflict and the resulting turmoil which paralyzed Laos, Cambodia (Kampuchea), and Burma.

Thailand is also blessed with an energetic labor force and abundant resources. Not surprisingly, outside investors—particularly the Japanese—have been attracted by the country's strengths and are moving strongly to make use of them. Much of that outside investment is for high-tech industries, especially assembly plants for consumer products.

On the negative side is Thailand's inadequate infrastructure which will retard growth during the early 1990s. Bangkok traffic jams can cause delays measured in hours. Making a telephone call from one side of the country to the other can often be impossible. Port and airport facilities are also inadequate even for present needs. Remaining political instability is also a factor, although it appears to be somewhat less negative than it may first appear. A recent coup removed Prime Minister Chatichai, but it was nonviolent and had the full backing of the King. Significantly, the Thai stock market rose strongly during the quarter when the Prime Minister was "persuaded to retire."

The Thai government is moving with all haste to improve the nation's infrastructure. Current plans call for a new deep sea port, an industrial estate, and a railway network. New telephone lines are also being installed across the country. In rugged jungle areas where lines won't reach, solar-powered cellular systems are planned. As each project is completed the Thai economy will be free to move ahead another notch.

Thailand's stock market rose 120 percent in 1989, a typical pattern for a small emerging nation. The overheated situation cooled off considerably in 1990, which was also to be expected. Growth from this point forward should be more gradual, although price volatility will remain a factor throughout the 1990s.

Thai Fund is a closed-end investment company that had 98 percent of its net assets invested in Thai common stock at the beginning of 1991, a strong vote of confidence in the country's future. The fund's biggest areas for investment were financial institutions and construction materials. The fund's policy is to keep at least 80 percent of its investments in Thai stocks. The portfolio may also contain convertible securities, warrants, and Thai debt securities. Investment advisors are The Mutual Fund Co., Ltd., and Morgan Stanley Asset Management Inc., which is also the Thai Fund's administrator.

Thai Capital Fund is a closed-end investment company that is quite similar to the Thai Fund. However, at the end of 1990 Thai Capital appeared to be somewhat less focused on selected issues within the country. For example, in December 1990 Thai Capital had about 17 percent of its assets in construction material stocks versus about 27 percent at the Thai Fund. On paper at least, the Thai Capital portfolio may offer better diversity. Of course, there is no guarantee that the difference between the funds will continue. Thai Capital's investment manager is The Mutual Fund Co., Ltd. The fund's investment advisor is Daiwa International Capital Management (Hong Kong) Ltd. It is administered in the United States by Princeton Administrators.

Central and South America Reach for Growth

Many Latin American countries have long histories of political unrest, rampant inflation, and generally poor business climates. However, there are changes occurring in that situation that hold promise for investors. The most important development is a move toward open markets. The coming unity in Europe, with its increasing trade and economic growth, is now being copied in South America. The pace-setting nations of Brazil and Argentina have agreed to lower trade barriers in 1994. Uruguay and Chile are looking into the prospect of joining them. Of course, American firms will also benefit from the pacts as they always do whenever trade barriers are lowered and the pace of commerce is increased.

There is also a growing trend toward free enterprise throughout Latin America. In several countries, state-owned industries are being sold to private interests in an effort to stop losses and reduce government debts. American banks are swapping government IOUs for part ownership of airlines, railroads, steel mills, oil fields, and even public utilities and postal systems. Private investors are also getting into the act through the purchase of shares on national exchanges. Although it will take some time for such investments to pay off, we should begin to see good results by the middle of the decade.

Of the many attractive opportunities in Latin America, Mexico offers the greatest promise to American investors. Not only is that country of over 88 million people one of the least developed in the region, but it is also next to the biggest economic powerhouse on earth— the United States. Perhaps most important of all, Mexico is now moving strongly to accept outside investment in order to transform itself into a modern nation.

Mexico Joins the North American Community
Most Americans are familiar with the European Community; the agreement between Western European nations that creates a homogenous economic region. Another term that is beginning to be heard is the *North American Community* (or *NAC*) to be comprised of Canada, the United States, and Mexico. As in Europe, the alliance will be mutually advantageous to all members of the group. In terms of raw growth, the biggest beneficiary will clearly be the Mexican economy.

Mexico is clearing the way for growth by getting bureaucrats out of the workplace. By the close of the 1980s, Mexico had swapped about $3.5 billion in bad debt for private ownership of what had once been government-run companies. The government intends to swap about $1 billion more per year throughout the early 1990s until most industries are in private hands. The Mexican government is also instituting sweeping new economic policies including tax reforms and the elimination of many antibusiness regulations. Specific steps will reduce the top marginal tax rate from 60 percent to 35 percent; change the tax status of small firms to encourage them to get bigger; abolish most restrictions on foreign investment; cut most of the remaining cross-border trade limits; and, of course, sell off state-owned industries. In July 1990 Mexico's business reform plan under Harvard-educated President Carlos Salinas was labeled the best in the world by *Wall Street Journal* editor, Robert L. Bartley.[10]

Mexico's moves toward private ownership and increased efficiency are already beginning to show good results. In 1987 the country's inflation rate was a crippling 132 percent, but it fell to 18 percent by 1990.[11] In addition, foreign investment is up sharply, providing thousands of jobs for Mexican workers. Ford Motor Company has put $1 billion into its Hermosillo export facility. Nissan Mexicana is building a new $1 billion facility in Aquascalientes with several Japanese subcontractors joining the move. Many U.S. firms including IBM, Hewlett-Packard, and Wang, are now looking for more advanced operations. High-tech suppliers are following suit by offering training to local laborers. If they are successful, said Mexico's chief trade negotiator Herminio Blanco in November 1990, "...the entire geography of industry in North America is going to change."[12]

The developments in Mexico which permit the formation of a North American Economic Community hold vast implications for the U.S. economy. David Fisher, President of the Capital Group, said in June 1990, "It can do for the United States what Thailand and Malaysia did for the Japanese: supplying low-cost labor. That would be good for Mexico and good for the United States. It's hard for the politicians to talk about this, but the direction is pretty sure."[13]

Of course, Mexico still shows many signs of its troubled past including third-rate roads, unworkable phones, contaminated water, and one-fourth of its people living in poverty. Those problems are the "Achille's heel of the economy," said Ernesto Warnholtz, head of Mexico's largest exporter's association, in July 1990.[14] However, most Mexicans now realize that economic development led by private enterprise, not socialism, is the way to solve those problems.

In response to growing optimism about Mexico's future, the country's stock market has more than doubled since 1989. Several U.S. analysts expect it to jump much more during the early 1990s. If so, Mexican investments could be among the best performing stocks of the decade. Although the safest way to invest in Mexico is through a country fund, many leading Mexican stocks are also attractive. That is particularly true of those in basic industries that will benefit broadly as the country grows. Of the group, Mexico's telecommunication company appears to be the most attractive.

Mexico Fund is a closed-end investment company with the goal of long-term capital appreciation through investments in Mexican equities. In the fall of 1990, over 90 percent of the fund's assets were in Mexican common stocks in the fields of development, retail sales, mining, electronics, construction, petrochemicals, and communications. As the Mexican government privatizes oil, gas, railroad, and electric companies, it is anticipated that this fund will take selected positions in those areas as well. The fund's investment advisor is Impulsora del Fondo Mexico, S.A. de C.V.

Mexico Equity and Income Fund differs from the Mexico Fund by seeking current income as well as capital appreciation. During normal periods, the fund maintains at least 50 percent of its assets in convertible debt securities issued by Mexican companies. The other half is held in equities and various debt securities issued in Mexico. The fund's investment advisor is Acci Worldwide, S.A. de C.V. with Advantage Advisors, Inc., a unit of Oppenheimer & Co., as its American co-advisor.

Telefonos de Mexico (often called "Telemex" in the United States) provides both local and long distance telephone services to individual and commercial clients in Mexico. The company was partially privatized in December 1989 when a 51 percent stake was sold to a group composed of Southwestern Bell, France Telecom, and Groupo Carso of Mexico. The balance of the company is being made available to individual investors through a series of stock offerings on global markets. The most recent offering occurred in the United States in May 1991. Telephonos is noteworthy because of its central position in the modernization of Mexico. Economic growth will provide the company with the opportunity to greatly expand its services. That is particularly true, because modernization requires first rate telecommunications not only for voice, but also for facsimile machines, computer networks, and other electronic devices. All in all, as Mexico prospers so will Telemex.

Cuba Will Turn from Fidel to Freedom

Cuba is becoming one of the most impoverished nations in our hemisphere. When the Soviet Union sharply reduced its economic aid in 1989, the country—which hasn't been self-supporting since its revolution—began a downward slide. By the spring of 1991, the situation had become so desperate that many Cubans began using inner tubes, oil drums, and even beach balls to float themselves to Florida.

Despite Fidel Castro's great personal popularity, it is clear that a major change is near in Cuba. The situation holds promise for U.S. investors, because thousands of Cuban nationals are waiting in the United States to help rebuild their homeland as soon as conditions permit. These Cubans are well educated, hard working, and generally very successful. Their talent and resources promise to turn Cuba into an overnight economic miracle. When the opening bell rings on that move, investors will need to act quickly or miss out on the best opportunities.

Investing Broadly in Less Developed Countries

For many investors, it may not be desirable to take positions in country funds or the individual issues of less developed nations. Such positions may be volatile because they can be influenced by events that have big impacts on small markets. Hazards include natural disasters, political unrest, currency devaluation, rampant inflation, and security fraud.

An alternative is to invest in funds that target a group of countries in one region. The added diversity of such funds can reduce risks considerably, while still allowing investors to participate in the growth of the area. Some regional funds are also open-ended. Because such funds are not traded on exchanges, their prices depend only upon the net asset values of their portfolios. Although that limits an investor's ability to use market sentiment to advantage, it can also reduce volatility.

Closed-end Regional Funds

Scudder New Asia Fund is a diversified, closed-end investment company that seeks capital appreciation from the stocks of Pacific Rim countries. The fund's management intends to place approximately 35 percent of its assets in smaller Japanese companies which appear to have the ability to grow significantly. At least 65 percent of the fund's assets will be devoted to the equity securities of Japan, Korea, Thailand, Hong Kong, India, the Philippines, Malaysia, Singapore, and others. Except for Japan, no more than 30 percent of assets will be devoted to any one country. Because the countries of the Western Pacific are among the most promising for the 1990s, the Scudder New Asia Fund should perform well. The fund's investment advisor is the respected U.S. firm, Scudder, Stevens & Clark, Inc.

Asia Pacific Fund is a closed-end investment company that is quite similar to the Scudder Fund with one important exception—it does not devote a fixed portion of its portfolio to Japaneses stocks. Under normal circumstances, at least 80 percent of the fund's assets are invested in Asian equities from Thailand, Singapore, Malaysia, Hong Kong, Korea, and the Philippines. The fund's investment manager is Baring International Investment (Far East) Ltd. The fund's U.S. administrator is Prudential Mutual Fund Management.

Latin American Fund is a closed-end investment company that seeks capital appreciation from the securities issued by various Latin American countries. Under normal conditions the fund expects to keep a minimum of 65 percent of its assets in the securities of Brazil, Chile, and Mexico. Equities of other companies which derive at least 50 percent of their revenues from Latin America may also be included. The fund's advisors are BEA Associates (equities and corporate debt instruments) and Salomon Brothers (debt instruments issued by Latin American governments).

Open-end, No-load Regional Funds

There are also many fine open-end regional funds which offer top prospects for growth. Representative samples from three respected companies are mentioned here. Because more are being added almost monthly, investors should consult a current mutual fund directory for an up-to-date list before making a final selection.

Financial Strategic Portfolio: Pacific Basin Fund is a no-load, open-end fund that invests broadly in the Western Pacific and the Far East. As of late 1990 securities in the fund came principally from Japan, Australia, Hong Kong, Malaysia, Singapore, and the Philippines. Under normal circumstances, 80 percent of the assets are held in equities. The balance is in various debt instruments from the Pacific Basin and the United States.

Vanguard International Equity Index Fund: Pacific Portfolio is a unique no-load fund that seeks to track the movements of the Morgan Stanley International Pacific Index. The index consists of more than

400 companies from Japan, Australia, New Zealand, Hong Kong, and Singapore whose economies lead the region. Vanguard also offers a European (index) Portfolio and a Combined Portfolio that tracks both regions.

T. Rowe Price New Asia Fund is a no-load fund that invests in both large and small companies of the Pacific Basin, outside Japan. This diversified fund holds equity securities from Australia, New Zealand, Korea, Taiwan, Indonesia, Malaysia, Singapore, Thailand, and Hong Kong. T. Rowe Price also offers the International Discovery Fund which holds equities from other emerging nations besides the Western Pacific and the Far East.

American Companies That Invest in Less Developed Countries

Generally, American participation in Third World development has not kept up with that of other industrial countries. Of the $22 billion invested in Malaysia, Thailand, and Indonesia from 1986 through 1989, only $3 billion was American. The remaining $19 billion came from Japan, Korea, Hong Kong, and Singapore. The U.S. companies that are investing in LDCs are those that are also taking strong positions in other parts of the world. Because the best of these multinational firms offer investors some of the best opportunities of the decade, the next chapter will cover these companies more completely.

NOTES

1. Nomura Securities International, "Monthly Reports," January 1990–January 1991.
2. Denis F. Simon, et al., "Globalization and Regionalization Of the Pacific Rim," *Business Week*, Fall 1990.
3. Andrew Tanzer, "What's Wrong With This Picture?" *Forbes*, November 26, 1990.
4. Ibid.
5. Ibid.
6. Ibid.
7. Dinah Lee, et al., "Rebuilding the Tiger: Who'll Get the Lion's Share?" *Business Week*, March 25, 1991.
8. Caspar W. Weinberger, "Three Strong Pacific Dragons," *Forbes*, April 1, 1991.
9. Robert M. Bleiberg, "First Philippine Fund: Unless Things In the Islands Improve There Won't Be Another," *Barron's*, October 22, 1990.

10. David Goodman, "A Revolution You Can Invest In," *Forbes*, July 9, 1990.

11. Ibid.

12. Stephen Baker, et al., "Mexico: A New Economic Era," *Business Week*, November 12, 1990.

13. Marcia Berss, "How to Buy the Third World," *Forbes*, June 25, 1990.

14. Matt Moffett, "Mexico Boosts Role of Private Investment," *The Wall Street Journal*, July 2, 1990.

CHAPTER 5

GLOBAL LIFESTYLES CREATE GLOBAL MARKETS

Nearly a century ago, during a severe downturn, J. P. Morgan warned investors, "The man who is a bear on the future of the United States will end up broke."[1] Although that statement is not witty or poetic, Morgan's bullish observation on America's long-term prospects remains accurate today. That's particularly true as a result of our nation's growing role in the rapidly expanding global economy of the 1990s.

Cross-border trading and international investing are already flowing at unprecedented levels which will increase dramatically as the decade progresses. As Unisys chairman W. Michael Blumenthal noted in May 1990, multinational corporations are establishing new manufacturing and distribution networks around the world "without particular reference to national borders."[2] The borderless firms are positioning themselves for the substantial profits which are becoming available as increasing world prosperity and freedom boosts the demand for every imaginable product and service.

Most of the new international businesses resemble stateless corporations that can pass for insiders in every country where they set up their offices. Nevertheless, the multinational firms remain powerful engines of prosperity for their countries of origin. Happily, the most promising of the new global powerhouses are American companies. During the 1990s they will generate billions of dollars for investors who have the foresight to take early positions in the leading firms and then hold them for the long term.

DEMOCRACY SELLS

There can be no doubt that American companies stand to receive the lion's share of the expanding global markets. The entire world is enamored with America's way of life—and it isn't just our affluence that is envied. Most people in other countries genuinely admire the freedoms that are available in the United States. Many of those people have historically suffered beneath ruling classes of one sort or another; all-powerful religious figures, dictators, old-world aristocracies, or entrenched political systems. For much of the world, America represents the hope for the future. In addition, America is the first truly international country. There is not a single ethnic group that does not have some representation in the United States. For all its social inequities and economic turmoil, America remains the land of opportunity.

America also remains the land of justice, however imperfectly it may be administered. Along with movies, midday soaps, and game shows, America's overseas television includes courtroom programs plus actual trials of every type. Many foreign nationals are astounded to see average citizens receive impartial treatment in our courts—something they don't always observe in their own countries.

Fortunately, the world is moving decisively toward democratic systems, economies that encourage private business, larger recognition of individual and civil rights, and "American" ways of doing things. And when people have the right to choose their governments, they usually have the right to choose the products they buy. Increasingly, they are buying American as a glance at our growing export figures clearly reveals.

AMERICAN CULTURE

Modern communication media has allowed the world to look into America and see its wealth; a situation that often stands in stark contrast with their own. Even former tribesmen in New Guinea regularly watch Disney movies and U.S. news broadcasts on televisions powered by portable generators. Since the United States is a racial melting pot, people in every part of the world can see members of their ethnic groups living in good homes, driving new cars, and holding positions of leadership in American business and politics.

It is now apparent that economic power by itself does not spread culture. Both Japan and Europe possess immense resources and rich, deep histories, but neither of their cultures are being emulated. In fact, Japanese and European youth copy America's latest fads in dress, music, and a broad sample of consumer products. American manufacturers clearly have the upper edge at capturing global markets. Of course, there are some exceptions. We will not become the VCR-makers of the world. In a general sense though, the successful sellers will be American. "When it comes to popular culture," said Boston University sociologist Peter Berger in March 1990, "I think we can talk about an almost absolute American hegemony, in anything ranging from music to clothing to food to lifestyles in the broadest sense."[3]

It is significant that the love affair with U.S. consumer products holds true even in anti-American countries such as Iran. On our television screens we often see mobs of angry people protesting U.S. foreign policy. But as millions of American viewers have noted, the protesters often march while wearing Levi jeans and Nike tennis shoes. After the protest, the demonstrators go home to other U.S. products and watch popular U.S. shows on TV.

What America's customers are buying, agree many economists, is their own piece, however small, of the American dream. As Jim Fisher, assistant professor of American Studies at Yale noted in March 1991, "It's about a dream, a utopian fantasy. It's rooted in the same kinds of dreams and fantasies that American advertising has been based on since the 1920s."[4] These dreams, portrayed in more than four decades of promotions by American companies, are dreams of freedom for the individual, freedom to start a new kind of life, and freedom to rise as high as drive and ability will allow.

These freedoms and dreams are tied to images of the American way of life and the products that we use. As American firms continue to move into the eager markets of developing nations, the seeds of 40 years of U.S. advertising and media exports will yield top profits for many leading U.S. firms.

THE WORLD IS BECOMING BIGGER

More people will be added to the world in the 1990s than in any prior decade, according to the Population Reference Bureau, a private research group in Washington, D.C.[5] It took 11 years for the last billion people to be born, but these analysts expect another billion people to begin life before the end of the 1990s. While some regions of the world will see more new children, other areas will decline in population. Bangladesh, Egypt, and China are seeing declining births, while Sweden, Germany, Iceland, and Finland are experiencing increases in fertility rates.

Depending on regional circumstances, both growth and decline in populations can be good news for investors. Some emerging nations have been held back by exploding populations. Declines will help them to develop and prosper. On the other hand, affluent nations will become bigger consumers by having growing populations.

The real potential that is revealed by world census figures can be lost in terms of millions and billions. A simple math calculation tells the full story. America's population broke 200 million during the 1980s. Global population will top 6 billion during the late 1990s.[6] This means that the actual size of the world's potential consumer market is 30 times what the domestic U.S. market was during the last decade! Of course, not all of the world's people have the income of 1980s Americans, but a surprising number are doing very well, particularly in Western Europe and the emerging nations of Asia. Most of the others are catching up with all due haste.

THE WORLD IS ALSO BECOMING WEALTHIER

Many investors don't realize how well much of the world now lives. Although we have fairly accurate views of Western Europe and Japan, our image of most other countries is too often based upon sensationalist news stories which show huge numbers of people living in abject poverty. Where modern cities are presented, they are thought to be atypical islands of affluence surrounded by illiterate, preindustrialized populations. However, as we saw in the previous chapter, dozens of emerging countries no longer fit their old stereotypes. American visitors who venture to many former Third World countries are often astounded by the emerging prosperity they encounter. Although such lands may be poor by Western standards, the inhabitants generally have an abundance of brand-name consumer products—and they want more.

From Budapest to Bangkok, there is also a rapidly emerging middle class that is doing well by anyone's standards. This affluent group represents a particularly important new consumer market for U.S. products and services. Overall, the 1990s will be an American decade for filling these expanding needs.

ADVICE FOR INVESTORS: BIGGER IS BETTER

Global markets are so huge and complex that only the strongest corporations have the financial muscle to capture its business. Not only does worldwide expansion cost money directly, but it can also take a long time before it begins to generate returns. During that period, new ventures are major financial burdens for their sponsors. Small firms simply do not have the resources to play the game.

Political considerations also favor large firms. Because they have the capability to establish complete operations, the big firms can more easily blend in with foreign landscapes. Local acceptance is achieved, and political troubles are avoided. It works so well that "going local" is now standard procedure among our most successful firms. As IBM World Trade Corp Senior Vice-President C. Michael Armstrong said about his company in May 1990, "IBM, to some degree, has successfully lost its American identity."[7]

Circumventing trade restrictions is another benefit of size. When protective regulations are bothersome, large companies simply make everything they need in their host countries using local labor and materials. Of course, that makes everybody happy. Operations on such a scale are beyond the reach of small firms no matter how excellent their products and management may be.

The advantages of large companies are reflected among both American and foreign institutional investors, and these companies all but guarantee that their stocks will perform well in the 1990s. Of course, a big reason large stocks are favored is that institutions can pour their billions of dollars into them without pushing their prices all over the board. Another factor influencing the attractiveness of larger U.S. stocks is that they usually pay much larger dividends than smaller stocks pay. As a result of the Tax Reform Act of 1986, dividends are now on an equal footing with capital gains, which makes them even more attractive.

The growing advantages of large corporations in the international business and investment worlds will be a dominant trend of the 1990s. It is one trend that should also dominate the minds of astute investors. Although many people may not expect blue chips to act like growth stocks, I believe investors will be astounded by their performance over the next few years.

A NEW NIFTY FIFTY FOR THE 1990s

The trend toward large stocks is bringing back the Wall Street phrase, *the nifty fifty*, which can be a misleading term, since the number of corporations with reserves deep enough to play in global markets is actually several times that number. The original nifty fifty were a group of stocks in the 1960s that were able to make money even during slow economic times when smaller companies floundered. The favored few were able to prosper because they had well established distribution systems, in-place manufacturing operations, and trained salesforces, as well as proven customer bases. They also had a habit of sticking to their main businesses, which they expanded steadily. What we are now seeing, and will continue to see in the 1990s, is a similar nifty fifty phenomenon. It is also directly related to company size and strength but is taking on a global scale.

The outlook for the new nifty fifty appears to be excellent. As money management advisor Roger Engemann, of Pasadena, California, forecast in July 1990, "We expect these stocks' earnings to grow at 20 percent plus per year for the next five years."[8] If so, the new nifty fifty stocks are likely to perform as they did in the 1960s and early 1970s. At that time their price-earnings ratios rose well beyond that of the market average and returned very attractive profits to investors.

Of course, the new nifty fifty cycle will eventually end as it did very sharply once before; but then cycles are a normal part of the investment scene. What counts is how they are played. Investors who buy wisely and don't overstay their welcome can expect to make a great deal of money as top U.S. firms make full use of the global economic expansion.

STOCKS TO WATCH

The best strategy for profiting from global economic growth is to buy leading stocks for the long term and hold on to those investments. Ignore temporary market fluctuations. Use economic downturns to increase positions at bargain prices. Always keep in mind that these stocks, in many ways, are the core of America's economic power in the

1990s. As such they should occupy central positions in the portfolios of every investor.

Entertainment: Our Biggest Export

The international love affair with American culture begins with our entertainment industry. Hollywood films have been exported since the invention of the carbon arc light. Television programs followed just as quickly. For better or worse, America's movies, television shows, and musical exports provide the long distance window through which the world views our culture. No other country has an equal to America's entertainment capabilities. Just as Americans seem equipped with an insatiable appetite for cartoons, shows, movies, and pop music, so goes the rest of the world's population. No matter how different their cultures may be, foreigners love nearly everything our entertainment industry produces.

Interestingly, overseas viewers often do not enjoy our shows for the same reasons we do. For example, French and Middle Eastern viewers watch the TV show, "Dallas," because they enjoy seeing J. R. get his just desserts. Scriptwriters for "Dallas" and other programs understand the differences in foreign interests and make sure the productions take them into account. Although it may surprise many American viewers, our preferences are only one part of the program equation for top shows that are worked out with near mathematical precision.

The market for U.S. entertainment is large and growing rapidly. As more of the world's population can afford television, radio, and stereo equipment, our entertainment industry will reap even more profits than they do now.

Walt Disney Company is a leading supplier of film and television entertainment to the world. Disney's wholesome cartoons, films, TV shows, and video programs are able to penetrate many tightly censored foreign markets that lock out other movies and shows. Even political radicals who profess to hate America are usually happy to take their children to see the Disney classics.

Disney is also noteworthy for its expanding theme parks. In addition to Disneyland in California and the Walt Disney World Complex in Florida, there is the prosperous Tokyo Disneyland. A new park is expected to open in France in 1992. Others will almost certainly be created to meet the expected demands of a rapidly developing world.

Finally, the company founded Touchstone and Hollywood Pictures to branch into more contemporary, adult markets. Both ventures are doing very well at home and abroad.

Disney would be attractive for its traditional entertainment business alone. With the additional potential of its theme parks and new film companies, the firm is almost a sure bet for the long term. (Readers who want more information about this excellent company may wish to read Ron Grover, *The Disney Touch: How a Daring Management Team Revived an Entertainment Empire*, Homewood, Ill.: Business One Irwin, 1991.)

Time Warner is the largest entertainment, media, and publishing company in the world. The company's film operations provide 17 percent of its revenue; cable TV, 16 percent; magazines, 24 percent; and books, 13 percent. Products owned include *Time, Sports Illustrated, Fortune, Asiaweek*, Warner Bros., Warner Cable Communications, and Home Box Office (HBO).

In 1991, Time Warner formed a 50/50 venture, The Columbia House Co., with Sony. The company also purchased global home video distribution rights from Pathe Communications for its MGM/UA, Pathe, and Cannon film libraries. Those moves gave the company the world's top position for home video distribution. All in all, Time Warner is very well positioned to profit in the 1990s.

Fast Foods and Drinks Find Ready Markets

Second only to the overseas passion for American entertainment is the popularity of our fast food and ever-popular carbonated beverages. Around the world, almost everyone associates these products with the "seen-on-TV-lifestyles" that Americans enjoy.

The world's infatuation with hamburgers and colas is disappointing in some respects because we offer cultural values that we think are far more valuable. But almost every other nation on earth has a longer history and a deeper culture than we do. What they don't have are the things that are unique to the American lifestyle of success, vitality, and freedom—and that is what they want to acquire.

Even in the most remote areas of the world, in places that appear to have little outside contact, the locals know about our foods and beverages. Curiously, the products also find enormous markets in advanced countries such as Japan and throughout Europe. Even in the formerly closed society of the Soviet Union, the first McDonald's was mobbed on opening day and has been the nation's most popular eating place ever since.

From an investor's standpoint our fast-food and beverage industries have great appeal despite the fact that the products they produce may seem like frills to us. Few other exports have as large a potential market. Moreover, that market is already presold before the products arrive. Its a marketer's dream. It is also important that almost everyone in the developing world can afford our fast foods and beverages. Although a cola may be expensive by local standards, it is nevertheless an affordable treat for millions of people. Each passing year of growing prosperity increases those numbers by additional millions.

Finally, most of the world is still wide open to the American fast-food and beverage industries. Despite all the jokes about creating a McWorld, the situation couldn't be better for long-term investors.

McDonald's is clearly the dominant player in the international fast-food industry. About three-fourths of its sites are located in the United States. However, the company is generating growing profits from its 3,227 foreign units. Around the world, these fast-food restaurants offer a universally popular menu of hamburgers, french fries, chicken, fish, specialty sandwiches, drinks, and desserts—as well as many local treats.

McDonald's is particularly noteworthy because it has a history of making long-range plans and sticking to them. The company's attitude is to do whatever it takes to become established in its target areas. For example, in the Soviet Union, McDonald's started farms and businesses to raise beef and make the supplies it needs. Although the payoff from such long-range programs may be years away, it promises to be substantial. I think the company is headed for a very successful decade.

Coca-Cola is the largest soft drink company in the world and makes the world's most popular bottled beverage. Other drinks include Diet Coke, Tab, Sprite, Diet Sprite, Fanta, Fresca, Cherry Coke, and Minute Maid. Coke is rapidly becoming an international company, perhaps even a "stateless" company. In 1989, over 50 percent of revenues and 76 percent of profits came from foreign operations. Both percentages are expected to increase as the company continues to expand its global operations into increasingly affluent markets.

Consumer Banking, a Uniquely American Idea

Many overseas countries have economies that are growing faster than that of the United States. Most such countries have rapidly emerging middle classes that are eagerly looking for ways to make better use of their increasing prosperity. One way they can do so is by using credit and other consumer banking services.

Unfortunately for millions of newly affluent people in many foreign countries, local banks are often reluctant to offer credit to ordinary working- and middle-class citizens. The very idea makes no sense to bank officials who live in nations where financial institutions exist solely to serve businesses. Of course, those banks are also unfamiliar with most other consumer services. Even personal checking accounts are usually unavailable to all but wealthy and influential clients.

American banks, of course, are the most consumer-oriented, mass-market financial institutions in the world. They have fine tuned their checking and credit card businesses to yield maximum profits. Not surprisingly, many of our banks are now expanding their services to overseas markets—and meeting with great success. H. Robert Heller, former Federal Reserve Board governor and later a Visa International executive, predicted in August 1990, that charge volume on Visa cards in Europe alone will hit $250 billion by 1993, a larger amount than is generated in the United States.[9] The potential for consumer credit in Asia is even greater. Combined they should approach three-fourths of a trillion dollars annually by the end of the decade. That is an attractive business by anyone's standards.

Citicorp, the largest U.S. bank and tenth-largest bank in the world, is moving quickly to create a substantial international presence. The company already has offices in 89 foreign countries and is continuing to expand as conditions permit. So far, credit card operations have been established in 18 foreign markets, with many more on the way.

Although Citicorp derives most of its revenues from consumer banking, it is also an important player in institutional and investment markets—both at home and abroad. The company's broad presence in all the world's financial affairs should pay off handsomely during the 1990s.

American Express Company is finding that its "travel related service business" is highly desirable in most foreign markets. The firm already has over 10 million charge card holders outside the United

States. More importantly, over 100 million more people in foreign countries could qualify for the card, a huge potential market.

As the world becomes more affluent, the leading edge of that wave will produce many new American Express customers. If that business grows as expected, and if the firm's investment and insurance businesses also do well, American Express should have a good decade.

Chase Manhattan Corp. owns America's third-largest bank, with established operations in international credit. The company also offers a wide range of financial services to larger corporations, governments, and other financial institutions. Chase carries about 10 million credit card accounts worldwide.

Although Chase is not a consumer banking pure play, the company should appeal to investors who desire a banking investment with diversified global interests. The firm's overseas income has quadrupled from 1987 to 1990. That growth should continue as the world becomes more prosperous and more involved in both commercial and consumer activities.

Growing Markets for Common Household Products

Although they are not as glamorous as Hollywood movies, there are growing overseas markets for America's ordinary household products. A fascination with American goods is not behind such sales. Instead, U.S. household goods are in demand simply because they are innovative and effective.

High production, shipping, and import costs have always made American products among the most expensive of their type in foreign shops. Until recently, the only overseas buyers for these products were the relatively small middle- and upper-class populations. Now, as prosperity finds its way to more countries, many millions of additional consumers will be able to afford these goods. That will be even more true as increased overseas production lowers costs and makes products more accessible.

Household product companies have the added advantage of being rather insensitive to economic cycles. Although one might expect that during tough times people would buy less expensive brands, they tend not to do so. Brand loyalty is very strong for everything from toothpaste to relish.

Growing worldwide prosperity, expanding populations, and improved U.S. product distribution systems are all coming together to provide an excellent sales environment for U.S. household products. The leading firms should have an excellent decade.

Colgate-Palmolive is a worldwide producer and distributor of many household products. The company's line includes detergents, household cleaners, bleach, toothpaste, laundry detergent, hair care products, shaving products, and bath soaps. Trade names include Colgate, Palmolive, Ajax, Fab, and Science Diet. In addition, the company has many regional tradenames.

Colgate-Palmolive is already well established in overseas markets, which contributed 64 percent of its income in 1989. Early 1990s reports indicate that total sales growth of 13 percent was made primarily in Europe, Canada, the Far East, and Africa. Colgate is particularly attractive because it should be able to increase its margins at the same time it increases overall sales. Of course, that would give an added boost to profits.

Procter & Gamble is one of the largest consumer products companies in the world with operations in more than 140 countries. Its highly diversified product line includes laundry and home cleaning products, personal care products, plus food and beverages. Tradenames in the laundry/cleaning category include Bounce, Cheer, Comet, Ivory Snow, Mr. Clean, Spic & Span, Tide, and Top Job. Personal care and cosmetics brands include Camay, Ivory, Zest, Charmin, Pampers and Luvs disposable diapers, Old Spice, Crest, Prell, Vidal Sassoon, Oil of Olay, Pepto-Bismol, and Vicks cough drops. This line of products appears particularly promising for P&G as millions of additional people around the world strive for the good life.

I expect Procter & Gamble to continue its climb through the 1990s, boosted by gains in production efficiency and greater expansion of its operations in foreign countries. Foreign sales accounted for 39 percent of company income at the close of 1990.

H. J. Heinz is a leading producer of food products which have long shelf lives, an important consideration for a food producer aiming for global markets. Heinz's products include ketchup and other condiments, pet food, frozen foods, and canned tuna. Products are sold under several labels including Heinz, Star-Kist, 9-Lives, Ore-Ida, WeightWatchers, California Home Brands, and Champion Valley Farms.

During the 1980s Heinz expanded into the pet food market and off-the-shelf diet foods, both of which are becoming top money makers. The company also began moving strongly into overseas markets which should pay off handsomely in the 1990s. The company is now established in Canada, England, Europe, Australia, South America, and Japan. Further overseas development is planned, since it is proving to be among the firm's most profitable operations. By the end of 1990 foreign sales were producing 38 percent of income.

Surprising Potential for U.S. Automobile Sales

Most American investors assume that U.S. automakers have little chance for significant sales in global markets. We consider most foreign cars to be better engineered, better crafted, and more fuel efficient than U.S. vehicles. Fortunately, such assumptions are incorrect, and overseas buyers know it. Consequently, in many foreign countries American cars sell very well. During the 1990s such sales should begin to have a big effect on American automakers' profits.

There are two principal reasons behind growing foreign sales of U.S. cars. The first is based on the very human "grass-is-greener" phenomenon that is at work all over the world. For example, in the United States, we perceive almost every product from Europe and Japan as being more desirable than domestic goods. This is why people will pay twice as much for a bare-bones German luxury car than they will for a fully equipped American sedan which is many times the value. Fortunately, the same thinking to some degree occurs overseas. For example, a posh American turnpike cruiser is considered a prestige car in almost every foreign market including those that produce excellent cars of their own. A big Lincoln will turn heads on the German autobahn every kilometer of the way. In Japan, people have been observed bowing to black Cadillacs and Imperials. However, the phenomenon will lead to very serious profits as people become more affluent and trade barriers collapse throughout the world.

The second reason for rising foreign sales of U.S. cars hinges on quality and price. American auto manufacturers have improved on both these aspects in recent years. As a result, most U.S. cars are now essentially on a level with most European and Japanese products.

From an investor's standpoint overseas sales are particularly important in assessing an automaker's prospects. That is because domestic sales are not growing significantly since the United States is becoming primarily a replacement market. Only foreign business has the potential for substantial growth. Because of the recession, the earnings outlook for U.S. automakers does not appear very good at present [Spring 1991] and stock prices are low. Interested investors could make good use of the attractive prices to take long-range positions.

Ford Motor Company is already on its way to becoming a global automotive powerhouse. In 1989 foreign operations accounted for 36 percent of vehicle sales. Products are made in Canada, Great Britain, Belgium, Brazil, Mexico, and Australia, to name just the principal areas. Exports go to nearly every country in the world.

The recession hit all U.S. automakers hard in 1991. Ford's first quarter losses set records. Nevertheless, this company's long-range prospects appear to be very good. When purchased at attractive levels, the stock should be well suited for conservative portfolios. This is especially true since over the past 15 years the company only skipped its dividend once, during the recession of 1982.

General Motors is the largest maker of automobiles in the world. As is the case with Ford, the 1990–91 recession created record losses. That decline is magnified by GM's position as the highest cost producer in the United States. Shrinking market share from Japanese competition also took its toll. However, GM's foreign operations have been very profitable, a fact that is not lost on the company's management. Foreign operations now account for 16 percent of sales, a number that will almost certainly be increasing in the future.

GM is also taking great steps to turn itself around at home. Large restructuring efforts were made in 1990. In addition, the firm's new, highly automated Saturn plant is now operational. Because of these actions—plus the greater foreign sales potential—General Motors appears positioned for a turnaround in the 1990s. That could make the stock a very big winner. Meanwhile, investors will have their dividends to keep them going—the company hasn't missed one in over 15 years. General Motors will also be discussed further in later chapters.

Demand Increases for Computers and Office Products

A few years ago the United States dominated the computer and office automation industry. Now, American firms are beginning to feel the heat of competition in the global market, especially from Japanese,

Korean, and Taiwanese firms. However, American makers of business computers and related office products still hold key positions in this field and will benefit substantially from increasing world commerce in the 1990s.

One of the most important moves that U.S. high-tech firms can use to increase their business in the 1990s is the formation of alliances with their overseas counterparts. The agreement between AT&T and Italy's Olivetti during the mid-1980s is an example of the kind of business arrangement that works to the benefit of each partner. AT&T provided Olivetti with badly needed telecommunications technology in exchange for its line of personal computers. The formation of international alliances is particularly important because it makes it possible for American firms to gain access to markets that would otherwise be very difficult to penetrate. Of course, alliances also help circumvent protectionist trade legislation that many countries set up to protect high-tech industries.

As is the case with automobiles, increased foreign sales are very important for the U.S. computer industry. According to InfoCorp, a market research firm, U.S. personal computer sales may grow only 8 percent in 1991. However, worldwide sales are expected to grow 15 percent.[10] Longer term, the foreign potential is particularly promising because it is based on new rather than replacement sales.

Unlike the situation in the automotive industry where all the players are huge, the computer and office automation area offers investors a full range of choices. Investors can stick with the bluest of the blue chips or go with smaller companies whose stocks could easily quadruple in price during the decade.

International Business Machines (IBM) needs little introduction. The company is the world's leading manufacturer of mainframe computers, workstations, and automated office equipment. IBM's other lines of personal computers, software, and peripherals also enjoy a large following. In addition, IBM offers data processing supplies, maintenance programs, support services, and financing.

IBM is known for its ability to blend into overseas markets. The firm is accepted everywhere, because it spends millions of dollars on infrastructure, hires foreign nationals almost exclusively, and supports many local suppliers. Foreign operations supplied 50 percent of revenues in 1989.

Industry seers sometimes predict that IBM will lose out to smaller firms that can be "more innovative and more responsive to changing market preferences." Although it is true that Big Blue can't change directions on a dime, it more than compensates with a superb product development program, a full line of systems, top support services, and an effective salesforce. Although IBM can have bad years—as is true at present—overall, the company can be expected to do well in the 1990s.

COMPAQ Computer is nearly at the opposite end of the size spectrum from IBM. Nevertheless, the company is the leading supplier of portable computers and is one of the top producers of personal computers. Growth has been rapid and sustained, a situation that should continue in the 1990s.

COMPAQ is doing very well in overseas markets which currently contribute about 45 percent of sales. Because the firm primarily supplies small, affordable computers, its foreign markets should expand significantly as more nations engage in more trade and become more affluent. Although COMPAQ should do well in the 1990s the firm's shares are best suited to aggressive investors who are willing to accept the wider price swings of a smaller company. This firm will be discussed more in Chapter 17.

NOTES

1. Richard Band, "Are You Wasting Your Wealth In Worry?" *Cogent Comments*, February 19, 1991.

2. William J. Holstein, et al., "The Stateless Corporation," *Business Week*, May 14, 1990.

3. Eric Felten, "Love or Hate It, America Is King of Pop Culture," *Insight*, March 25, 1991.

4. Ibid.

5. Alan L. Otten, "Growth Will Make '90s a Billion-Person Decade," *The Wall Street Journal*, June 21, 1990.

6. Ibid.

7. Holstein, "The Stateless Corporation."

8. Douglas R. Sease and Craig Torres, "Growth Stocks Take a Pounding, Showing Market's Vulnerability—Rerun of 'Nifty Fifty' Feared," *The Wall Street Journal*, July 24, 1990.

9. Robert Guenther, "Citicorp Pushes Its Bank Cards Overseas," *The Wall Street Journal*, August 20, 1990.

10. John W. Verity and Sunita Wadekar–Bhargava, "PCs: What The future Holds," *Business Week*, August 12, 1991.

SECTION 2

DEMOGRAPHIC CHANGES CREATE OPPORTUNITIES

CHAPTER 6

AN OLDER, MORE AFFLUENT POPULATION

A very significant trend that will come into full bloom in the 1990s is the accelerating wealth and population of older Americans. Already the "50-plus" population is our most affluent consumer group. As they further reap the rewards of their lifetime's efforts, they will become our largest market. As that market develops, it will present today's investors with many outstanding long-term opportunities.

WHEN EVERYTHING CAME UP ROSES

It is not difficult to see how America's senior citizens became our wealthiest. They began their careers during the booming postwar economy between 1947 and 1973. At the time, America was the center of the industrialized world. Our competition had been reduced to ashes during the war. Both Japan and Germany were in ruins, and before they fell, the Germans destroyed much of the industrial capacity of the British and the French.

Consequently, after World War II nearly anyone in the world who wanted a consumer product or a machine tool bought from an American company. The United States was the world's principal supplier for almost everything. At the same time worker productivity increased 3.3 percent a year, a rate 50 percent greater than from 1900 to 1947.[1] It is no wonder that almost every American business and occupation made money in the 1950s and 1960s.

At the same time Americans' income was going up, their living costs remained in check. The postwar years were a time of low inflation and low taxation. I remember my father complaining when his federal income tax rose to 7 percent. There was no state income tax when I was a child, there was only a property tax and a small sales tax of 2 percent. Inflation remained in the 3 to 4 percent range. Under these circumstances it was not particularly difficult to save some of the money that was earned.

Today's seniors also found themselves riding an investment tidal wave during the postwar economic boom. They watched their $5,000 bungalows sell for $25,000, $50,000, $100,000, and then $150,000! Stock market investments during that period did even better. It was a golden time for anybody with a few dollars to invest.

Following that economic advance was a huge transfer of wealth from the young to the old primarily through soaring real estate values and by funding growing Social Security and Medicare benefits. Retirees now collect between 2.5 and 4 times the money they contributed during their working years. By contrast, today's 25 year olds will have a hard time getting back 98 cents on each dollar contributed during his or her working life. In addition, the elderly received more than 75 percent of the $450 billion in social entitlements in the 1986 federal budget.[2]

NUMBERS TO WARM THE HEARTS OF INVESTORS

There can be no doubt that seniors are a rapidly growing economic force. Bureau of Census records published in 1989 show that wealth of the 65 to 69 age group increased, in constant dollars, from $169,366 per person in 1973 to $321,562 per person in 1983.[3] In March 1987 Robert England of *Insight* summarized various studies that showed that Americans in the age group 65 and older had become the second-richest group in U.S. society. The richest group were those aged 55 to 64. Total assets of the aged are almost twice that of the median for the nation. The median net worth of their households in 1984 was $60,266, while the median for all U.S. households was $32,677.[4]

People born before World War II are also proving to be big savers, which means they have the cash to finance their needs. According to Mr. England's report, certificates of deposit with a median value of $20,000 were held by 37 percent of elderly families in 1983. Although the data are not conclusive, the median value of CDs for the upper third of the elderly is almost certainly twice as high today.

Analysis of individual wealth statistics reveal the surprising result that today's retirees are actually earning more than workers, a historical reversal. This growing income difference between workers and the retired is adding to the generation gap and is leading to some ill feelings. Conflicts aside, the point remains that America's aging population represents a potent economic force that is of prime significance to investors of the 1990s. Their every whim will translate into millions of dollars in profits for the leading suppliers, and their investors.

Of course, there are also many poor elderly. Census Bureau figures tell us that among the elderly are some of the nation's most destitute people whose retirement plans were scattered by renewed inflation, bankrupted pension programs, or catastrophic illness. Nevertheless, since 1982 people over 65 have reported a lower poverty rate than the rest of America's population. More importantly, they continue to gain ground every year—another reversal of historical trends.[5]

Census Bureau statistics for low income people confirm this trend towards elderly affluence. During the late 1950s more than 35 percent of those 65 and older had incomes below the federally defined poverty line. By 1987 the figure had dropped to 12.2 percent. In November 1988 Economics Professor James Schulz at Brandeis University stated, "Poverty among the elderly as measured by the poverty index and adjusted for non-money income, has virtually disappeared."[6]

HEALTHIER AND MORE NUMEROUS TOO

Not only are the elderly richer, there are also more of them. In fact, census data show there are more Americans aged 65 and older than there are teen-agers. The proportion of the population aged 65 and older is up 50 percent since 1950, and will increase another 75 percent in the coming four decades. Census data also indicate that the age group 85 and older is expanding faster than any other. It will increase another 50 percent by 1998. During the same period, the 45 to 54 group will increase about 45 percent, and those 75 to 84, 21 percent. By the year 2000, 40 year olds will outnumber 20 year olds—exactly opposite of the present age distribution.[7]

Several university studies suggest that the 85 and older group will grow far larger than government predictions. In November 1989 demographers James Vaupel and Dennis Ahlburg at the University of Minnesota indicated that the census projections may badly underestimate a continuing decline in mortality rates in later life.[8] Edward Schneider, dean of the Andrus Gerontology Center at the University of Southern California, has data that support a similar conclusion.[9]

Whatever the final number may be it will be substantial and will have a big impact on the U.S economy.

The bottom line for investors is clear. An older, affluent America will be a durable and continuing trend beyond the year 2000. People who take solid positions in this major demographic event can expect to reap very substantial rewards.

STOCKS TO WATCH

Medical Supplies, Medicine

An aging population will be particularly good news for many drug companies because the use of prescriptive medicine doubles between the ages of 30 and 60. After the age of 70 prescriptive medicine use rises another 24 percent.[10] Clearly, the growing numbers of seniors will have a significant impact on the drug industry.

Their biggest impact will be on the growing generic drug industry. In almost all cases, generic drugs work as well as higher priced brand names. Despite a highly publicized scandal in 1988–89, the economic case for generic drugs all but mandates their increased use in the 1990s. Seniors will also help boost the profits of low-cost mail order pharmacies. Medications for ongoing conditions such as high blood pressure and arthritis can be provided at substantial savings by firms that fill prescriptions through the mail.

Mylan Laboratories is a leading generic drug company that appears headed for an outstanding decade. The company is now well established and is quite profitable. In addition, Mylan is developing a line of products for the elderly market including drugs for Parkinson's, Alzheimer's, and other neurodegenerative problems.

Medco Containment Services, the leading provider of mail order medications, is also a leading contender for decade-long profits. The company operates primarily through benefit plans such as retirement systems, HMOs, and insurance companies. Through a network of participating pharmacies, Medco can even fill prescriptions for short-term illnesses at reduced costs. Medco is positioned to do well in the 1990s.

Medicine Shoppe should also benefit from the effects of the senior boom. This rapidly growing firm is already America's seventh-largest franchised drugstore chain and is by far the most tightly focused on prescription products. I think the company will move up a notch or two over the next few years.

An Exploding Need for Implantable Medical Devices

Our aging population will also substantially increase the need for many types of implantable medical devices. Since various parts of the body tend to fail years before death occurs, artificial substitutes of every type will be more and more common during the 1990s.

Medtronic appears to have the brightest future among the many companies that make personal medical devices. The firm has a very broad array of products, some of which are industry leaders. A top salesforce rounds out the company's prospects. Products include pacemakers (both implantable and nonimplantable), artificial heart valves, and other cardiac devices. Several neurological products are also produced. The company has been profitable for at least 10 years. With the exception of a small dip in 1985 those profits have increased steadily since 1981.

Nursing Home Demand to Surge

Millions more Americans in their older years, followed by the "graying" of the baby boomers, will bring a corresponding increase in demand for nursing homes. The federal government's Agency for Health Care Policy and Research calculates that more than half the women and almost one-third of the men turning 65 in 1990 will spend time in a nursing home before they die.[11] Present data reveals the need for a new 100-bed nursing home every *day* for the next ten years.

Unfortunately, nursing homes have been plagued with high operating expenses, high employee turnover rates (some as high as 100 percent per year), and reduced Medicaid payments. Rising construction costs in the late 1980s added to their troubles. Nevertheless, I expect this field to be a promising one for the 1990s and beyond, because the compelling need for these institutions will demand a solution. Possible scenarios include expanding care for presently hospital-bound patients needing only routine care; designing group wards where patients with similar ailments can be more efficiently treated; and releasing more nursing home patients to in-home assisted living situations.

Nursing homes will benefit from substantially increased government aid for the elderly. As the aging end of the nation's population continues to increase so will its political power. This trend will be enhanced by the dwindling percentage of younger people. We can expect a lot of funding to come down the political pike to support seniors' needs.

Much of that funding will flow into the private sector. Today's wiser, more practical Americans look to the government to provide a stimulus to pay some of the bills, but they look to the private sector to deliver the goods and services. This will prove to be a very significant trend for investors, most of whom assume that our social problems offer few opportunities.

Beverly Enterprises is America's largest provider and operator of nursing homes with over 860 facilities. The company has a history of problems resulting from tight Medicaid reimbursements, excess debt, and a few unprofitable facilities. Nevertheless, Beverly appears to be turning the corner. Medicare payments for nursing homes have recently been increased, a trend that I expect will continue during the 1990s simply because there is no alternative. The company is also paying down its debt and streamlining its business by selling off losing operations. Beverly Enterprises isn't out of the woods yet. However, the company offers investors considerable potential for the 1990s.

Manor Care is also an important nursing home supplier with over 160 facilities. Because it has the highest private pay clients in the industry, the company is in better financial shape than Beverly Enterprises. In addition, Manor Care operates Econo-Lodge motels, Rodeway Inns, and Choice Hotels which are presently doing well. Although Manor Care isn't a pure play, as the national situation improves for nursing homes the company will profit considerably from the trend.

Angelica Corp. is a major supplier of linen and laundry services primarily to nursing homes and other medical facilities. In addition, the company provides uniforms to the health care industry. Although I don't expect Angelica to soar in price quickly, it should have a very profitable future in its unique market niche. The company should be of particular interest to conservative investors who wish to play the growth in the nursing home market indirectly and at a minimum risk.

Assisted Living and Home Health Care Are Other Top Fields

A greater need for assisted living will also rise. As the number of people growing older increases, so will the demand for those needing help in daily living, according to the Urban Institute's analysis of two large government surveys. During 1984 nearly 5 million people age 65 and older needed help in one or more basic daily activities: dressing, eating, bathing, going to the bathroom, and particularly with medication and therapy. By 1990, the number is predicted to grow to 6.2 million, then rise to nearly 14 million by the year 2030.[12] Companies that can meet the needs of that growing market can expect to see their profits increase substantially throughout the 1990s.

Invacare Corp. is rapidly emerging as one of the nation's leading suppliers of assisted living equipment. Products include a full line of wheelchairs, three-wheeled electric "scooters," home care beds, recliners, bath safety equipment, and related devices. A major competitor is now in serious financial difficulty which should benefit Invacare considerably.

Healthdyne is moving rapidly into the growing home health care market that is being heavily influenced by our aging population. The company manufactures several medical products for use in the home, primarily by licensed practitioners. It also offers several in-the-home services through a majority-owned subsidiary (see the next entry). The company is profitable and had solid growth during 1990. Healthdyne represents a broad play on development of the in-home health trend.

Home Nutritional Services, of which Healthdyne owns 66 percent, offers investors more focus. The company provides several in-the-home medical services including nutritional therapy, intravenous therapy, pain control, oxygen services, and several treatments for AIDs patients. Home Nutrition is presently one of the largest players in its field and appears to have a very bright future.

Lifeline Systems also looks fondly at the new decade and its legions of aging citizens. The company makes emergency response devices for people with medical problems that could become critical without notice. Patients receive a small transmitter which has been programmed to send a series of prearranged signals when activated by the user. The issuing hospital or clinic has the necessary receiving and decoding equipment to enable emergency teams to respond appropriately. This small company has been profitable since 1985 and has been growing steadily.

A Growing Need for Adult Day Care

The growing economic squeeze that is affecting all Americans is forcing many seniors into the homes of their children. Often the seniors need supervision to ensure their safety, to get their medications on time, and to help maintain their mental health. This is creating an enormous need for adult day-care facilities which provide the essential services while the senior's children are at work. This new service and the opportunities it offers will be discussed in the next chapter.

Insurance Needs Expand

Older people, because they know they are more vulnerable to life's downturns, will pay handsomely for good coverage of their health, homes, possessions, and everything else in their lives. Medical supplemental policies, such as those providing the so-called medigap coverage—paying what Medicaid fails to pay—will find a particularly healthy market.

Triple-digit levels of daily nursing home costs will add to the push for more insurance. As affluent as the 50-plus group is, full-time nursing home care can quickly wipe out the assets of this age group. A study by the Harvard Medical School revealed that 45 percent of those 75 and older in Massachusetts would be reduced to poverty after just 13 weeks in a nursing home. After a two year stay, 80 to 90 percent would have exhausted their savings and sold everything they owned to cover the full-time care.[13]

American Integrity Corp. is a leading supplier of health and accident insurance. A majority of the firm's business comes from supplemental policies which are designed to fill in the gaps left by Medicare and Blue Cross, such as excess doctors fees, uncovered nursing home stays, private rooms, and so on. I think this company has the right products for the demographic and medical trends of the 1990s.

Pioneer Financial Services isn't as pure a play in supplemental policies as American Integrity. However, Pioneer is becoming an important supplier of medigap insurance. In addition, the company handles other special accident and health policies which appeal to the

50-plus population. Products are marketed through 40,000 agents, and the company has been profitable since 1983.

Unique Housing Needs

Census Bureau statistics indicate that people tend to stay in private housing until their mid-70s. It is not until their later years, as they approach 80, that they move into retirement or nursing homes. The trend is reflected by University of Rochester data which indicates that more than 90 percent of the elderly live alone or with their spouse.[14]

While many retirement communities are exploding in new areas—usually ones known primarily for tourism—an opposing trend has become evident. Most older people tend to stay put while their children leave in search of better opportunities. As a result, both the Midwest and parts of the Northeast are actually getting "grayer" than most of the Sunbelt states. Investors should keep this little-known demographic trend in mind when evaluating retirement investments in the Frostbelt. Trends always come with exceptions, and Florida is that exception. It has the oldest average population of any state, and is felt to be representative of what the rest of the nation will look like by the year 2020.

In all areas where seniors are found in large numbers, there is increasing demand for group living arrangements. Complexes that provide on-site personal security, communal meals, and a low-maintenance lifestyle will have a golden decade. Spacious mobile home parks with security fencing and sites for double- and triple-wide models are particularly in demand—a situation I would expect to soar in the 1990s. Once considered a second-class way of life, trashy trailer parks have given way to attractive planned mobile home communities, as an increasing number of affluent retirees opt for these high-end mobile home parks.

Some seniors clearly have the money to get just what they want in retirement housing. The cash usually comes from selling their city homes for several times the original investment. For example, a $300,000 suburban home usually costs less than $100,000 in many retirement areas. Of course, the difference is even greater for seniors who buy mobile homes. The money that is left over from the switch can be put to good use generating extra income—an added inducement to make the switch.

Oakwood Homes is a manufactured housing company that appears particularly well positioned for the future. The company offers everything from mobile homes to complete communities which are designed expressly for them. The company also offers in-house financing. Most products are upscale double-wide models. Housing communities are located primarily in the Sunbelt. The company is profitable, but earnings vary from year to year as is common throughout the housing industry. Long term, Oakwood's ability to offer complete housing services to its customers should continue to make it attractive.

Del Webb is a real estate developer in the Sunbelt that specializes in upscale adult retirement communities. The company has been hammered by the weak real estate market plus tough times in the Sunbelt but managed to return to profitability in the first quarter of fiscal 1991. Recently, the company also sold many unprofitable operations. Once the economy turns around this company should be in position to do very well.

Marriott Corp. is best known for its large hotel chain. However, the company is moving strongly into retirement communities and senior citizen centers which it sees as a strong growth area for the 1990s. Of course, the tough real estate market is leaving its mark on Marriott as well, causing profits to be down. But that situation should reverse itself once the economy permits the company to move forward again.

Conventional Travel Heading Toward Dollarville

A December 1989 *Wall Street Journal* survey revealed that 45 percent of retirees or their spouses would pay for an annual railway or airline pass for unlimited travel at peak times at bargain prices. And 43 percent would pay for a club membership offering trips for cultural, educational, and recreational purposes.[15]

This older, affluent group will have a lot of disposable income to make their travel desires possible. In addition, this generation is also healthy. Unlike their parents who became bedridden early in their old age, today's seniors can be about as active as they wish. It is true that the younger 35 to 54 age group travels the most. But the 55 to 64 group takes the longest, most expensive trips.[16] Travel companies, especially those that offer cruise ship packages that include airline passage to and from the port of departure, will do well with the growing senior market. Hotels and destination resorts—especially resorts that provide everything—will be big winners.

Several companies have excellent recreation hotels in various places. Some also have casino resorts in Atlantic City, Las Vegas, the Bahamas, and elsewhere. The lineup includes Caesars World, Circus Circus, Hilton Hotels, Ramada, Showboat, and Marriott.

Marriott is a company presented earlier for its careful move into retirement communities. Although Marriott is not as flashy as some of the sizzle stocks in this industry, I like the diversity it offers. The company is also expanding into many promising markets.

Carnival Cruise Lines is the world's largest passenger ship company. Although many ships cater to younger people on short vacations, several others are favorites of the older set who go for a week or more and want every luxury possible. The company also operates the Crystal Palace Resort, a top recreation and casino in Nassau, Bahamas. Rapid expansion at any cost during the 1980s and a cyclical economy put Carnival's earnings on a roller coaster. However, Carnival is becoming a more mature company with new ships and experienced management. The result should be greater and more stable earnings over the next few years.

Security Services Will Soar

Security services will be an especially big growth area in the 1990s. Because seniors are not as strong as they once were and have lost the fine edge to their senses, they feel particularly vulnerable to crime. To help even the odds older people are eager to install high-tech security systems and live in supervised housing units.

ADT Limited is the clear front-runner in the security monitoring and surveillance industry. The company operates from coast to coast and has commercial as well as residential accounts. The company has a ten-year history of steadily rising earnings which should continue through the 1990s.

Funeral Services Also Grow

Finally, since no one gets out of this game alive, funeral services will also prosper during the decade. The most notable trend in this area is against expensive funerals. More and more elderly people are deciding that burial expenses are not something they wish to pay for themselves or bequeath to their offspring. Simple memorial services followed by cremation is the plan that is becoming popular.

Another trend that is coming on strong is "cycle of life" interment that takes place in a cemetery that will become a dedicated forest or future park. Headstones are small and flat to the ground, if they are used at all. This ecologically sound "return to the earth" philosophy doesn't preclude future use of the land as a traditional cemetery does. This niche market should see continued strong growth in the 1990s.

Service Corporation International is the nation's leading operator of funeral services and cemeteries. The company recently streamlined operations by dropping unprofitable businesses that included a funeral supply subsidiary. The trend toward cremation and low-impact interment hurt profits, but the firm has adjusted by acquiring crematoriums, mausoleums, and modern cemeteries. Earnings are back on an upswing which promises to be long term.

A LONG, STABLE OUTLOOK FOR INVESTORS

Fortunately for investors, the senior industry promises to be as long lasting as it will be profitable. Census Bureau data reveal that by 1998 people aged 45 to 54 will increase 45 percent. And by the year 2000, 40 year olds will outnumber 20 year olds.[17] This demographic group, the current baby boomers, follows immediately behind today's 50-plus group and ensures that the senior industry will continue growing for at least another decade.

Another attraction to the senior market is its relative insensitivity to normal business downturns and recessions. After all, retirement income usually comes from secure sources such as pension funds, fixed income obligations, and Social Security. Since the checks keep coming regardless of what the economy is doing, most seniors don't need to cut spending during tough times. That gives the growing senior industry a great deal more stability than is generally found among investments. On the other hand, seniors are very sensitive to inflation. Since their monthly incomes tend to be fixed, any erosion in spending power hits them heavily. If high inflation returns during the 1990s the discretionary side of the senior market will not be the place to put your money.

NOTES

1. Subrata N. Chakravarty, with Katherine Weisman, "Consuming Our Children?" *Forbes,* November 14, 1988.

2. Ibid.

3. Ibid.

4. Robert England, "Greener Era for Graying America," *Insight,* March 2, 1987.

5. Chakravarty, "Consuming Our Children?"

6. Ibid.

7. Ibid.

8. Alan L. Otten, "Oldest Old May Outstrip Government's Forecast," *The Wall Street Journal,* November 28, 1989.

9. Ibid.

10. Daniel M. Kehrer, "5 Population Trends Every Investor Should Know," *Changing Times,* September 1988.

11. Alan L. Otten, "Nursing Homes Factor into More Futures," *The Wall Street Journal,* April 23, 1990.

12. Alan L. Otten, "More Old People Face Disability," *The Wall Street Journal,* March 20, 1989.

13. England, "Greener Era for Graying America."

14. Alan L. Otten, "The 'Young-Old' Often Stay Put," *The Wall Street Journal,* July 21, 1988.

15. Eugene Carlson, "Graying Market May Not Be So Golden," *The Wall Street Journal,* December 27, 1989.

16. Kehrer, "5 Population Trends."

17. Subrata N. Chakravarty, with Katherine Weisman, "Consuming Our Children?" *Forbes,* November 14, 1988.

CHAPTER 7

BOOMERS AND BUSTERS STRIVE FOR GOALS

In any decade the size, makeup, and economic strength of the working population are the most important factors for investors to consider when making long-range plans. Taking stock of our working population is particularly important now because our most powerful consumer groups are changing dramatically. Fortunately, investors can expect to be very successful over the next few years if those changes are reflected in their portfolios.

In one of the most important trends of the 1990s, America's postwar baby boomers will enter middle age. They will begin to see their careers mature and pay off. As that event occurs, the boomers will become an even more powerful economic force in our nation's population than they were in the 1980s. Coming up behind the boomers are their children the "baby busters." Although the busters are fewer in number than their parents, they too will have a big impact on the economy. In the coming decade the busters will start families of their own and begin to exert their particular preferences on our vast consumer industry.

As both the boomers and the busters strive to reach their goals they will create excellent opportunities for long-range investors.

BABY BOOMERS REACH THEIR PEAK EARNING YEARS

The previous chapter dealt with the good health and great wealth of America's elderly. Next in line are the well-known baby boomers, the 76 million people born between 1946 and 1964. They represent one-third of the entire U.S. population. Because the boomers tend to work hard and earn good money they had a great impact on the economy of the 1980s. In fact, the baby boomers were the principal driving force behind our prosperous consumer sector. Fortunately, the boomers will also have a huge impact on the 1990s. That is because they are just now entering their most productive earning years. The result will be another enormous wave of healthy, generally wealthy, and better educated consumers.

However, the maturing boomers will impact very different markets than they did during the 1980s when they were young, impulsive, and focused on material goods. By their own admission, the aging boomers are becoming more reflective, more mellow, a little wiser, more conservative, and a little less hedonistic than they were in the prior decade. These changing attitudes will have a big effect on their spending patterns over the next several years.

It is particularly important to note that boomers are becoming less focused on money and careers. It isn't that affluence and success are less important to them; they are still priorities. The difference is that the boomers are already quite successful economically and are now turning their attention to other aspects of life. Now that they have advanced well above the entry levels of their careers, they also have more time to spend on other pursuits.

It is worthwhile for investors to realize that the boomers already have many of life's major acquisitions. They purchased their homes in the 1980s and have acquired most of the furniture they need. In addition, the boomers have their families well underway. Finally, as may be seen from the collapsing sales of prestige products which started two years before the 1990–91 recession, the boomers are finally losing interest in the shallow symbols of status that they once thought were so important.

Instead, the maturing boomers are trending toward more traditional goals. They are borrowing less, saving more, and shopping more cautiously than ever before. The shift is becoming so pronounced that it is already showing up in the economy, no doubt pushed along by the recession. For example, Department of Commerce statistics indicate that consumer spending was flat during the first half of 1990, consumer debt fell by 4.6 percent, and the savings rate topped 6 percent for the first time since the early 1980s.[1] Although some analysts dispute those numbers, most of them agree that lower debt and higher savings are becoming popular. The boomers are clearly becoming a more realistic, more back-to-basics generation.

It should come as no surprise that the aging boomers are becoming home bodies, often called cocooning, in the 1990s. Former yuppies who lived at work during most the 1980s are now staying home much more. An October 1988 *Wall Street Journal* study reported that our corporate professionals, whose lives were once focused totally on their careers, now balk at late hours, frequent travel, and family neglect.[2] Company expectations that result in more time away from the family are particularly out of favor. Business people are opting for a more balanced work and home life even if it results in missed promotions or increases in salary. More than 50 percent of men polled by Robert Half International in 1990 said that they would take up to a 25 percent salary cut in exchange for more family or personal time.[3]

The increase in personal interests, homes, and families will have a large and immediate impact on the marketplace. Later in the decade when most children have left their nests, the boomers will shift focus once again. All in all, the boomers promise to help make the 1990s a very different decade than the 1980s. For knowledgeable investors those differences should also make the 1990s even more profitable.

AND THEN COME THE BABY BUSTERS

The population group coming up behind the boomers are their children, the baby busters. Because they are fewer in number than their parents, the busters' influence in major markets will cause severe problems for companies that rely heavily on the 20- to 35-year-old set. Generally, the baby busters are people who were born after 1964, the year when the U.S. birthrate began to fall after the postwar baby boom. The leanest years, between 1972 and 1978, came to be known as the "birth dearth," a period of time that saw 800,000 less new babies per year than during the boomers' birth years.

In the 1980s there were vast differences between the boomers and the busters. Maybe it was just the usual rebellion of any younger generation or perhaps it was rooted in economics, but all the designer wares, status cars, and prestige interests of their parents turned the busters off. The busters also took great exception to the money-oriented career fanaticism of their parents. In a 1988 Roper Organization poll of more than 1,000 college students, the opportunity to be creative or to exercise initiative ranked well above starting salary in evaluating job prospects. The busters also indicated strongly that they want their work to be satisfying and their lives to be meaningful. Also important were leisure time activities, family matters, homes, and outdoor experiences.[4] All in all, the busters were considered by most psychologists to be much better balanced than their parents.

TWO GENERATIONS COME TOGETHER

As we look at the attitudes of the boomers and the busters we find that a very unusual event is occurring. In a complete reversal of the usual pattern of children becoming more like their parents, we are instead seeing the parents—the baby boomers—becoming more like their children. That is to say, the boomers are backing away from their youthful hedonism with its single-minded focus on money, careers, and toys and are beginning to look upon life as their children always have.

For investors the merging of lifestyles between the boomers and the busters is extremely important. It means that all the demographic data of the past decade which shows the chasm between the values and interests of the boomers and busters must now be set aside. Instead, boomers and busters must be increasingly considered as a very potent economic force that will have a huge influence on the 1990s. I believe that investors who understand this development—and place their money accordingly—can expect to make a great deal of money in the current decade.

STOCKS TO WATCH

A New Do-It-Yourself Movement Gets Underway

As people move back to their homes we will see sales of many classic hearth and home products soar once again. This movement will get an added tailwind from the trend toward self reliance and financial conservatism. Put those trends together and you have the makings of another strong do-it-yourself movement in the 1990s.

Workshop tools of every type should do particularly well over the next several years. That includes purchases of both stationary and handheld tools, i.e., everything from table saws to handsaws. Specialized tools for home additions, furniture making, household repairs, appliance repairs, and routine automobile maintenance will be at the top of the list.

Homemaking tools and supplies should also prove to be very popular in the 1990s. Making clothes, drapes, and other fabric items is becoming popular again. Even men are getting into the fact which should be no great surprise to investors over the age of 40. Until the early 1970s tailors—like chefs—were almost always male. Now the cycle is coming back again at the same time that women are rediscovering the pleasures and the savings which come from increased reliance on home skills. A typical comment about the trend came from Alan Rosskamm, chairman of Fabri–Centers of America, who observed in July 1990 that his company's powerful growth was due to renewed interest in making things from scratch.[5]

Black & Decker is the world's largest maker of power tools primarily intended for the home and small shop. The company also makes many commercial products and has an impressive line of home appliances. Because of its broad product mix for do-it-yourself enthusiasts from the workshop to the kitchen, Black & Decker should benefit from the full range of the hearth and home movement.

Black & Decker is also becoming a multinational company. The firm presently sells its products in over 100 countries. A recent problem with excessive debt seems to be in hand but investors should wait to see before making a commitment.

Stanley Works is also a diversified tool company with many products for the do-it-yourself market. In addition, the firm makes a large number of commercial tools for professional home builders. Because Stanley's professional sales account for about one-half of their revenues, the firm isn't a pure play on the do-it-yourself movement. However, Stanley will benefit substantially from the trend. Dividends have increased steadily from 1974.

House of Fabrics owns and operates America's largest chain of home sewing stores. To date over 600 retail outlets are in operation from coast to coast. In addition to offering fabric products of every type, the company is now the biggest U.S. dealer for Singer sewing machines. House of Fabrics is particularly noteworthy for its long term move from small stores to super stores. The company should do very well in the coming years as the transition to super stores continues at the same time the hearth and home movement matures.

Fabri–Centers of America competes directly with House of Fabrics. The company has a chain of approximately 600 retail outlets which it is upgrading to larger stores. In addition, Fabri–Centers owns a smaller chain of stores that sell housewares. Fabri–Centers had a loss of $0.98 in 1988 but bounced back strongly to a $1.01 profit in 1989. Since this company may be on the rebound it could outperform House of Fabrics over the next few years. Investors should run updates on both companies before making a final selection.

Homeowners Adding on and Pushing out

Closely related to the new do-it-yourself movement is the growing home remodeling market. It is being fueled by falling wages and soft housing prices which make it more difficult for people to switch houses as their needs change. Consequently, if they require more space they will add a bedroom, home office, study, or mother-in-law unit instead of moving on to something bigger and better. Clearly, the 1990s trend will be to upgrade and remodel existing homes rather than to trade up. The trend is expected to pump millions of dollars through the home remodeling fields in the 1990s.

Building material stores that cater both to homeowners and to small contractors will benefit most from the remodeling trend. Likely to do best are stores that have everything from how-to books to the materials themselves. The best stores offer knowledgeable salespeople and even classes in how to get jobs done efficiently.

Home Depot operates a successful chain of over 120 building material and home improvement stores in the Sunbelt and in the Northeast. The company handles virtually everything the do-it-yourself homeowner and small contractor might need from tools and lumber to upscale bathroom fixtures and fireplaces.

Home Depot was a superior stock in the 1980s. Prices went from under $10 in 1987 to over $40 in 1990 before easing back in reaction to the 1990–91 recession. Fortunately, the earnings outlook continues to be very good as Home Depot adds stores at the same time the hearth and home movement develops.

Waxman Industries is a distributor of electrical, plumbing, and hardware products to retail stores which cater to the do-it-yourself and home repair markets. The company is particularly strong in the broad plumbing market, from pipes to upscale faucets, where it is now a leading supplier. The recent acquisition of U.S. Lock Corporation gives Waxman a new position in the rapidly growing home security business. As a distributor Waxman is in position to make money no matter which retail chain of home building centers proves to be the most successful. I think the company represents an attractive way to play the cocooning trend.

Knape & Vogt Manufacturing is a leading supplier of home storage products. The company makes a wide variety of shelves and shelf-hanging systems for both decorative and utilitarian uses. Drawer slides, closet rods, kitchen storage products, and closet hangers round out the product line. Some items are sold to the commercial market—mostly retail shops—as well. Knape & Vogt may not be glamorous, but its future should be prosperous. Earnings have been on a gradual upturn since 1987.

The Home Office—Even Bigger in the 1990s.

Many boomers and busters who are getting out of the rat race are establishing home businesses. Electronic information technology such as faxes, powerful personal computers, clear long distance telephone lines, and inexpensive copiers are making the home office possible. Some production work can also be done at home. Everything from custom quilts to electronic assembly is becoming a cottage industry throughout America.

The idea of a no-commute, home workplace has captured the attention of millions. According to the Bureau of Labor Statistics, there were 18.1 million part- or full-time Americans working at home in 1985 and 24.9 million in 1988. The survey projects the numbers working at home to rise to 30.8 million by 1992.[6] The increasing desire of the nation's workforce to enjoy more family time is an added factor fueling this movement. I expect this trend to create continued strong sales for home office equipment and furniture, especially more professional, efficient, compact and affordable business-oriented computer furniture systems.

Of course, the personal computer industry will also benefit from the growing home office trend. This area is so important that it will be discussed separately in Chapter 17.

HON Industries is a popular maker of affordable wood and metal office furniture ranging from desks to freestanding partitions. The company is best known for its sturdy file cabinets that are priced well below the competition's products and are very popular with small businesses. In addition, HON supplies the well-known Heatilator brand prefabricated fireplaces to the building supply and home remodeling markets. HON's office products are marketed through over 18,000 office furniture and stationery stores nationally.

Hunt Manufacturing is to small office products what HON is to office furniture. The company makes the well-known Boston brand of desktop items such as pencil sharpeners, paper trimmers, and paper punches. In addition, Hunt makes computer furniture and other computer accessories. Lastly, the company has a growing presence in the craft market that includes picture framing kits and tools. All in all, Hunt appears well positioned for both the home office and the broader hearth and home markets.

Simpler, More Comfortable Clothing—and Better Sources

Today's more conservative Americans are giving up the high-end razzle-dazzle buying interests of the 1980s. The developing trend is toward simplicity, comfort, and home-oriented merchandise that is fairly priced. Nowhere may this trend be seen more clearly than in changing clothing styles. Store labeled goods are already beginning to replace high status merchandise. Ordinary brand jeans will replace designer label jeans. Some large department store chains, such as Macy's, have already begun removing many designer labels and are replacing them with their own.

Although many stores will adapt to the growing trend toward simpler and more inexpensive merchandise, the change does not bode well for many others. Particularly shaky are inefficient stores that prospered only because their high-margin products of the 1980s made up for their problems. Now that those margins are collapsing in the face of stiff competition from factory outlets, discount stores, and catalog shopping, I think we will see many famous retailers disappear from the scene. In fact, the consulting firm Management Horizons expects more than half of the present retail firms to fail by the end of the 1990s.[7]

On the other hand, the new environment will be very kind to stores that are up-to-date not only in terms of merchandise but also in terms of management, inventory control, marketing, and distribution. Many of the biggest winners will be smaller specialty shops that focus on just one segment of the market. Those shops will handle their piece of the retail pie with the flair of a Paris boutique and the efficiency of a military campaign.

Merry-Go-Round is a highly efficient, upscale clothing chain that appears to set the standard for apparel shops of the 1990s. The company has a highly automated warehouse and order processing system that keeps its 600 stores supplied at minimum cost. The addition of trendy but private label merchandise keeps margins high while saving the customers money over designer brands. The company is expanding rapidly and appears to have a bright future.

Nordstrom is a West Coast apparel and accessory retailer with over 50 specialty and clearance outlets. The firm is famous for its high quality service, yet prices are very competitive. A high level of repeat business indicates that Nordstrom has what customers of the 1990s want. The company is now expanding its operations to the East Coast and Midwest which should be a very successful move.

Conservatism Hits the Automobile Market

Nowhere are the boomers changing values becoming more apparent than in the automobile market. Auto industry statistics reveal that reasonably priced sedans that are safe and reliable are beginning to replace the prestigious "yuppiemobiles" of the 1980s. Some of the indicators of change are quite striking. For example, Porsche sales in the United States dropped 69 percent from 1986 to 1989,[8] although they recovered somewhat in 1990. Some of the drop may be attributed to increased competition from Japanese car makers, but there is no doubt that powerful social and economic factors are also at work. It seems that in some groups showing up in a BMW can now be considered a sign of being successful but immature.

Another trend also promises to have a big impact on the auto industry of the 1990s: the move away from imported products. The switch toward domestic goods is not being fueled by patriotism but by economics. Rising costs overseas and a moderately priced dollar are making many imports increasingly expensive. At the same time the quality of many U.S. products is soaring. The result should be a slow but significant shift to stylish but cost-effective models made by Ford, Chrysler, General Motors, and U.S. branches of Honda. Of the group, I like GM and Honda the best for long-term accounts, because they have well established products and should remain profitable even during normal economic downturns.

General Motors is the world's largest automobile manufacturer. The company has its share of problems but it also has a strong balance sheet and the necessary talent to solve those problems. GM's new Saturn plant is considered state-of-the-art even by Japanese standards. Although it will take some time to work the bugs out of the new Saturn facility, I am convinced that GM can do the job. Then the company will adapt the new technology to the rest of its line. From that point forward GM should become a money machine.

Honda Motor Company, of course, is a Japanese auto maker— their third largest. However, Honda is rapidly becoming an important U.S. manufacturer of vehicles that are made in American factories. Some models, such as their station wagons, are made *only* in the United States. Hondas from America are regularly exported to Japan and other countries which is a sure sign of the quality the company has been able to achieve in the United States.

Because of Honda's strong U.S. presence and their product's affordable price, the company's autos are seen as practical and smart by American consumers. They are also increasingly viewed as domestic products that are becoming as common as apple pie. I think the company has a bright future in the United States, no matter what happens with the dollar or world trade.

Babies Are an Unexpected Source of Profits

One bright spot for growth in the 1990s is children—and it was completely unexpected. Most experts predicted that America's population would grow only about 1 percent per year throughout the 1990s. However, thanks to a delayed baby boom by our aging boomers, it now appears that the number may be much higher. Although the new children won't boost the adult market for several years, it is good news now to producers and sellers of baby foods and baby clothes. Many excellent firms make goods for babies and infants. However, there is one company that makes nearly everything. That makes it quite easy for interested investors to take a broad position in the new baby boom.

Gerber Products needs little introduction—it is the biggest and perhaps best known supplier of baby foods in the world. Less well known is the company's full line of baby clothing from sleepwear to playwear. Diapers, toys, and baby care items round out the line of this very successful and highly focused company. Gerber should do well in the coming years as America produces a far bigger crop of babies than was originally predicted.

Child Care Growing Stronger

With the increase of babies, comes better child care and more effective preschools. Besides the growing birthrate, the numbers of employed parents also point out the need for increases in this area. A Census Bureau report indicates that dual-employed couples with children increased by 61 percent from 1976 to 1987, to a total of 13,446,000. In comparison, dual-employed couples without children increased in number by only 31 percent.[9] And almost two-thirds of all women with a child less than one year old were employed. This powerful trend, with its demand for child care, will soar in the 1990s.

Because Americans are shifting their life's focus from their work to their families, they are clearly willing to pay for private, upscale child care. The "smarter baby" trend of the early 1980s developed thousands of the nation's preschools into finely-honed factories where even infants received structured early education and accelerated developmental skills. These preschool "academies" are now being seen by millions of new parents as the necessary first step to their children's education and a successful life.

In the 1990s child centers of every type will continue to expand their services to dual-income families whose after work time and energy are minimal. Drop-in care for just a few hours is also becoming available for evening outings by parents. Flexible weekday schedules meet the needs of part-time working parents. Some facilities specialize in weekend care so that parents can have a getaway trip. Others offer gym classes and transportation on preschool outings. A few are arranging for immunization visits by a physician. In many ways, child care is becoming America's answer to many social and economic problems.

On-site child care at the business place will also grow by leaps and bounds in the coming decade despite problems with liability and soaring costs. A survey by Hewitt Associates of more than 250 major companies in 1990 revealed that 55 percent already offered some form of day-care aid.[10] In some communities such as Minneapolis where employer-sponsored child care is becoming established, the unfortunate company that does not have it simply cannot get top people. Now we are seeing the start of a race to "out child care the competition." That is good news for millions of parents—and savvy investors.

La Petite Academy is a major owner and operator of day care and preschools in America. In the fall of 1990 the company had over 700 centers which served over 80,000 children in 30 states. Centers provide a wide range of care and educational services depending on the preferences of parents. A big plus for this company is its strong move toward providing child care for major corporations. La Petite has been profitable since 1983.

Kinder–Care Learning Centers is the nation's largest operator of child care centers. In September 1990, Kinder–Care was serving over 140,000 children in more than 1,200 centers in both the United States and Canada. Unfortunately, Kinder–Care experienced major difficulties recently which were undoubtedly related to its rapid expansion program. The stock reacted sharply downward. However, a new emphasis on efficiency and debt reduction is now under way, which may prove to be successful. Consequently, I urge investors who are interested in the growing child care industry to carefully check current numbers for Kinder–Care before making a final stock selection.

A Growing Need for Adult Day Care

There is also a rapidly growing need for centers that provide weekday care for elderly adults. A little more than 30 percent of those same 250 companies noted in the Hewitt Associates study were also providing some assistance for elderly care in 1990.[11] As the family unit regains some of the ground it lost in recent decades, as housing costs continue to increase, and as money becomes more difficult to make, the combined effect will lead to more and more elderly parents living at home. Caring for an elderly parent during working hours will demand a solution, which will be met by drop-off day-care centers for the aged.

Senior Service Corp. was started in 1985 to provide specialized products and services to older Americans. For several years the company earned most of its revenues from large print books for the visually impaired. Now most of the publishing operations have been sold and the company is shifting its focus to senior day-care services. By late 1990 seven centers were in operation in the Northeast under the name "Almost Family." Many more centers are planned for the coming years.

By the end of fiscal 1990 Senior Service had yet to become profitable. When and if it turns the corner, the company should have every chance for a bright future by serving the growing market it shares with few competitors. This investment is quite speculative but worth careful consideration.

Teen-Age Market to Revive

The 1980s saw a decrease in the population of teen-agers in America. After all, many baby boomers were too busy with their careers to have many children. However, the offspring the boomers did produce—the baby busters—had many children of their own during the decade. Many of those youngsters are now entering their high school years which will revitalize the market for teen products.

What makes the potential of the growing teen market even greater is that the successful parents of the 1980s have a considerable amount of money to spend per child. In addition, we are entering a 1950s type economy where a shortage of low-cost help is creating ready jobs for teen-age workers. All in all, the teens of the 1990s are becoming more numerous and more affluent than was true of teens in the past. That should translate into top profits for the growing teen industry.

Handleman Company is a leading distributor of products for the home entertainment market. A full line of videos and compact disks (CDs) gives the company strong exposure to teen-agers who are reached through national chains such as Wal–Mart and trendy specialty stores. The bankruptcy of a customer and the recession had a big impact on sales recently, but the long-term outlook should be good.

PolyGram N.V. is one of the largest recorded music companies in the world. The company has a strong orientation to popular music which it distributes on a variety of labels. Artists include Janet Jackson, U2, and Bon Jovi. Some 60 percent of revenues are from Europe, but the company is aggressively expanding its U.S. operations. I think the firm is well positioned to profit from the growth in numbers and affluence of American teens.

A National Savings Spree Impacts Wall Street

During the 1990s millions of Americans, particularly the baby boomers, went to the brink of excessive debt and didn't enjoy the view. The free spenders are now paying their debts, and will continue doing so for two to three more years. After that, they are likely to "spend" the money on secure savings instruments. This change marks a major shift in focus from the consumption of goods to the accumulation of wealth.

Since the emphasis is on safety, I am convinced that a major trend in the 1990s will be a return to money funds. Top quality fixed income obligations should also do well as will the financial service firms that specialize in them. Almost all major financial service firms offer a variety of safe savings and retirement plans. Two companies appear to be particularly well positioned with such programs and should do well in the coming years.

Dreyfus Corp. is a major mutual fund management firm with nearly $60 billion under its care. The company is noteworthy because of its heavy orientation toward fixed income and money funds which are ideal for current trends and attitudes.

Dreyfus spends heavily on advertising and is not above using a loss-leader to bring in business. The firm's earnings rose from $0.38 per share in 1980 to $2.04 per share in 1989. An expected drop during the 1990–91 recession may provide an attractive buying opportunity for long-term investors.

Franklin Resources is also a large mutual fund management company that emphasizes fixed income and cash investments. Approximately $45 billion are now under administration. Although the company makes certain that investors know of its products and services, its advertising program is not as aggressive as that used by Dreyfus. Margins are high thanks to Franklin's low overhead. Earnings increased steadily from $0.40 per share in 1983 to $2.28 per share in 1990. Over half the stock is owned by Franklin's officers and directors.

Traveling to New Experiences

As Americans cut down on their material needs they are increasing their interest in life experiences. For the most part people spent most of their adult lives either in school or working. Now they are beginning to realize that there is another world, and other rewards, out there. They want to see and experience some of it. Consequently, the entire travel and leisure industry looks very good for the 1990s.

Particularly popular will be trips that offer new opportunities or new life experiences. Archaeological digs, science tours, ecological awareness excursions, and other trips well off the usual tourist trails will be well attended in the 1990s. Also popular will be "theme tours" where everybody travels with an expert on the area at hand. Trips to Antarctica and the Amazon are examples of theme tours that will find additional success in the 1990s.

Another notable trend in travel and recreation will be increased demand for family-oriented activities. We are already seeing this trend reflected in the industry. For example, of 17 resort villages operated in North America by Club Med, only 3 still focus on single adults. The other 14 now cater solely to family vacations.

Club Med is doing more than re-orienting itself to family vacations. The company is also catering to people who are interested in visiting unique areas all over the world that are well away from the usual tourist trade. Study tours at resorts located next to top nature and archaeological areas are also growing in popularity. Prepaid, all-inclusive rates make the Club Med tour packages attractive to today's cost conscious travelers.

Carnival Cruise Lines is also well positioned to profit from the vacation trends that are emerging. As mentioned in Chapter 6, this cruise company is quite popular with seniors as well. Wide use by group tours and seagoing conferences is another plus for Carnival.

Eating Out Brings a Different Course

The end of the boomers' fascination with trendy, costly things in general will spill over to the restaurant industry. The stylish places that used to serve one green bean, a slice of poached cactus, and a bottle of Mongolian beer for double-digit prices are on the way out. What will be seen instead will be a move back to more traditional meals, with the sole difference being that the food will be more healthy. Restaurants that offer that fare will find millions of eager customers lining up at their doors.

Chili's, Inc. (to be renamed Brinker International) has over 175 restaurants in 31 states. They cater primarily to those customers who enjoy both traditional foods plus lighter dishes and salads. The number of customers who return is high, which indicates that the sale of food and atmosphere rather than the sale of franchises is boosting the bottom line—which is an important point when evaluating any franchise operation.

In addition to its own restaurants Chili's has acquired two competing chains, Grady's Goodtimes and Romano's Grill. Additional acquisitions—and expansion of the new chains—are probable in the future. Although competition in the restaurant business is stiff, Chili's appears to have the winning plan for success in the 1990s.

Spas Are Out—Family and Individual Sports Are In

The boom in exercise salons will turn into a bust over the next few years. Although specific figures were not made public, a 1989 survey by the National Sporting Goods Association indicated that the number of people who jog, swim, do aerobics, or play racquetball is already falling drastically.[12] In January 1989 Krystyn B. Spain, a researcher for the President's Council on Physical Fitness said, "Our best estimates are that less than 10 percent of Americans regularly do what the cardiovascular community calls exercise."[13] Falling just as fast are sales of big ticket exercise equipment. Such gear declined from $1.22 billion in 1985 to $1.06 billion in 1987 according to the association. Although current figures have not been released they are also very likely to be disappointing.

While many people are giving up exercise altogether, most others are only changing its form. Interest is now moving toward activities that people can do themselves without spending a lot of money. In particular, sports that can be done with the family are becoming more popular such as cycling and walking. This trend means good news for sales of walking shoes, bicycles, tennis rackets, and other individual sports equipment.

Huffy Corp. is America's largest maker of bicycles, most of which are sold through mass merchandisers. In addition, Huffy makes other leisure products such as basketball backboard assemblies for both homes and schools. A juvenile products division makes cribs, gates, car seats, and strollers. A line of garden tools is also offered. All in all, Huffy is in the business of serving active, sports-oriented families. I believe the firm is well positioned for the future.

Stride Rite Corp. isn't as famous as NIKE, Reebok, or L.A. Gear. Nevertheless, this maker of athletic shoes has an excellent chance for top profits over the next few years as two major trends—family sports and conservative spending—make Stride Rite, Sperry Top-Sider, and Keds brands very smart again. Stride Rite operates nearly 200 stores which market its products that are made in the United States and Puerto Rico or are imported from overseas. In addition, the company leases space in major department stores. Earnings have increased steadily from $0.18 per share in 1984 to $2.11 per share in 1990.

DARK CLOUDS ALSO EXIST

Unfortunately, there is also a dark side to the demographic outlook of the 1990s. Powerful forces are at work which are pushing millions of formerly middle-class Americans into lower economic positions. This erosion of the middle-class is of enormous importance to investors and will be the subject of the next chapter.

NOTES

1. Janice Castro, "Hunkering Down," *Time*, July 25, 1990.
2. Amanda Bennett, "New Generation Asks More Than Its Elders Of Corporate World," *The Wall Street Journal*, October 26, 1988.
3. Cathy Trost, "Careers Start Giving In to Family Needs," *The Wall Street Journal*, June 18, 1990.
4. Compiled by the staff of *American Demographics*, "Today's Students Say Money Isn't Everything," *The Wall Street Journal*, September 7, 1988.
5. Castro, "Hunkering Down."
6. George Garties, "Baby Boomer's Working At Home," *Eugene Register Guard*, November 20, 1988.
7. Jeffrey A. Trachtenberg, "Largest of All Malls in the U.S. Is a Gamble in Bloomington, Minn.," *The Wall Street Journal*, October 30, 1990.
8. Castro, "Hunkering Down."
9. Alan L. Otten, "Forget the DENKS; Look at the DEWKS," *The Wall Street Journal*, July 21, 1988.
10. Trost, "Careers Start Giving In to Family Needs."
11. Ibid.
12. Joseph Pereira, "The Exercise Boom Loses," *The Wall Street Journal*, January 9, 1989.
13. Ibid.

CHAPTER 8

A SHRINKING MIDDLE CLASS BRINGS PROBLEMS AND OPPORTUNITIES

Almost from the beginning the economic, social, and political backbone of America has been our middle class. Unfortunately, that critically important group is beginning to shrink in size and vitality. That development has huge implications for all of us, particularly investors. It is especially alarming that there is almost no chance that the trend has been misdiagnosed or will be short-lived. Data reported in May 1990 by economist A. Gary Shilling confirm that the middle class is clearly eroding. In 1975, 53 percent of American households were in the $20,000 to $60,000 income range. By 1985 the figure fell to 49 percent. Even worse, the number is expected to drop to 38 percent by 1995.[1] For the entire business community—and its investors—those numbers demand attention and careful changes in planning.

MOVING TO EXTREMES

Where is the middle class going? It is dividing and moving toward its two opposing ends—the upper- and lower-income classes of America's population. The spread in growth rates between the top 20 percent and bottom 20 percent of American income groups was 13.4 percent greater in 1987 than in 1979. The good news from economist Shilling is that the upper end of the scale—households earning more than $60,000—are expected to represent 13 percent of the population by 1995—up 5 points from an 8 percent share in 1973. And many of the older baby boomers discussed in the last chapter will inherit a vast windfall from their parent's generation, an unusually affluent group. Of course, this expanding upper middle class will be an excellent market for many industries.

Unfortunately, an even greater number of the middle-class Americans are sinking. Particularly hard hit are young blue-collar workers who were earning $22,000 to $23,000 on average during the early 1970s. By the end of the 1980s when good-paying manufacturing jobs were scarce, that group was earning only $18,500. Unfortunately, during the 1990s the wage squeeze is expected to spread to white-collar workers as well.[2]

Of course, our shrinking middle class represents an ominous development for all of us. However, all big changes create equally big opportunities. This one will be no exception.

IMPLICATIONS FOR INVESTORS

Marketers have been talking about the enormous consumer potential of the middle class for the last four decades. The fulfillment of that potential is now behind us. Trotting out the same old wares and services that made money in years past won't work as well in the 1990s. In many cases, aiming for the middle will result in almost certain failure.

While this is a disturbing trend, the growing extremes of the middle class offer many excellent investment opportunities. The companies that adapt early to the changes will reap top rewards. The same will be true for their investors.

STOCKS TO WATCH

Successful Retailers Look to Both Ends

Few retail outlets are likely to successfully address both ends of the marketplace that will develop as the middle class separates further into upper- and lower-income groups. The affluent shun discount stores, and the poor can only window shop at high-priced stores. Therefore, the most profitable businesses of the 1990s will target one or the other extreme.

High-end luxury products will continue to do well, as our upper middle-class population continues to grow. Fine jewelry, high-quality clothing, and special vacation trips to new and strange places should all prosper. At the same time more and more people find their budgets shrinking, discount department stores will see their customer base expand rapidly. Those stores that understand that their new customers are often quite refined and well educated are the ones that will do the best. In the 1990s discounters that manage to create an upbeat atmosphere in their shops will attract customers in droves.

Who will lose from the shrinking middle class? Stores that serve the very core of the group. Many of those stores have been around for as much as a century and have become American institutions. Nevertheless, they can't hope to remain healthy by serving a declining market.

One type of upscale shop is expected to benefit as the budget bite hits additional millions of people: those which supply affordable luxuries. Although many people will no longer be able to buy the car of their dreams, they will be able to buy an excellent ice cream cone or similar small extravagances. Such products should be extremely popular with people who are under increasing economic pressure, because the psychological boost these products give more than justifies their low cost.

Many retailers and suppliers are well positioned to profit from current socioeconomic trends. Here are four such businesses that should pay top rewards over the long term.

Tiffany & Co. is one of the world's best known designers, manufacturers, and sellers of high-quality jewelry and gifts. Although the company has some modestly-priced goods, its primary market is affluent customers. Tiffany's is expanding at a moderate pace and presently has stores in Europe and Asia in addition to shops in several U.S. cities. Current plans call for one new store a year to be opened in selected areas. Growth has been very good and should become even better in the 1990s.

Wal-Mart Stores is a successful discount merchandiser that operates nearly 1,500 stores primarily in small towns in the Sunbelt and the Midwest. Growth has been spectacular as the company applied highly efficient retailing practices to serve the needs of growing numbers of budget-minded customers. Since many sections of the country remain available for expansion and Wal-Mart has a proven formula for success, I think the company will continue to prosper in the 1990s.

Kmart Corp. is the nation's second largest mass market retailer. In recent years the firm lost market share to Wal-Mart and other chains that offer similar merchandise without making people feel that they are in a welfare office. However, Kmart recently began a long-term store modernization program that will cost over $2 billion. The result will be a mass retailer with a more upbeat atmosphere and more name brand products—at discount prices. I think Kmart is right on track with socioeconomic trends and has every chance to be very successful.

Dreyer's Grand Ice Cream makes premium ice cream and other treats which it sells primarily through supermarkets in the West and Midwest. Although Dreyer's high-end products cost more than those offered by the competition, few customers seem to mind. After all, the difference is often just a few pennies which even the budget-minded can afford. I think that businesses like this—including **Ben & Jerry's Homemade**—that offer low-cost, moral-building luxuries have just the ticket for the 1990s.

Automakers Think Big or Think Small

The middle class squeeze will also have a big impact on the automobile industry. Many automakers have already started reducing their variety of middle-class autos while increasing their lines of both luxury cars and smaller "commuter cars." For example, **Honda** brought out its high-end Acura at the same time it boosted production of its affordable Civics. **General Motors** launched the Cadillac Allante to compete with Mercedes and shortly thereafter introduced the inexpensive Geos. Both firms, which were introduced in the previous chapter, are moving strongly to position themselves to profit from current demographic trends.

Another auto industry that should do well in the 1990s is the repair market. Car prices are continuing to go up at the same time economic pressures increase. People are adjusting by keeping their cars longer than they did a few years ago. I would expect that a growing number of American automobile owners will begin to resemble their European counterparts who take good care of their cars and keep them for seven to ten years. Of course, that will be good news to auto parts suppliers.

Genuine Parts should be a major winner from the growing auto repair business. The company distributes NAPA brand replacement parts to about 6,000 stores in North America. Many stores are owned outright and have a similar exterior which makes them easily recognizable to customers. New streamlined sales and ordering systems help make Genuine Parts very efficient. This successful company is the McDonald's of the auto parts business.

Sun Electric sells computerized diagnostic equipment for popular automobiles and light trucks. Because modern vehicles are becoming very sophisticated, it takes specialized equipment to analyze problems and repair them. Sun makes some of the finest products for that task.

Since each new vehicle requires a different plug-in module for Sun's machines, the company appears to be well positioned for continued profits.

Champion Parts is one of the nation's major rebuilders and refurbishers of used automobile and light truck parts such as water pumps, alternators, starters, clutches, and dozens of others. Sales are primarily to distributors. A loss occurred in 1989 which prompted several internal changes. Profits returned during 1990. Continued increases in efficiency at Champion Parts could be very profitable.

Housing to Expand in Opposite Directions

Our increasing income disparity will also become more visible in America's housing patterns. Because the upper middle class is growing rapidly, upscale home builders appear to have an excellent future.

As the decade progresses, demand should also soar for low-budget homes of every type. The manufactured housing industry should do particularly well because they deliver a great deal of comfortable space for the money. In addition, manufactured housing suppliers and dealers usually offer their customers fast, convenient financing.

Kaufman & Broad Home is a leading builder of upper middle-class homes in California and France. The company is noted for its innovative styling, the many extra amenities it includes in each home, and its ability to offer convenient mortgages to most homebuyers. Although the California housing market was impacted by the recession, the state's strong economic base all but guarantees another decade of prosperity. The company appears likely to profit from prevailing economic and demographic trends.

Clayton Homes is one of America's leading suppliers of manufactured housing in the low to medium price range. The company sells its products through a chain of company-owned stores and independent dealers. A mortgage subsidiary makes it easy for customers to finance their purchases and, of course, provides Clayton with ongoing revenues from each sale. Clayton appears to be well positioned to profit in the 1990s.

Increasing Demand for Security Services

Unfortunately, the growing division between our economic classes will almost certainly result in a corresponding increase in anger, hostility, and crime. As a result, private security services and home protection systems should see big increases in business over the next few years.

Security companies that offer modern antishoplifting systems should also prosper in the 1990s. Not only will demographic trends favor their systems but so will shrinking profit margins in many retail stores. Competition is becoming so stiff and profit percentages so thin that most stores simply can't afford shoplifting or employee theft.

Sensormatic Electronics is the world's leading supplier of security tag and detection equipment for use in retail stores. In addition, Sensormatic supplies closed circuit video surveillance systems to prevent employee theft of merchandise and to monitor cash handling at sales registers. Foreign sales account for about one-third of revenues. The company has been very successful and should continue to prosper as socioeconomic trends continue to make crime a leading problem of the 1990s.

Knogo Corp. is also a leading manufacturer of in-store security systems. The company offers antitheft tags and detectors for libraries as well. In addition, systems have been adapted to monitor and control the movements of patients in nursing homes and hospitals. The company uses different technologies depending on the need. Rising foreign sales also look good for this innovative company.

Checkpoint Systems competes with Sensormatic and Knogo in most markets. In addition, the company makes area entry and control systems which restrict access to authorized personnel. A new system not only identifies tagged merchandise but it also registers prices. The system permits self-checkouts in many applications and could prove to be very popular with efficiency-conscious retailers.

ADT is a leading home and business security company that was first mentioned in Chapter 5. I give it another vote here for having good prospects for the next several years.

NOTES

1. A. Gary Shilling, "Winners and Losers," *Forbes*, May 14, 1990.
2. Survey of experts, "What's Really Squeezing the Middle Class?" *The Wall Street Journal*, July 26, 1989.

SECTION 3

NEW AND REBOUNDING INDUSTRIES FOR THE 1990s

CHAPTER 9

OPPORTUNITIES IN OVERSOLD REAL ESTATE

Several years ago I gave a speech at an investment conference at the beautiful Del Coronado Hotel in San Diego. After my presentation a gentleman in the audience rose to ask a question. The revealing conversation that followed was typical of dozens I have had over the years and is worth repeating.

GUEST:

"How do you think I should invest my money for the long term?"

JBP:

"How did you make your money in the first place?"

GUEST:

"Oh, I bought a duplex several years ago."

JBP:

"And you just sold the duplex?"

GUEST:

"Not exactly. The rents payed the darn thing down at the same time the market went up so I wound up with a lot of equity."

JBP:

"Then what?"

GUEST:

"Well, it didn't seem like a good idea to leave all that money tied up in the duplex so I borrowed on it when the market was soft again and I bought a fourplex."

JBP:

"So you have a duplex and a fourplex?"

GUEST:

"Well, no. After a few years I borrowed on the fourplex and I bought an eightplex."

JBP:

"And now?"

GUEST:

"Well, you know how it is with real estate, I just kept the system going and now I have 108 units—all of them generating income I need to do something with."

JBP:

"And you want to buy stocks?"

GUEST:

"What else?"

It didn't take long for me to gently suggest to my guest that he might consider buying more real estate. I also suggested that he hire a professional manager to run his growing empire. I understand that he took my advice and has become more successful than ever.

My guest was typical of hundreds of investors I have met over the years who have done very well with their real estate. Some of them purchased property directly and managed it themselves. Others did so by means of local partnerships. An even larger group took long-term positions in publicly traded real estate companies. All three methods, when handled conservatively and held for the long term, have a solid track record for returning top profits.

THE CASE FOR REAL ESTATE

As it turns out, the outlook for many segments of the real estate industry is beginning to look especially good for the 1990s. In fact, many of the highly publicized troubles in areas such as overbuilding, loss of tax advantages, more frequent recessions, and adverse demographic trends are the very reasons that real estate should be among the best performing investments of the decade. As always, the top profits will go to the best informed investors who make their plans early and then act on them.

One of the biggest reasons real estate should perform well in the 1990s is that overbuilding in the 1980s pushed prices down severely. In many regions everything from highrise office buildings to single family homes were built well in excess of market needs. Of course, when demand didn't keep up with the exploding supply, prices collapsed. In 1990 residential investment alone contracted 5.3 percent—the third straight year for a decline.[1] In some cases values have dropped so low that it would be very difficult for long-range investors to take conservative positions and not make money.

The 1986 Tax Reform Act was also responsible for many of today's real estate opportunities. Before the act was passed, tax write-offs from real estate losses were so valuable to high income investors that they rarely cared whether or not deals made sense from a normal business standpoint. Naturally, prices soared. In addition, the buying pressure led to even more overbuilding.

Now that huge write-offs from real estate losses are no longer permitted, prices have become more reasonable. For the first time in decades, real estate opportunities are likely to be profitable right from the start. As an experienced real estate investor in my area told me recently, "I still need to negotiate aggressively but it's almost always possible to set up deals that make economic sense from the day the papers are signed. That wasn't true a few years ago."

The recession of 1990–91—and the promise of still more economic trouble in the future—also helped push prices down to attractive levels. The effect of the economic downturn was particularly striking because it came on top of real estate's other problems.

As you may expect, many individuals and corporations are now beginning to ease back into real estate. Although these early bird investors don't expect overnight results, they feel strongly that they must move now or miss out on the biggest profits. David Webb, head of real estate banking at Merrill Lynch, summed it up in June 1991 when he expressed the opinion that at the time there might only be a 12 to 24 month buying window in the domestic real estate markets before prices start moving up again.[2]

Perhaps best of all, more frequent turns of the economic cycle in the 1990s can be expected to create a succession of attractive real estate opportunities. The normal boom and bust real estate cycle of three to five years may be replaced by a two to four year pattern. If so, "compounding up" will become easier and more profitable than ever before.

Demographic trends are also increasing the potential of many real estate investments. It is true that most of America's baby boomers have already purchased their homes and have raised their families. It is also a fact that the baby busters are fewer in number and are having a tough time economically. And, yes, the busters are often electing to stay single or marry later in life and often decide not to have children.

However, those demographic trends are already reflected in current real estate prices. In addition, many analysts have overstated the effect of those trends and have failed to see a few advantages they present. For example, economic troubles and fewer children will increase the demand for affordable apartments and smaller homes. Lower marriage rates will boost those demands even further because a population of singles needs more places to live than does a population of married people. As for the effect of delayed marriages on real estate sales, Barbara K. Allen, housing analyst at Prudential Bache observed in January 1989, " . . . instead of a peak of 44 million in 1990 you get over 60 million peaking in 1995."[3]

Finally, as the 1990 Census clearly reveals, the U.S. population is expanding much more rapidly than was expected (see Chapter 7). That growth is creating more demand for every type of real estate—from housing to shopping malls to industrial parks.

OTHER ADVANTAGES OF REAL ESTATE

Specific economic and demographic considerations aside, real estate deserves a place in most portfolios because it offers needed diversification. Real estate serves as a hedge because it often behaves contrary to other investments. It also serves as a buffer against shocks because its values tend to change slowly.

For example, during the stock market crash of 1987 stocks fell an average of 20 percent, while real estate securities fell less than 10 percent according to Karel McClellan, who co-authored the book, *From Main Street to Wall Street: Making Money in Real Estate* (John Wiley & Sons, NY, 1988). Properties themselves barely budged at all. The lesson was not lost on growing ranks of real estate converts who noticed how well the industry held its value during the crisis.

In most situations real estate also offers tax advantages whether investors own property directly or do so through publicly traded companies. Actual business costs plus depreciation, taxes, and interest payments are deductible when real estate is purchased and managed directly. In addition, owner/managers who make under $100,000 a year can still apply up to $25,000 in losses against ordinary income. From $100,000 to $150,000 the $25,000 phases out on a sliding scale. Many real estate companies and partnerships also offer useful tax breaks to their investors.

Real estate also provides investors with one of the world's best hedges against inflation. Although inflation is not currently a problem and may not be for several years, many economists expect to see its return later in the decade. Those economists argue that today's runaway budget deficits all but guarantee another inflationary spiral. If they are correct, once current market conditions have run their course real estate can be expected to offer needed protection against inflation as it has always done in the past.

Finally, real estate can be a fine producer of current income. This is especially true when properties or publicly traded real estate companies are purchased during recessions at bargain prices. In today's more business-oriented real estate market, cash flows generally run about 7 to 8 percent—the same as [Spring 1991] Treasury bonds. Of course, real estate offers greater potential for capital gains than is true of Treasuries, and real estate is more likely to go up rather than down during inflationary times. All in all, real estate deserves a place in the portfolios of nearly all long-term investors.

THE BEST WAYS TO INVEST IN THE 1990s

There are many types of real estate, each of which differs significantly from the others. The combination of size and complexity has produced a variety of ways that investors may choose to participate in the industry. Here are the methods which I think look best for the 1990s.

Direct ownership is the traditional way that individuals make top profits in the real estate market. In the usual situation an investor buys a property—usually a rental but sometimes a small commercial building—during slow economic times and rides it up during one or two turns of the economic cycle. At that point, equity in the property is used as collateral to make a second, usually larger, purchase.

After 20 to 25 years one's real estate holdings will usually have grown to substantial proportions. Growth is then frequently given a back seat to income. Properties are paid off at which point profits soar. Alternately, properties are sold and the proceeds are invested in secure fixed income securities. Either way the long term real estate investor comes out a winner.

For many years robust economic growth and explosive birth rates practically guaranteed profits to every real estate investor. Those years are over. However, our expanding population and the effects of our economic cycle continue to create opportunities that can make direct ownership of real estate a promising investment. As Allan Parker, portfolio manager of the U.S. Real Estate Fund said in August 1989, "Real estate isn't a get-rich-quick investment anymore, and never will be again, but you can [still] find quality and make a lot of money, especially if you buy big publicly traded companies like REITs."[4]

The best way to get started in direct ownership is to see a qualified investment realtor. Although it's true that an investor is unlikely to obtain a great bargain from a realtor, a good professional is worthwhile, particularly for first-time buyers. Often an investment realtor will give what amounts to private lessons in the essentials of rental economics— pricing, choosing tenants, and trading up. Several books cover the same topics but only a professional will know how the rules apply to the local situation.

Partnerships make a great deal of sense provided they are composed of local people whom an investor knows and trusts. The typical successful arrangement consists of eight or ten individuals who give a competent attorney a share of profits in return for legal help throughout the life of the partnership.

Some partnerships are very long lived. Others are set up for a specific investment that the group expects to sell within 7 to 10 years. Because it may be difficult if not impossible to sell one's share in a partnership before it matures, the arrangements are best suited to investors who can remain for the duration.

On the positive side, a partnership typically has more money to invest than an individual. Generally it starts out with a medium-sized property that can be managed by a professional agency. Short-term partnerships generally dissolve after their investment is liquidated.

Long-term arrangements ratchet up their holdings as would an individual investor.

Almost every area has successful real estate partnerships. In many towns they dominate the rental or commercial real estate markets. Although it can be difficult to be accepted into such a group, doing so can be well worth the effort. A call to your attorney or realtor should put you on the right path.

Limited Partnerships (LPs), large investment groups that are registered with the Securities and Exchange Commission, are an entirely different proposition from local partnerships. LPs pool money from many investors nationwide, and the money is used to buy large properties, sometimes many of them. The partnership's sponsors put the real estate deals together and arrange for them to be managed. Investors have a passive role throughout the usual 7 to 10 year life of an LP.

LPs have several disadvantages which, in my opinion, make them poorly suited for most investors. The first is high sales and other upfront costs that can total 25 percent of an investment. High ongoing fees are also common. In order for such expenses to be justified, the returns from the partnerships must be extraordinary. Usually they fall well short of that mark.

Although limited partnerships are beginning to offer investors attractive opportunities, I feel that most people would be better off with other types of real estate investments. At the minimum, I would urge readers to give the LP industry another year or two for the aftershocks of the late 1980s to settle out.

Master Limited Partnerships (MLPs) are usually formed by consolidating smaller LPs into larger entities that have the financial muscle to make major real estate investments. MLPs offer investors a big advantage over LPs—they are traded just like stocks on major exchanges. Not only can MLPs be easily liquidated at any time, but they also prepare uniform financial reports that make them easier to evaluate. Even though MLPs are a step in the right direction, the jury is still out on their long-term potential. Few of them have been around for more than six years, not much time to establish a track record.

Real Estate Investment Trusts (REITs) offer most investors one of the best ways to take attractive positions in virtually any part of the real estate market. REITs are publicly traded securities that tend to behave like ordinary stocks. That allows investors to buy and sell them as they wish. Because REITs have active markets, investors can also evaluate and monitor them using well understood principles of technical and fundamental analysis.

REITs are somewhat reminiscent of closed-end mutual funds. The most popular type, equity REITs, pool investor's money to buy large properties, usually several of them. Most of the better REITs offer attractive yields, a realistic potential for capital appreciation, and professional management. And they do so without the high sales fees which are common to LPs.

REITs also offer tax advantages to investors without incurring the IRS problems which can often go with partnerships. Because 95 percent or more of profits are passed on to their investors REITs are not required to pay corporate taxes. Consequently, earnings are taxed only once instead of twice as is the case with stocks. That may sound trivial but it generally results in yields of 6 percent or more, a level that is very uncommon in stocks.

Because REITs have been around for many years, a proven strategy has emerged for picking likely winners. Of course, no formula is perfect and almost no investment meets all the criteria. Nevertheless, top REITs specialize in just one or two types of property; they stick with the basics such as apartment buildings rather than amusement parks, and they don't borrow much more than 50 percent of their property's purchase price. In addition, the top REITs don't wait for normal appreciation to increase the values of their holdings—they make significant improvements.

Equity REITs, the only type we will consider here, generally have good track records. From 1978 to 1987 their dividends and price appreciation totaled 269 percent.[5] Then from 1987 to 1990 they lost nearly 30 percent as overbuilding and the recession hammered real estate prices in most parts of the United States. However, once the last of the oversupply passes through the system and real estate prices stabilize, many REITs should do very well. In April 1991, three analysts from different firms predicted that the better REITs are likely to provide returns of 13 to 15 percent a year for the next few years.[6] I believe this is a conservative prediction.

Real Estate Stocks are also attractive for the 1990s. Top homebuilders, developers, and suppliers will benefit substantially from an upturn in the real estate market. As with other real estate investments, how soon real estate stocks perform will depend largely on which segment of the market they serve and in what part of the country they are located. Housing in strong cities should do well early in the 1990s while office building in recessed areas should emerge later.

Real estate stocks from established firms look particularly good for the 1990s. The building market in particular has become so competitive that only the largest companies can do well. They buy building materials by the carload and hire workers who are used efficiently year round at affordable wages.

Large builders and contractors also make real estate transactions both easy and affordable. Many firms now offer "turnkey deals" that come complete with builder-supplied financing. Buying a house or an apartment from such a firm can be no more trouble than buying a car. One of my clients from Southern California reported that his last house purchase took less than a day from start to finish, "and the sales team handled all the red tape."

It's no wonder that during healthy market conditions the top real estate companies can sell an entire development in a week. We will see it happen again and again throughout the 1990s as the real estate cycle continues to develop.

Real Estate Mutual Funds offer a particularly attractive way to invest but unfortunately they are few and far between. To date, there are less than a half dozen of them. I will review two of the best of these funds later in the chapter.

INVESTMENTS TO WATCH

After four years of a tough bear market in real estate, there are many reasons investors might list for *not* taking positions. For example, the market is awash in red ink, there's a glut in many areas, sales by the Resolution Trust Corporation (RTC) threaten to depress the market further, tax laws have reduced real estate's appeal, many investments are illiquid, the field is full of crooks, and so on.

However, investors who allow current negatives to sway their moves risk missing out on the next upturn in the real estate cycle. That upturn is expected to begin once the combined effects of overbuilding, tax law changes, and the recession work through the system. I think that will begin to happen in 1992 for many sectors such as housing and strip shopping centers. Other sectors, including office buildings and industrial parks will emerge later. Here are the specific areas and the ways to play them which I believe look best for the 1990s.

Housing to Lead the Way Up

House prices and new home construction dropped sharply in the late 1980s which created the weakest housing market in a generation. The drop was fueled primarily by overbuilding, the recession, and the market's reaction to the sharp price increases which occurred earlier in the decade.

Not all areas were hit equally hard. The Northeast and Southern California suffered the most followed by the Southwest and the Mountain states. On the other hand, the Midwest market remained quite firm. In the Pacific Northwest, particularly in Seattle and Portland, a strong local economy and an influx of people from California permitted housing to gain ground.

At the conclusion of the Persian Gulf War in early 1991 it appeared that housing was in the process of bouncing back sharply. However, when the euphoria ended so did the boomlet. By May of 1991 it appeared that nationwide housing starts for the year would actually be lower than at any time since 1988. Although it was cut off prematurely, the early 1991 housing surge carried a valuable message. The event demonstrated that housing is likely to be the first real estate sector to recover once conditions improve. Investors should use that knowledge to place the housing sector high on their list of promising real estate opportunities.

Lennar Corp. (stock) went into 1991 as one of the best positioned and strongest home builders in the nation. The company has benefitted from its central position in the Florida market, where housing remained healthy during most of the post–1987 real estate bust. More importantly, the Florida market should become even stronger once the economy turns around decisively. That event will also help Lennar's smaller stake in the Arizona market, which did drop during the real estate slump.

Lennar is also noteworthy for its growing emphasis on financial services which it provides to its customers. In particular, the company's strong mortgage business promises to become even more valuable in the future. Moreover, the mortgage business should provide the company with a cushion during periods of slow economic growth.

Kaufman & Broad Home (stock) was first mentioned in Chapter 8 for its central role in the California housing industry where it sells upper middle-class homes in several growing communities. Although parts of the company's territory were hit hard by the recession, the housing market in that region showed considerable strength during the aborted recovery in early 1991. That bodes well for Kaufman & Broad once the cycle actually turns up again.

Toll Brothers (stock) is an important builder of upscale single family homes primarily in the Northeast. Because that region was among the hardest hit during the recession, the company had several very lean years. However, a recovery should have the opposite effect and make Toll Brothers among the biggest winners. That is particularly true since the company used the recession to pick up land to use for future developments at bargain prices.

Apartments Will Also Do Well

Apartment building suffered from all the problems common to new home construction plus a few of its own. Chief among them was the credit crunch that made money unavailable at any price. On the positive side, the various problems facing the apartment market cured the overbuilding problem that occurred in many areas. In the four years since the industry hit the skids, much of that oversupply has been absorbed by the market. As a result, the outlook is now improving dramatically.

Already there are signs of recovery. From November 1989 to November 1990 the value of multifamily property rose 3.8 percent according to the *Liquidity Fund* publication of the National Real Estate Index in Emeryville, California. That is not a great increase, but it stands in sharp contrast to the losses which occurred previously. In addition, it beats the 0.8 percent gain for office buildings and the 0.6 percent rise for warehouses.[7]

It appears that the apartment market will follow housing out of the basement in 1992–93. I think it should fully recover by 1995. Well before that point savvy investors will have taken key positions in the leading players.

United Dominion Realty Trust (REIT) earns approximately three-fourths of its income from apartments, most of which are located in the Southeast. The trust's remaining holdings consist of shopping centers and office buildings. United Dominion is particularly adept at finding apartment buildings which can be renovated for increased income. Profits also benefit from the trust's professional marketing and aggressive leasing programs. The formula should work even better when the real estate cycle turns up again.

BRE Properties (REIT) specializes in owning and operating high-grade, income-producing properties in the West. Apartments are the firm's largest holding. BRE also owns and operates two shopping centers, three office buildings, and other assorted real estate.

Despite the real estate slump, BRE is doing quite well. The trust reports an average occupancy rate of 90 percent for all its holdings. In addition, the trust made modest increases to its rents even during the slump. When the slump ends, BRE should see substantial increases in the value of its portfolio.

Hovnanian Enterprises (stock) builds condominium apartments and townhouses primarily in the Northeast, one of America's hardest hit real estate markets. Not surprisingly, the company sustained a large loss in 1990–91. However, Hovnanian should bounce back just as strongly when the economy turns around.

Building Supply Companies Offer Secondary Plays

Frequently the best way to profit from a trend is to ignore the leading players and invest in their suppliers instead. There are two principal advantages of shifting focus to top suppliers. First, the suppliers make money no matter which of the front line players becomes the biggest winner. Whoever leads the industry buys the most supplies. If one customer falls behind or fails altogether, its business goes to someone else. The biggest problem a key supplier needs to worry about is the health of the industry itself. As long as the industry continues to grow so will its suppliers.

As housing and apartment markets recover in the 1990s, the new wave of building should create very attractive profits for the construction materials industry. Everything from lumber, glass, brick, plumbing, and grass seed will be needed in huge quantities. Consequently, the leading suppliers appear to offer a promising way to take a broad and relatively conservative position in the new construction trend.

Owens–Corning Fiberglass Corp. (stock) is a major producer of fiberglass products including insulation, roofing shingles, heating and cooling ducts, and raw materials for makers of shower stalls, tubs, and dozens of other products. The company has been hit hard in recent years due to the recession and a costly hostile takeover attempt which was finally defeated. Because of its troubles and its strong ties to the real estate construction industry, Owens–Corning should appreciate strongly once conditions improve.

Republic Gypsum (stock) manufactures wallboard and related products for the housing construction industry. Of course, the company was heavily impacted when that industry dropped sharply in the late 1980s. However, the company has a strong balance sheet—much stronger than most of its rivals—and should weather the storm until better conditions occur. At that point the company should do very well.

Justin Industries (stock) is one of America's largest suppliers of bricks. The company also produces industrial cooling structures and owns four companies that makes Western boots. I'm impressed with the potential of Justin's brick business which I think will grow steadily as U.S. timber supplies dwindle and become much more expensive. Environmental problems, overharvesting, and poor management by the U.S. Forest Service have devastated the timber industry which is unlikely to fully recover. Of course, that situation should shift a great deal of new construction business to alternative materials of which brick is the leading player.

A Growing Outlook for Manufactured Housing and Mobile Home Parks

In earlier chapters about the greying of America and our shrinking middle class, I discussed many demographic and economic factors which point to a positive outlook for the manufactured housing industry in the 1990s. Those points will not be repeated here. However, I will mention that the prefab housing industry is capitalizing on the trends which promise to bring good fortune. Newly designed units are becoming difficult to distinguish from site constructed homes. New models are also more solid and more energy efficient than earlier units. Of course, the improvements are attracting additional buyers.

Zoning changes are also attracting prefab customers. In many communities, prefabs can now be set up in most neighborhoods provided they are placed on foundations. Although existing residents often object to the relaxed rules, the regulations are much more likely to be expanded than rolled back.

Finally, prefab housing stocks offer investors two plays with one ticket. That is because the top manufacturers are also among the leading developers of mobile home parks in growing areas. The leading makers make money on the sale and they continue to make money from rent and appreciation of their properties. In summation, I urge you to again investigate **Oakwood Homes** and **Clayton Homes** as you plan your long-term portfolios.

Regional Shopping Centers Bounce Back

From coast to coast America is becoming "malled out." Even before the recession began, our fascination with huge shopping malls was beginning to wane. As reported in Chapter 6, the baby boomers are maturing and giving up their devotion to material goods and outward displays of "success." In addition, it appears that millions of people are simply tired of crowds, security concerns, ho-hum merchandise, and the carbon copy franchises common to malls.

At present many shopping malls are in trouble and few new ones are being constructed. However, there is a growing business converting older properties to mixed use complexes. It now appears that the malls of the future will resemble small indoor towns complete with apartments, shops, and offices.

There is also a resurging interest in small strip shopping centers that first became popular in the 1950s. Unlike many older centers, the new facilities are upscale without being ostentatious. Usually they are "anchored" by a first class supermarket or retailer and include a mix of smaller shops that people tend to use frequently. The most profitable strip centers are carefully structured to make shopping both attractive and efficient.

Of course, there is a lively business creating the new strip shopping centers. And, since so many older centers are available there is also a booming business rehabilitating them. Frequently, that task requires little more than a face-lift but it can greatly increase the value of the property. Adding a top anchor can boost it again. All in all, rehabs can be very profitable.

Federal Realty Investment Trust (REIT) is one of the nation's leading owner/operators of shopping centers, mainly in the East. The trust specializes in older properties which it acquires and rehabilitates. The process usually involves making structural changes, changing the tenants to effect a better mix, and attracting a major anchor. Since most acquisitions are in mature areas which have no open land available, there is little opportunity for others to compete with a totally new facility. Federal Realty appears to be in good position as its sector prospers in the 1990s.

Western Investment R.E. (REIT) operates principally in Northern and Central California and Nevada—areas which largely escaped the real estate slump and have very good prospects for future growth. The trust invests primarily in shopping plazas which have top anchors like K mart and Safeway. Aggressive leasing practices provide the trust with a share of gross sales or other sliding incentives. Western Investment should do well thanks to its cental position in a geographic area that has considerable potential.

Weingarten Realty Investors (REIT) owns and develops shopping centers primarily in the Southwest and the southern Midwest. Many holdings are in Houston and other Southwest cities that were hampered by the general recession and lower oil prices. The problems in its region notwithstanding, Weingarten is doing well. Revenues from rents went up over 9 percent in 1990 while occupancy rates topped 93 percent overall. Now that the Southwest appears to be coming out of its slump, Weingarten is building again—a strategy that should pay off within a few years.

Office Markets to Offer a Series of Opportunities

No part of the real estate industry saw more overbuilding than offices, particularly in some of our biggest cities. Because class A offices in major urban centers are much more expensive than housing developments and apartment buildings, they promised much greater profits. They also promised big ticket investors enormous tax shelters. All told, the market attracted billions of dollars and surged during "the decade of business."

Then the tax axe fell, the economy slowed down, oil prices dropped, and growth in the service sector began to falter. From its peak in 1985, office construction fell 35 percent overall according to a February 1991 article by economist A. Gary Shilling.[8] Drops of over 80 percent were common in some cities. The oversupply in many areas is sufficient to meet expected market needs until late in the decade. Boston, New York, Los Angeles, San Francisco, and Chicago appear to offer especially poor prospects for new office construction in the near future.

As with housing and apartments, a few areas either missed the slump or are beginning to come out of it. Houston and Dallas with their famous "see-through buildings" may be turning the corner this year. Seattle is already moving up as is most of the Pacific Northwest. The inland cities of California also look very good, particularly those in the central Valley. Many fast-growing areas in Florida will see new construction soar as will several regional centers such as Richmond and Louisville.

The office market is particularly attractive because its regional nature promises a long play. Investors can take positions in first one area and then another as the cycle unfolds from place to place. Here's what looks best now.

Koger Equity (REIT) invests in office buildings which are located in suburban business centers in the Sunbelt. The buildings are developed by Koger Properties—a NYSE company—then sold to the trust, no doubt to avoid the double taxation on profits that would occur if they remained in the corporation. At the close of 1990 the trust owned over 125 fully leased buildings and had the right to acquire over 50 more from Koger Properties. This prearranged ability to expand quickly should pay off handsomely when the office market turns upward again.

Washington REIT has an unusually tight geographic focus since it invests almost exclusively in the Washington, DC, area. The trust has a broad mix of properties but emphasizes office buildings and business centers. The balance of the portfolio consists of apartments and shopping centers. This well-run trust has not had a down year since 1986. That should not be surprising since the trust's fortunes are indirectly tied to the most recession-resistant organization on earth, the federal government. Due to its unusually secure niche, the trust should be particularly well suited to more conservative real estate investors.

Health Care Properties Offer Continuing Prospects

One real estate sector that bucked the late 1980s downtrend is the development and management of health care properties. That is less of an achievement than it may seem, because most of the industry didn't come on stream until after the 1985 real estate peak. Nevertheless, the health care property industry has since shown that it is much more resistant to recessions and industry downturns than other real estate sectors. In addition, health care properties were never overbuilt to the extent of housing and offices.

Developers of health care real estate also benefit from the long-term nature of their associations with their tenants. Most properties are leased rather than sold which provides the owner/operators with continuing revenue streams. Since leases commonly run for 10 years or more, the occasional recession has little effect on income. That's not to say that health care real estate is without its problems. As will be discussed in some detail in Chapter 12, the hospital industry is undergoing a shakeout, particularly in rural areas. Many hospitals have gone bankrupt. However, there is an equally strong trend toward major urban medical centers and various specialized clinics which helps to balance the scale.

Government health care cutbacks are also a potential problem. Hospitals and nursing homes that rely heavily on Medicare and welfare reimbursements are having a tough time. Although I would expect payment increases rather than cutbacks during the 1990s, they won't come quickly. In the meantime, health care developers are beginning to stress markets that have a substantial percentage of private-pay patients.

All in all, the health care real estate industry looks very promising. It should appeal to investors who wish to emphasize steady gains over the chance for large cyclical profits.

Health Care Property Investors (REIT) invests in a broad range of specialized medical facilities from nursing homes to substance abuse clinics. The trust also has a broad geographical distribution with properties from coast to coast. At the end of 1990, the total value of the trust's holdings approached a half billion dollars. The trust is also noteworthy for its strong performance during the late 1980s when most of the real estate industry did poorly. Earnings increased steadily from 1987 to 1990, a trend which I expect to continue.

American Health Properties (REIT) has a similar business and performance record to that of Health Care Property Investors. However, in addition to owning specialized facilities, American Health has seven acute care hospitals. A March 1991 agreement in principle should lead to the acquisition of another hospital, this one located in Irvine, California.

As mentioned previously, specialized clinics rather than general care hospitals are the current trendsetters in medicine. However, hospitals are fighting back by establishing efficient clinics of their own. By 1995 the tables may be turned. For now, Health Care Property Investors appears to be the most promising of the two trusts reviewed here. However, the longer term may favor American Health.

Mutual Funds Offer Broad Plays

As we have seen, property development and management is a diverse field that is also very cyclical. That makes it difficult for individual investors to take broad positions and then monitor them knowledgeably. The task is much better suited to a team approach which good mutual funds can offer. Of the few real estate mutual funds available, two appear to be particularly attractive.

United Services Real Estate Fund is the only major no-load real estate fund in the United States. The fund's manager, Mr. Allan Parker, has been a guest on *ValuTRAC* and impressed everyone with his knowledge of the real estate industry. The fund's portfolio is oriented toward long-term capital gains and includes a broad spectrum of real estate plays from housing to office buildings. The portfolio appears well positioned to profit from the cyclical recovery of the real estate industry in the 1990s.

Fidelity Real Estate Investment Portfolio is a low-load (2 percent), income-oriented fund that is conservatively managed. The fund holds a variety of real estate securities including those of major lending companies. In addition, up to 35 percent of the fund's portfolio may be invested in nonconvertible debt securities including bonds and mortgages. The fund appears to be well suited to investors who wish to emphasize income while participating in the broad recovery of the real estate industry.

NOTES

1. Charles E. Babin, "The Turnaround Is At Hand," *Forbes,* May 27, 1991.
2. Neil Barsky, "Real-Estate Funds Raise $1.3 Billion—Wall Street Begins To See Opportunity In Depressed Market," *The Wall Street Journal,* June 10, 1991.

3. Kathleen Madigan, "What's Pulling The Rug Out From Under Housing," *Business Week,* January 23, 1989.

4. Barbara Donnelly, "Finding Real Estate Opportunites Despite Recent Woes of Market," *The Wall Street Journal,* August 28, 1989.

5. Author's calculations based on data from "The National Association of Real Estate Investment Trusts."

6. Howard Rudnitsky, "The REIT Stuff," *Forbes,* April 1, 1991.

7. Jim Carlton, "Developers of Apartments Face Adversity," *The Wall Street Journal,* January 17, 1991.

8. A. Gary Shilling, "Thirteen More Lean Years," *Forbes,* February 4, 1991.

CHAPTER 10

AMERICA REBUILDS ITS INFRASTRUCTURE

Most Americans are painfully aware that much of our country is literally falling apart. We regularly bounce down deteriorating roads and inch our way across failing bridges. We ride commuter trains that are in such bad shape that we are tossed around like rag dolls. When we fly, we are at the mercy of a system that is horribly overstressed. And when we open a faucet we are never sure what we'll get with our water—provided we get anything at all. In many parts of the country we can't even be certain the electricity will be on when we need it.

We have clearly reached the point where our deteriorating infrastructure can no longer be ignored. During the 1990s we must catch up on more than 20 years of deferred public works maintenance. Moreover, we must expand our infrastructure to meet the needs of a growing population. In the words of the National Council on Public Works Improvement in their far-reaching February 1988 *Final Report to the President and Congress*, "...our infrastructure is inadequate to sustain a stable and growing economy. As a nation we need to renew our commitment to the future...."[1]

To bring our infrastructure up to date we will need to spend at least four times what we spent during the 1970s and 1980s.[2] That will create boom times for public works engineering firms, contractors, construction material suppliers, and a host of others. Of course, that will also create excellent investment profits for people who take early positions in this trend. In fact, rebuilding our infrastructure should be one of the most profitable, long-term trends of the 1990s.

To understand the scope of the problem—and its investment potential—we need to look at what we have lost, what it is costing us, and how we are likely to cure the problem.

A HISTORY OF DREAMERS, BUILDERS, AND MOUNTAIN MOVERS

America has set the world standard for infrastructure development for more than 150 years. We set new records every decade in the construction of bigger dams, longer roadways, and higher bridges. A brief list of notable accomplishments includes our deepwater ports, many international airports, transcontinental railways, and a public health system that is the envy of the world. Add to that list many individual achievements such as Hoover Dam, the Erie Canal, the Great Lakes Seaway, the Golden Gate Bridge, and even the Panama Canal.

It is critical to note that America's extraordinary economic success and rapid rise as a world leader over the last two centuries would not have been possible without our immense, complicated infrastructure. Its fundamental importance to our future success is now being recognized by business leaders and politicians alike, especially in light of recent international economic developments which demand that we become much more competitive.

In fact, a growing number of economists lay a substantial part of the blame for our slumping nation's productivity on the doorstep of our failure to maintain our infrastructure. We have reached the point where it is costing us more to live with the problem than it will to fix it.

GUNS AND BUTTER REPLACED INFRASTRUCTURE NEEDS

Since the late 1950s, both federal and local governments began to reduce budget allocations for public works. Both upkeep and expansion projects were set aside in favor of matters which were more pressing. The Vietnam War was a big factor behind delayed infrastructure spending. During the war our administration limited its focus to the basic needs of guns and butter. Social programs also began receiving greater funding by 1960 and grew even more through the 1970s. At the same time, the cost of servicing the rising federal debt took an increasing percentage of tax revenues.

Balancing local budgets proved to be no easier. Most municipal officials chose to defer almost all infrastructure expenses. The practice was benign at first. Government leaders felt they would just put public works repairs aside for a few years. Unfortunately, a few years grew into 20 years.

Rising taxes caused additional problems. When taxpayers showed signs of revolt—as in California's Proposition 13—governments eased off a notch or two. At the same time rapidly rising maintenance and construction costs made infrastructure projects more expensive. These forces worked together to close and bolt the door on significant public works funding.

The numbers tell the tale. In 1950, spending on America's public works accounted for 19.1 percent of all government dollars spent. That figure fell to 10.1 percent by 1970, then to 6.8 percent by 1984.[3]

HIGHWAYS PAVED WITH POTHOLES

Probably the most visible sign of America's infrastructure problem is the ever-increasing time it takes to drive to work. Bumper-to-bumper traffic is more than an aggravation. It is also expensive in terms of both lost resources and reduced productivity. Government officials report that traffic congestion wasted 1.4 billion gallons of gasoline in 1984; and 20 minutes lost in commute time per day over a 45-year career equals about two working years.[4]

A 1987 study by the Los Angeles County Transportation Commission revealed that the cost of traffic congestion was about 485,000 hours per day wasted by commuters and shippers. That number equals "a minimum of about 507 million per year in wasted time, and about 72 million gallons of gasoline. . . ." And that was just for Los Angeles County.[5]

It is estimated that truck operating expenses increase by 6.3 cents per mile when road conditions drop from good to fair. The Department of Transportation projects that if the country's roads are allowed to continue deteriorating, the economy will forfeit increases of 3.2 percent in the gross national product, 5.9 percent in disposable income, 2.2 percent in employment, and 2.7 percent in manufacturing productivity.[6] We simply cannot afford such losses.

Americans presently travel two trillion miles by car, truck, bus, and mass transit. That figure is expected to double by the year 2020. However, it is not unusual for an interstate highway project to take twenty years or more from inception to completion. Clearly, if we are to have the roads needed in the future, we will need to begin building them now.

Of course, a great deal of money is already being spent every year on highways—about $13 billion. But even that impressive amount turns out to be grossly inadequate in the face of repair estimates that run from $560 billion to more than $650 billion spread over the coming two decades.[7] And that's just to bring America's roads up to minimum engineering standards. The problem and its costs are staggering; but those numbers make the investment potential equally impressive.

ONCE ABUNDANT, FRESH WATER NOW GETTING SCARCE

The increased rationing of drinking water in drier regions of the nation is another indication of the depth of the infrastructure problem. Some communities are reduced to using no more than 50 gallons of water per day per household. That is about enough water for one load of laundry and one short shower.

Blame for the shortage is usually placed on drought cycles that leave many reservoirs with less than one-fourth of their normal capacity. However, water experts say that enough water falls each winter to serve our needs many times over. The trouble is with our outdated and inadequate water collection systems. The fact is that our water systems have not been expanded along with the growing population. High growth areas have been especially hard hit. Many communities, notably in the West and in Florida are trying to serve their residents with systems that were originally designed for half as many people.

Leaks compound the problems. In most underground water systems, leaks have gone without attention for so long that one-fourth to one-half of the supply is lost enroute. We have reached the point where the leaks waste more money than it will cost to fix them.

Similar troubles, with dangerous implications, have surfaced in the nation's reservoirs. About 3,000 dams above populated areas have been found to be unsafe by the U.S. Army Corps of Engineers.[8] Here, too, the cure will cost less than the problem, since a single dam failure could destroy billions of dollars in property and almost certainly kill hundreds of people.

UNCLE SAM BEGINNING TO ACT

It should be evident that we can no longer serve the America of the 1990s with 1950s public works systems. We have to fix and expand because the systems are falling apart. They are also costing us a lot of money. Workers can't get to jobs, products are slow to get to the market, and fuel is wasted. The lack of a decent infrastructure prevents us from expanding industry and commerce in many areas.

Although the situation is bad, there is a bright side to the picture. Uncle Sam will be forced to act—and soon. In fact, the federal government is beginning to do so already, even though we have a growing budget deficit. State governments are also gearing up for action.

Currently the bulk of the new money that is being raised for our growing infrastructure needs is coming from higher user fees. Already, gas taxes were raised sharply earlier this year. More hikes are on the way. Federal matching funds for local projects, though presently at low levels, are also likely to be boosted over the next few years. It is important to note that the government's role in funding infrastructure projects is favored by most elected officials. Such spending is increasingly seen as an excellent way to get federal money back to hometown voters. In addition, big ticket public works projects help prime the economic pump during downturns. Not only do they put people back to work, they get them off unemployment and welfare.

Completely new funding sources are also in the works. Public-private partnerships hold particular promise. Private roads are now on the drawing board in California and Virginia. Lockheed recently expressed an interest in buying the Albany County Airport in New York. The list goes on and on. Because private involvement takes much of the burden off taxpayers, I think we will see much more of it in the 1990s.

Whatever the source, money for rebuilding America's infrastructure must be, and will be, found. As the trend generates momentum it will create many profitable opportunities for investors.

STOCKS TO WATCH

Engineering and Design Firms Start the Biggest Projects

It is estimated that it will take about $200 billion per year during the next two decades to bring America's infrastructure up to date.[9] Work of this magnitude must begin with experienced engineering firms. In fact, the bigger the project, the more essential the planning becomes. Since engineering and design companies usually charge a percentage of a project's total cost, their profits are all but assured.

Michael Baker Corp. is not a pure infrastructure play. However, two-thirds of the firm's income comes from government agencies which utilize the company's exceptional design and engineering services as well as its construction management capabilities. Projects include water and wastewater systems, solid and hazardous waste, highways, bridges and airports, seaports, mass transit, energy, and mining. The company has also acquired a leading role in the design of military bases. Lastly, Michael Baker recently opened an office in Germany—just in time for the 1992 debut of the European Community.

Michael Baker's strong position as a leading engineering and design firm steadily increased through the second half of the 1980s. The company's size and diversity allow it to respond favorably to virtually any substantial project that the infrastructure rebuilding boom might present. The firm appears to be extremely well positioned to profit during the 1990s.

Greiner Engineering derives approximately 75 percent of its income from publicly funded projects. The firm offers a full array of planning, engineering, architectural, and construction management services. Greiner's special strengths are in transportation systems. Road, bridge, mass transit, and airport development projects are all specialties of the firm. Greiner is also keeping its other capabilities active. These include water and floor control systems, waste treatment, and marine facilities.

Greiner has shown a generally improving financial condition through the last few years. That is due in part to the firm's history of involvement in large private construction projects including industrial plants, shopping centers, and health care centers. Greiner should continue to benefit from future projects from both the public and private sectors.

Public Works Construction Firms See Rising Orders

Once engineering and design work has been done, public works projects are handed over to appropriate construction firms. Many such firms are highly specialized. However, several large companies operate in many fields. Because of their broad range of capabilities, the bigger firms are often able to keep busy when more focused firms are idle.

Larger public works construction firms should find the 1990s to be particularly profitable as more and more public works projects are funded. Not only do public projects help insulate contractors from economic downturns, but they also tend to be big ticket items that take many years to complete. All in all, the long term outlook appears quite good for America's well established public works contractors.

Morrison Knudsen is a leading construction firm offering a full range of building capabilities from basic design to project management. The company is able to handle nearly every type of job from installing pipelines to building nuclear plants. Public works projects are a major source of revenue, and contracts from the private sector also contribute to the bottom line.

Morrison Knudsen is noteworthy for its efforts to fine tune its operations for the 1990s. A shipbuilding business was sold in favor of greater efforts with rail systems. Environmental capabilities were boosted considerably. In fact, the company is moving strongly into hazardous waste abatement projects—an area with considerable promise of its own. Morrison Knudsen's strong and diversified position in the public works market should allow it to respond easily to growing contract awards in the coming decade. It may represent the single best way to invest in the broad infrastructure trend.

Granite Construction is also a leading heavy contractor but with more geographic focus than Morrison Knudsen. The company operates primarily in the southwestern market that includes Nevada, Arizona, and California where it is a major builder of both public and private projects.

Granite's history in the infrastructure business is impressive. The company has been involved in the interstate freeway system, California's aqueduct, and San Francisco's impressive Bay Area Rapid Transit (BART). In addition, Granite builds dams, tunnels, canals, and airports. I think the company will find its capabilities in increasing demand in the coming years.

Kasler Corporation is an important California-based heavy construction contractor that has the capabilities to do nearly any type of large public project. However, in recent years more than 90 percent of its work has been in road and bridge construction. Almost all operations are in the high growth areas of the Southwest where road building budgets have been increasing and will increase even more in the future.

Kasler excells in freeway projects, including rural, desert, and urban systems. The company also builds complicated interchanges with several levels of traffic and ramps as high as 175 feet above ground. Kasler is currently the contractor for the Los Angeles Century Freeway project which is the largest highway project currently underway in America.

Kasler experienced subcontractor troubles during the late 1980s, but these appear to be over. I think the company is well positioned for the growing infrastructure trend.

Astec Industries makes specialized mixing machines that combine liquid asphalt, a heavy petroleum product made by CalMet (see the following section) and other refiners, with the proper aggregates for use in highway construction. The company also owns Barber–Greene, a major producer of road paving machines that are used throughout the world. Astec's management owns about 40 percent of the stock.

Increasing Demand for General Construction Materials

When compared to the companies that span rivers, build superhighways, and create dams, the makers of construction materials look pretty dull. That undoubtedly explains why few investors bother to take a good look at the materials industry.

However, any investor who overlooks the construction materials industry in the 1990s will probably have cause to regret it. That is because cement and aggregates will form the backbone for almost every public works project we will see. Highways, dams, airports, power plants, and so on use millions of tons of materials, and generate millions of dollars for their suppliers.

Because of their great weight, most construction materials are obtained from companies close to the projects that need them. Consequently, investors must be conscious of which regions of the country are getting the most building activity and invest accordingly. Here are the major companies located in regions that look especially promising.

Texas Industries is a major manufacturer of concrete products in the American Southwest, an area that has seen the largest growth in the nation in the last decade. Its 81 percent-owned subsidiary, Chaparral Steel (see Chapter 13), is a rapidly growing firm that provides Texas Industries with about two-thirds of its revenue.

Texas Industries is unique because it supplies two very different but essential construction materials—steel and concrete. Since almost every public works project requires mass quantities of both products, the company is in a particularly strong position to profit. The firm's location in the Southwest is also fortunate as that section of the country should see a great deal of construction activity during the 1990s.

CalMat Co. is a top producer of asphalt, construction aggregates, and concrete. Although the company's materials are used in a variety of construction projects, its use in highways is a major contributor to revenues. In fact, CalMat is the largest producer of hot mix asphalt in its region, operating more than 40 such plants from California to Arizona. The company also rents paving equipment to highway and airport contractors. CalMat is in a good position to respond quickly to orders for new road building material. The company could be one of the first firms to profit from any upswing in highway construction.

Florida Rock Industries occupies the leading position in the Southeastern United States, producing concrete and many construction aggregates. Two recent acquisitions reinforce its market role. Revenues come from highway and government projects, the rest from the private sector. Florida Rock's revenues fell during 1990 due to the softening construction market in its home territory. However, a resumption in the 1990s in the normally robust Florida economy should create many new public and private contracts for this well placed firm.

Vulcan Materials is America's largest supplier of construction aggregates—primarily crushed stone. The company also produces industrial chemicals, which contribute about 40 percent to revenues. Vulcan's 120 aggregate plants are strategically located in 14 states, primarily in the central and southwest region, that have a history of large public and private construction projects. Vulcan should do very well when new infrastructure spending occurs at the same time the economy will support the company's private sector operations.

Southdown, Inc. is one of America's biggest manufacturers of cement, the binding agent that turns sand and gravel into concrete. The company operates plants from California to Pennsylvania. Unlike aggregates, which are rarely shipped very far from their source, cement is often moved great distances to plants that create concrete for local projects. Consequently, Southdown can profit from any regional upturn in the heavy construction industry.

The company is also noteworthy for its move into the environmental sector. Using special combustion processes, the company can now burn contaminated oils in its concrete kilns. Of course, that disposes of the toxic products at the same time it supplies the company with heat. Southdown's presence in both the infrastructure and the environmental areas could prove to be quite profitable over the next few years.

Heavy Construction Equipment Manufacturers

Nearly every construction project requires the use of heavy equipment. Even small jobs need specialized gear if they are to be done efficiently. It is important to note that existing inventories of equipment are not sufficient for the expected upturn in heavy construction activity. During the recession, financially pressed contractors scaled down their inventories to save money. They also squeezed most of the remaining life from what little gear they kept. As a result, many firms—including some that are quite well known—will need to go on a buying spree when construction orders start coming in again. Of course, that will be good news for equipment makers.

Caterpillar, Inc. is famous for its bulldozers, road graders, and related equipment. It is the world's largest heavy equipment manufacturer. The company also derives about one-fourth of its income from the production of diesel and natural gas engines for truck manufacturers. In addition, electric power generators and related infrastructure systems contribute to profits. All in all, Caterpillar is ideally positioned to profit from increasing public and private construction projects.

Caterpillar can hold particular promise for investors because it is quite cyclical. The company has a habit of periodically frightening Wall Street which results in very low stock prices. Investments made during such periods have a history of paying off handsomely.

Ingersoll–Rand construction equipment is found at nearly every public works project as well as almost every large private sector development. The firm's primary line is air compressors which supply power to tools such as jackhammers. However, the company also makes pavement cutters, heavy rock drilling tools, mining and tunnel machinery, air filtering systems, and other equipment.

Ingersoll–Rand represents a broad construction investment that can profit from weaker activity than is needed to benefit heavy equipment makers like Caterpillar.

Millions of Dollars for New Water and Sewer Systems

In many parts of the country, the infrastructure is more than a century old, especially its sewer and water systems. A recent emergency repair to a street in a major city in Oregon actually uncovered a redwood pipe that dated from the 1880s. It leaked more water than it delivered, but it was still in use!

Throughout the United States, the situation has reached the point where even when the systems are working properly, they don't serve our needs. It is estimated that about half of America's communities are unable to allow additional building permits because their water and sewage systems are operating at maximum capacity.

The size of the problem is staggering, as is its investment potential. In 1988 the Environmental Protection Agency released an estimate of more than $60 billion to bring water treatment facilities into compliance with the 1972 Federal Clean Water Act.[10] Even tougher standards are on the way.

It is clear that upgrading and expanding our water and sewer systems will be one of America's biggest public works projects of the 1990s. Two firms stand out from the handful of firms that are likely to benefit from this trend.

Insituform of North America is particularly interesting. The firm holds the patent for a unique technology that installs a new resin-impregnated pipe through existing pipes, sewers, and tunnels that have failed. Most importantly, the Insituform process does not require excavation with all its attending costs and disruptions. In a single day, cities can often fix a pipe for a few thousand dollars that might otherwise cost many times that amount and leave a street torn up for months.

I can't be certain that Insituform will be a big winner in the 1990s. However, I can say that the firm's use of new technology to solve old public works problems is an example of the kind of innovation that will receive an attentive hearing by public officials from coast to coast.

Davis Water & Waste supplies a full range of municipal water and sewage distribution products. The list includes pipes, valves, pumps, fire hydrants, fittings, and flow meters. The company also provides specialized materials that are used in municipal treatment plants. Davis operates primarily in the Southeast, where it is the largest supplier in the industry. The company serves its market through a network of over 30 service centers in key areas. This firm is a well positioned pure play that should do well.

Electric Utilities to Upgrade and Expand

As the nation continues growing, there will continue to be an increasing demand for electric power generation—by any means possible. More efficient power production and an increased trend toward conservation will have its impact, but probably not enough to balance the effects of growth.

Late in the decade I would expect nuclear plants to stage a comeback. Even with the best pollution controls, fossil fuels create vast quantities of carbon dioxide which is thought to be the cause of the greenhouse effect. By contrast new technologies appear to make nuclear power virtually safe. Finally, the problem with nuclear waste disposal will finally be solved. This will be discussed in greater detail in Chapter 14.

For the first part of the decade, new power plant production will make use of fossil fuels. In particular, natural gas will be favored because we happen to have it in great quantities. It is also our cleanest fossil fuel and can meet current clean air standards with modern pollution control equipment.

Upgraded distribution networks are also in the works. Many of our transmission lines are out of date. Some of them lose nearly as much power as they deliver. That situation won't be allowed to continue.

The biggest demand will be for private power generation. Many industries either can't tap into the public power grid or they find it uneconomical to do so. A few companies need private power plants in order to turn their waste products into energy.

The stage is set, therefore, for an increase in the construction of power plants and electric distribution systems. I expect orders to build slowly but steadily as the decade progresses.

Powell Industries is a leader in electrical power plant equipment design and manufacturing, primarily for private industry. Clients include chemical plants, offshore oil platforms, and paper mills. Public utilities and government agencies are also important customers. In addition to generators, Powell supplies electrical monitoring and switching gear that is used in power distribution systems. As a result, Powell is one of the few companies that is able to offer complete electrical systems from generation to final use.

L.E. Myers Co. Group is a specialist in large-scale power distribution systems that are sold primarily to electric utilities. Products range from transmission lines to complete substations. In addition, the company acts as a prime contractor for most jobs. The firm services customers throughout North America. Myers is so well established that it may get a substantial portion of the contracts to upgrade our electric distribution network. The jobs should be worth millions of dollars to the company.

FlowMole Corp. is somewhat reminiscent of Insituform, which was presented earlier. FlowMole specializes in making small diameter underground tunnels used primarily to hold power cables. The process uses high pressure water jets and high-tech guidance techniques to create tunnels as long as 400 feet. Jobs are done with a minimum of surface disruption—a small pit at each end is all the excavation that is generally needed. In many applications FlowMole offers the least expensive way to expand or extend electric service. Over one-third of U.S. utilities have used the company. Many European firms are also becoming customers.

Infrastructure Exports on the Rise

An often overlooked source of infrastructure business in the 1990s will be from foreign markets. Undeveloped countries and newly emerging industrial countries are both in great need of roads, bridges, airports, water and sewer systems, power plants, and everything else. Where will they get the money for the work? The United States will undoubtedly lend it to them.

There is sound economic justification for the United States to help friendly countries develop their infrastructure. One of the reasons the United States is not number one in the world market any more, according to the General Accounting Office, is that other countries devote more resources to developing Third World public works projects. According to its report, Third World countries with new roads and bridges tend to buy cars and trucks from the people who help fund them. Improving a country's infrastructure also tends to boost its economic health which creates new markets for everyone.[11]

America is now attempting to make changes in our foreign policy to favor greater infrastructure development. We already require countries receiving foreign aid to spend most of their funds on U.S. products. In the 1990s we will insist that much of that money be spent on improving basic services. Although that policy will not favor any particular group of stocks, it will give added power to the infrastructure trend. It makes the industry all the more attractive for long-term investors.

NOTES

1. Joseph M. Giglio, "Fragile Foundations: A Report on America's Public Works, Final Report to the President and the Congress," *National Council on Public Works Improvement*, February 1988.
2. Ibid.
3. Ibid.
4. Jonathan R. Laing, "The Rebuilding of America," *Barron's*, November 14, 1988.
5. Giglio, "Fragile Foundations."
6. John Voo, "As Highways Decay Their State Becomes Drag On The Economy," *The Wall Street Journal*, August 30, 1989.
7. Ibid.
8. Laing, "The Rebuilding of America."
9. Giglio, "Fragile Foundations."
10. Laing, "The Rebuilding of America."
11. Eric Felten, "GAO Urges Foreign Aid to be Tied to Trading," *Insight*, July 30, 1990.

CHAPTER 11

THE UNITED STATES TURNS TO PRIVATE EDUCATION

If one of America's Founding Fathers traveled forward to the present time to see how this country turned out, he would recognize very little. Our factories would be fantastic to him. He would be stunned at our transportation system and shocked to disbelief at our medical advances. Generally, he would feel completely out of touch and out of place. However, if he walked into a public school he would feel at home, because our education system has not changed significantly in the last 200 years.

To educate our young we still put 25 to 30 children in a room to be lectured by a teacher in front of a chalkboard. Given the needs of the twentieth century, this outmoded format is just not getting the job done. The problem is not lazy teachers or a lack of money; it's the system that is deficient.

To see how bad our educational system has become we have only to look around us. Start with our technology needs. According to Senator Mark Hatfield of Oregon, the demand for scientists and engineers in America during the last 13 years increased 85 percent, far exceeding the supply. The senator reports that our graduates are so ignorant of technical subjects that current trends will produce 700,000 fewer scientists and engineers than we will need by the year 2000.[1] A separate study reveals that about 13 percent of our 17 year olds are illiterate. In Japan and Germany the rate is about 1 percent. In 1950, about 3 million Americans could not read.[2] Today, somewhere between 30 and 40 million cannot make sense out of a printed page, according to education commentator, Regna Lee Wood.[3]

Now look at economics. According to the 1988 Commission on Youth and America's Future, from 1973 to 1986 the income of Americans 20 to 24 who had finished high school dropped 28 percent, from $15,221 to $10,924.[4] In the 1990s that decline will continue. Former U.S. Labor Secretary William Brock said in July 1990 that if nothing changes to halt the slide, many parts of our society will soon take on the characteristics of a Third World country.[5]

The social costs are just as bad. Our schools are so unsuccessful that many children give up in frustration, usually without knowing exactly why, except that they conclude that there is little real-world value in continuing. America's dropout rate of 14 percent is soaring up to as much as 50 percent in some inner city schools.[6] Unfortunately, there is little indication of an end in sight. Of course, the failure contributes to America's huge problems with drugs, alcohol, broken families, and the loss of human potential.

POOR EDUCATION CREATES POOR COMPETITORS

It is now clear that America's dismal education system is doing more than creating a permanent underclass—it is hurting the future of the nation. Poorly skilled workers are a major contributor to the decline of American goods in the global market. If nothing changes, it is estimated that the cumulative shortfall in America's gross national product between 1990 and the year 2010 will be more than $3 trillion, according to a December 1990 projection by Cornell University economist John Bishop.[7]

Meanwhile, our competitors continue to upgrade their already successful educational systems. According to a December 1988 article by Gary Becker, professor of economics at the University of Chicago, Japan, South Korea, Taiwan, Hong Kong, and Singapore have all learned that with the right skills their people can compete with anyone in the modern world. Professor Becker says our competitors also pay more attention to on-the-job training, work habits, and methods of improving worker skills.[8]

LIFELONG LEARNING COMPOUNDS THE PROBLEM

To make matters worse our educational needs are growing exponentially. The days are long over when a person can learn a trade then practice it for 30 years. Today's workers will be trained an average of five times in their lifetime according to a November 1988 projection by Hewlett–Packard President John Young.[9]

The bottom line is clear: not only is our educational system inadequate for today's needs, it is also totally unsuited for our future needs when millions of Americans will need to go back to school again and again.

TOP HEAVY TEACHING TO TOPPLE

Many people, especially within the education industry, believe that the problems with our schools can be solved by the simple application of large sums of money. But a closer look reveals that more money simply produces more expenses. Nationally, overhead costs during the 1980s rose 110 percent, while teachers' wages rose 24 percent.[10] The more the nation spent on education, the more its administrative bureaucracy grew; and proportionately less money made it to the students.

According to Bruce Cooper, a Fordham University professor, and Robert Sarrel, budget director of the New York City Board of Education, less than one-third of public school funds made it to New York classrooms during 1988–1989. Where did most of the money go? About half was spent on administration. The public affairs office is staffed by 60 people, the office of strategic planning by 161.[11] Incredibly, there appear to be more school administrators in the state of New York than there are in the entire European Community, which contains 12 countries and a total of 320 million people!

PRIVATE SCHOOLS WILL BE THE CHOICE AHEAD

The American public, its government, and industry appear to agree that our public education system will not improve quickly enough to adequately address our current problems. It is simply too resistant to change. Consequently, America is looking to the private sector for solutions—and it is finding them.

There are several reasons that private education is becoming the way out of our educational dilemma. The first is the greatly increased efficiency. A good example is provided by America's Catholic schools. According to New York based education policy consultant Thomas Vitollo–Martin, Catholic schools in 1988–1989 managed to deliver at least half of their funds to the classroom.[12] At the same time Catholic students scored higher than public school students in reading, math, and the sciences.

The situation with private vocational schools is even more dramatic. Less than 10 percent of funds go to administration. In addition, vocational schools do a superior job of teaching people what they need to know to get hired and fit into the modern workplace.

A large part of the private sector's advantage comes from being removed from the typical civil service malaise that infests all public institutions. Private educators can be more innovative and more adaptable to fast-changing industry needs. They can also make quicker use of new technology, which will be a major trend in the 1990s. Finally, most private schools can hire and fire as they see fit, which keeps people on their toes and the educational process in high gear.

VOUCHERS WILL BENEFIT PRIVATE SCHOOLS

In the 1990s we will undoubtedly see the widespread adoption of a voucher system to support education. It will be established to force the public school system to upgrade its services and be more responsive to public desires. However, the voucher system will actually do the private educational system far more good in the long run.

A voucher is a certificate issued by the state which entitles a taxpayer's children to an education. The voucher can be "spent" at any school in the system which meets the parent's approval. Even if the desired school is across town, the child may attend it. There were many gloom and doom predictions about vouchers when they were first introduced but they appear to be groundless. A mass exodus from poorer school districts did not occur. However, there have been instances when parents pulled their children from schools that were ineffective. Of course, the right to do so benefits the public because these unsatisfactory schools have been forced to improve their teaching skills or close their doors.

In places such as Minnesota where vouchers are already being tried, many people are expressing the desire to use them for private schools as well. Most of these requests are from families who want to send their children to religious schools. However, an increasing number of people want their children to attend private vocational schools.

Perhaps more significantly, the students themselves are expressing the desire for the more focused education that the public sector offers.

I have no doubt that as the voucher system continues to prove its worth, and as more states adopt it, taxpayer demands will ultimately expand the system to include private schools. That will provide the schools, and their investors, with very attractive profits.

BIG BUSINESS BECOMES TEACHER

For awhile, industries supported local public schools in the hope of gaining better-trained graduates as employees. Many still do so. But sadly, an increasing number of corporate leaders realize that their millions of dollars in contributions have largely been in vain. Employers are still deluged with applicants who lack the basic skills needed for entry-level training programs.

Unfortunately, it is more than basic education skills that are lacking. Not only do many new employees not know how to read and write well, but they don't even know how to sit down and listen. And this is occuring as companies adopt progressive new programs that ask employees to think, solve problems, and communicate their ideas effectively to the group. With many of today's workers the innovative new plans won't work according to a June 1989 observation by Robert Fraser, associate director of Michigan's industrial training program.[13]

Industry, for the most part, is now giving up trying to get the public school system to teach basic education, much less specific job skills. Instead, many firms are offering their own classes to their employees, at the cost of $30 billion per year on remedial education, according to a 1990 estimate by Cornell University economist John Bishop.[14] For example, when Corning discovered that two-thirds of their 20,000 employees were weak or seriously deficient in reading and math comprehension, management established a goal of devoting 5 percent of all work hours to classroom training. The payoff: the firm's return on equity jumped from 9.3 percent in 1984, at the start of the program, to 15.9 percent in 1989. Said Chairman James R. Houghton in December 1990, "A large part of our profit increase has come about because of our embarking on this way of life."[15]

Industry forecasters predict that corporate life in the 21st century will include employee recruitment programs not at the college level, but for high school graduates. Selected young people will attend company schools then go on to college on company scholarships. They will learn specific job skills tailored to promised positions after graduation.

For older employees, businesses will provide enrichment reading, math, communication, and high-tech courses. For immigrants, employers will offer classes in English as a second language. Already, corporate giants such as IBM, Citicorp, and 3M are giving these ideas serious thought. Many of them already have such programs. Businesses are learning that if they want educated employees, they will often have to provide for themselves. That task will ultimately cost billions of dollars and will create another large market for our growing private education industry.

PUBLIC SCHOOLS WILL FINALLY RESPOND

No system, no matter how entrenched it may be, can withstand pressure to change if that pressure is sufficiently strong and long lasting. The public school system is no exception to that rule.

In many areas public schools are working overtime to meet the demands of the 20th century. Although progress is slow, it can be measured. The better schools now have at least some computers. Vocational education programs are being established. New textbooks are on order. Nonteaching staffs are getting trimmed. Budget managers with business rather than education degrees are being hired. Although these changes are occurring very slowly, public school reform will add power to the huge trends that are starting in American education.

STOCKS TO WATCH

The education industry offers a wide variety of choices to investors from blue chip multimedia publishers to little educational computer companies. Many of the smaller firms sell for only a few dollars a share and offer great promise. Consequently, our emerging education market is one area where even the most prudent investors can justify an occasional speculation.

Vocational Schools See Rising Enrollments

One of the most promising areas in the private education sector are vocational schools. Although they are not a new idea, changing conditions in the workplace plus inefficient public schools are making many vocational schools increasingly attractive. Many modern vocational schools have exactly what millions of students need in the 1990s and they are prospering from rising enrollments.

The big advantage vocational schools have over the public competition is their much greater efficiency. Unlike the broad approach to learning used by public schools, vocational students focus only on the specific job-related skills they need to get and hold a job. That results in much lower costs, shorter terms, and earlier graduation. In fact, vocational schools tend to do their job so well that many employers are beginning to look upon a trade school certificate as just as valuable, if not more so, than a public school degree.

Public schools often criticize vocational programs for not creating well rounded students who can speak knowledgeably about art, music, politics, and other subjects. That is a valid charge. However, the better vocational schools do at least teach many basic subjects such as reading and computation along with the work-related subjects they offer. In fact, many observers believe that trade schools do a better job teaching basic skills than do our public schools.

Vocational schools stand to benefit from the growing lifelong learning trend. As mentioned earlier, the average high school graduates of the 1990s will have as many as five careers during their working lives. Once a person has a basic education degree, the recurring need for further training will be only for specific skills. Consequently, we can expect to see growing demand during the coming decade for training in many specialized subjects. Vocational schools are already showing that they will be at the head of the class in filling those demands.

Vocational schools will also see more demand resulting from current labor contracts. Most work agreements now contain provisions that require employers to retrain employees who are laid off. Vocational schools are proving to be the instructors of choice for contracted retraining programs.

As new skills are needed in the workplace industry will also turn to vocational schools. Many schools are offered contracts to come into the workplace and hold classes onsite. Because vocational schools are in the private sector and have learned to compete, they can offer much more efficient instruction than can public schools or community colleges.

The growth of vocational education represents a growing trend which will include high school students as well. Less than 10 percent of our nation's high school seniors have the skills needed for demanding jobs or college level work, according to a multi-year analysis of tests given by the National Assessment of Educational Progress.[16] Many kids are dropping out of public schools to attend trade schools that teach them something they see as useful in the job market. When the public school system voucher program is extended to vocational schools, the trend will explode.

During the 1990s vocational schools should become even more popular than they already are. Driven by competition, they will continue to keep abreast of new teaching skills, new machines, and new ways to deliver more information in a shorter time for less money. Their clients, from corporate giants to individual students, will respond accordingly which will benefit today's investors.

National Education is the largest technical training firm in the United States, supplying services to both private and government markets. The company runs 53 schools that focus on turning out skilled entry-level workers for high demand industries. Ten of its centers are "super schools" which provide state-of-the-art equipment and teaching techniques. The company also offers independent study courses and publishes educational works.

National Education is noteworthy not only for its size and success but also for its innovative instructional methods which are often copied by others. Courses make full use of multimedia instructional aids including print, video, computers, and simulators. All in all, the company is well positioned to profit from the developing trends in American education.

Concorde Career Colleges is a smaller firm than National Education but it has considerable promise providing vocational training for fast-growing medical and dental fields. Medical technicians will be in rising demand during the 1990s. Particularly needed are dental assistants, EKG technicians, laboratory assistants, pharmacy technicians, opticians, and certified nursing assistants; all of whom can receive training at Concorde. The company operates 21 schools in 10 states.

Concorde is also moving into the professional market. With the acquisition of Person/Wolinsky Associates the company offers CPA review courses. Paralegal training is also being added. A travel school rounds out the new offerings. Concorde appears to be on track for a profitable decade.

Innovative Textbook and Multimedia Publishers to Do Well

One part of the education sector that investors must not ignore is the textbook industry. Although that industry appears to be unexciting, with an outlook to match, nothing could be further from the truth. Textbook companies have enormous promise because they have learned that the owner of information can repackage it in a variety of ways. Smart textbook companies are coming out with software, videos, audio tapes, educational television shows, and a big new trend—computer information services. Such multimedia products are becoming very popular in both private and public schools. As you may imagine, they are bringing in top profits to their producers.

Educational computer networks offered by top publishers are particularly promising at present. A student can sit down at a computer terminal and enter a network outside of the school system. Once logged on, the student can interact with dozens of programs no school could possibly afford to purchase. The school does not have to buy anything but the end user equipment—inexpensive PCs serve nicely. Of course, the school is billed for each student's network time but the per pupil cost is very low.

The new multimedia technology will not mean an end to textbooks. That demand will remain. In fact, the need for textbooks will increase as the rapid pace of change calls for more frequent revisions. The number of new books needed just to reflect the recent changes in Europe will be staggering. Similar changes exist in nearly every subject.

The demand for multimedia products will also increase as large companies develop more in-house educational programs. Aetna, for example, began a two-month long training program in 1989 to bring 130 new entry level employees up to hiring standards. Many of the firm's student/employees had previously been welfare cases.[17] Similar programs, including hundreds that are less socially ambitious, are being started from coast to coast. Of course, each new classroom and each new program boosts the need for teaching materials. The outlook is very good for the handful of companies that dominate the textbook and multimedia industry.

Houghton Mifflin is one of America's most established and respected textbook publishing houses. The firm's emphasis is on reading, math, science, social studies, and foreign languages. The company also provides trade books, educational software, electronic databases, and testing materials. Houghton Mifflin is noteworthy for its attractive sales terms which allow customers to acquire the textbooks they need on three- to six-year contracts. Although the costs are spread out over time, the books are delivered early in the contract period.

Houghton Mifflin is beginning to use its information to increase revenues in very creative ways. For example, the firm recently started licensing its reference data to firms that create electronic language aid systems for students, businesses people, and doctors. Many popular spelling checkers, foreign language translators, and so on now contribute to Houghton's bottom line. This company should do even better in the 1990s that it did in the 1980s.

McGraw-Hill, Inc. is an information giant. Although the company is not a pure play in education, it is marketing more and more of its information to schools of every type. Sometimes it does so directly through its line of textbooks and multimedia products. In addition, the company benefits from selling many of its mainline products to schools that find it contributes to the instructional process. This is particularly true among secondary schools, vocational schools, and colleges.

McGraw-Hill's educational potential increased recently when the company started a textbook customizing system. With the push of a few buttons the company's editors can now alter and update texts for changing conditions. Modern presses make it economical—and profitable—to print the special texts in relatively small quantities. McGraw-Hill's huge information base, plus its ability to use and reuse it in a variety of ways, should pay off handsomely in the 1990s.

Educational Technology Lives Up to Its Promise

Many education experts predict that the present lecture method of instruction will not survive intact into the coming century. It is too wasteful of America's resources to continue to have one well-paid person for every 25 students. Somehow, the student/teacher ratio must be made much greater or we will not be able to afford any meaningful improvements in our schools.

The trend in education will be towards the kinds of advances that we have seen in every other American institution that has learned to deliver more products and services for the dollar. It may sound crass to apply that commercial principle to teaching children but it results in more good for more children. We must have these advances, and we will have them.

One solution that is already showing considerable promise is the use of computers and computerized systems to help students learn many skills. Research done by Charles L. Blaschke, president of Educational Turnkey Systems shows that computer-taught students learn 30 percent more in 40 percent less time, compared to traditional teaching methods.[18] Other studies have uncovered about 125 programs that at least double the learning rate of students.

Industry is leading the way to more efficient teaching methods. It is presently spending much more money on computer-based instruction than public schools, based on a percentage of compared budgets. But schools are beginning to play catch up. I believe we will see enormous progress in the 1990s.

The potential for further expansion of educational equipment sales is enormous. Less than 1 percent of America's companies are spending 95 percent of the total job training money, according to former Labor Secretary Brock. As employers recognize the compelling benefits from in-house training in the 1990s, that small percentage will grow substantially. In public schools the potential for high-tech growth is about the same. As late as June 1988 the ratio of computers to students was about 1 to 35, according to John Schram, senior vice president of Houghton Mifflin.[19]

All in all, the untapped markets in both the public and private sectors represent extraordinary opportunities for the emerging educational equipment industry. Here are the areas within the education technology field that should be watched by astute investors during the 1990s.

Demand Grows for Educational Computers and Software
When computers hit the education field early in the 1980s many experts predicted that we would see an almost instant revolution in learning. Clearly, that did not occur. However, it did start a transformation

that is beginning to deliver good results. As the movement gathers momentum in the 1990s it will create many profitable opportunities for investors.

So far the biggest demand in educational computers is for use in computer literacy classes. It isn't difficult to see why the demand is so powerful. Industries are so short of trained employees with computer skills that their ability to expand is becoming severely limited. The shortage is especially critical in technically advanced occupations. But, even the most low-tech business is now equipped with a computer of some sort for handling administrative and product management systems. Those companies are also hard pressed to find properly trained workers.

The result is a trend that cuts across both private and public educational institutions. It requires that modern equipment be found in virtually every classroom. The demand for the hardware will be great—the demand for software will be even greater. In fact, for every dollar spent on computers about $2 to $3 more is spent on software programs. Stanford's professor of education Henry M. Levin reported in July 1989 that about $260 million was being spent annually on educational software.[20] I expect that number to increase steadily for several years.

The next, and by far the biggest, demand for computers will be for instructional applications. That use is presently in its infancy. However, the groundwork has been laid for more computerized instruction in several fields, especially in math and science. Teachers in those subjects are not only comfortable with computers, but they are happy to have them take over the load of teaching routine skills. As their use of computers begins to pay off word will spread throughout the schools. It's only a matter of time before today's trickle of interest becomes a flood.

The market for school computers is already big and it is getting bigger. Its development will not be an overnight event but a steadily growing, long-term trend. Because these high-tech educational systems provide one of the few ways that educators can boost their productivity, their adoption is assured. I think the industry will have a golden future in the 1990s.

Apple Computer is by far the world's leading supplier of educational computers. To date, the company has over 60 percent of the school market. Moreover, the company is likely to maintain its dominant role despite the best efforts of IBM and others. Not only are Apple's products easy to learn—especially the Macintosh line—but they are also inexpensive. In addition, most schools have considerable investments in Apple compatable software which they are unlikely to abandon for a competing system. Lastly, Apple provides top support services to the education market.

Of course, Apple is not a pure play in educational computers. Nevertheless, the company will win in two ways as the education technology market expands. First, it will sell many more systems to schools. Second, and often overlooked, the company will sell large numbers of its computers to adults who trained on Apples as children. All in all, Apple stands to be a very big winner in the 1990s.

Jostens Inc. is a major supplier of many educationally oriented products including class rings, yearbooks, certificates, and diplomas. In addition, the company is moving strongly into large computer-based instruction systems—called Integrated Learning Systems or ILS—through Jostens Learning Corp. The company also supplies staff training and consulting services for computer aided instruction.

Jostens is noteworthy not only because of its excellent systems, but because the company is already well established in the education industry. Although the firm is not a pure play for integrated learning systems, it should benefit substantially from the trend toward improving educational efficiency through the adoption of advanced technology.

WICAT Systems supplies a wide line of advanced computer systems for the education industry. It is nearly a pure play in the ILS industry which it helped found in the early 1980s. WICAT has a varied history. The company went public during a great deal of fanfare about the future of educational computers. When that trend was slow to develop, WICAT fell sharply on lower earnings. The future brightened when IBM purchased a small stake in the company, but obscurity has returned.

For all its past problems, the company's products are very good— it is just waiting for the schools to catch up to what it offers. When that happens, as it should in the 1990s, WICAT could be in the limelight again. I think the company represents an attractive low-cost speculation.

High-Tech Simulators Find Many Applications
The majority of modern vocational, factory, and military training programs teach the operation of complex devices such as automated production equipment, power plant controls, or aircrafts. To do so efficiently, most training programs use high-tech simulators which often combine video laser discs and computers to duplicate actual machines under different operating conditions. Simulators offer many advantages over training with on-line equipment. For example, simulators for nuclear plants can be programmed to present crisis events that could never be tried with an actual plant. Likewise, student pilots can walk away from being shot down and bad weather crashes, having learned from their mistakes.

Simulators also have the advantage of being less costly than most of the actual machines they represent. The devices save additional money because hands-on learning is both fast and thorough. Most simulator trained employees become so skilled with their machines that they are able to move directly into a productive job without long break-in periods.

Simulators have historically been used only for very technical fields. However, they are beginning to find much larger markets to teach more ordinary skills like factory assembly. These expanding applications will provide the simulator industry with growing revenues over the next several years.

Of course, the rapidly expanding role for vocational schools will also boost the demand for simulators of all types. As employers increasingly demand that new hires bring specific skills to the workplace, we will see simulator sales climb steadily.

FlightSafety International provides a full line of high-tech simulators for training airplane pilots and technicians. Customers include the aircraft industry, airlines, government agencies, and the military. The firm also makes training simulators for shipping, steam generating plants, and other advanced training applications. FlightSafety is rapidly becoming the top company in the growing simulator industry. It currently operates more than 100 on-site systems at about 35 training centers in the United States, Canada, and France. As technology oriented education needs explode in the 1990s FlightSafety should continue to expand and prosper.

Perceptronics is a small firm providing simulators to train personnel to operate various types of military equipment. Most of the firm's orders come from research and development contracts with the government. Its product line includes simulators for tanks, armored vehicles, and other defense equipment. The company is also involved in team performance measurement, decision assisting software, and robotic weapon systems as well as specialized simulators.

As a pioneer in its field, Perceptronics has an up and down history. However, its products are considered to be quite effective. It wouldn't take many more orders to turn this company up sharply. I feel it is speculative but worth watching.

ECC International makes computerized simulators that train military personnel to operate and service various weapon systems. About 90 percent of the company's income comes from the U.S. Department of Defense. Several foreign markets are also served. As we learned in the Gulf War, the military is constantly employing newer, more advanced weapons, as well as training its constant turnover of new recruits. In addition, our success in the war boosted the demand for U.S. weapon systems. Consequently, ECC appears likely to see rising orders in the 1990s.

Automated Testing Systems Improve Productivity

It isn't just the lack of modern teaching systems and strategies that retards America's public school systems. The lack of rather ordinary office automation equipment also contributes to high costs and overall ineffectiveness. Most schools still muddle along with electric typewriters and rooms full of paper records. Local real estate offices are more efficient by a wide margin.

The biggest problem created by the lack of modern office systems is the diversion of expensive professional time from teaching to record keeping. Although many teachers may not be paid enough for their professional skills, they receive far too much to be used as clerks. Nevertheless, many teachers use one-third or more of their time bogged down in routine work. Fortunately several school clerical tasks are now being automated. Of the group, computerized test grading and tabulating is the most promising for both schools and investors.

National Computer Systems is the leading supplier of computerized scanning systems used primarily for scoring and analyzing tests. The company's principal customers are educational and government teaching institutions. The firm's high-volume computer-based equipment "reads" pencil marks on examination sheets then fully processes the information in whatever ways are needed.

National Computer's scanning and processing systems can also be used to track surveys, keep attendance records, monitor inventories, and do market research. The company is also moving into school administrative software and medical data processing, fields that also have growing potential. National Computer is also noteworthy for its large trade in scanning supplies which include scoring sheets, tally sheets, and test answer sheets—all of which are machine readable. The supply business provides the firm with a steady flow of revenues which follow each hardware sale.

Basic Equipment and Services Are Also Needed

Although high-tech educational systems offer great promise for the future of America's schools, there is also a growing need for less exciting products and services. Classroom equipment and tutoring companies offer investors particularly attractive opportunities.

Growing Orders for Classroom Fixtures and Equipment

The explosion of industry job skills programs, private vocational schools, and the revamping of public institutions is leading to the creation of more classrooms. Those classrooms need specialized fixtures and equipment. Filling that demand will bring millions of dollars to the leading suppliers.

Kewaunee Scientific is a major producer of scientific lab equipment and furniture. The company supplies workstations for the education market, as well as for governmental, industrial, commercial, and health care laboratories. Specific science fields served include chemistry, physics, and biology. Kewaunee's products range from chemical-safe table tops to cabinets and display cases. Although Kewaunee doesn't supply products that make headlines in the investment media, its outlook appears to be good. The stock should provide investors with gradual long-term gains for the next several years.

Tutoring Businesses Earn An "A + "

Bridging the gap between the public and private schools are firms that offer tutoring services to both elementary and high school students. Most firms started out as day-care centers for preschoolers. Gradually they added some early education features to help children get off to a good start in school. Before long parents were bringing older children back for remedial help. That led to the development of enrichment programs for students who simply want to learn more than public schools can offer.

The leading companies in the tutorial field are **La Petite Academy** and **Kinder-Care Learning Centers**. Both were introduced in Chapter 7 for their growing potential in the day-care industry. Of the two, La Petite Academy remains my top choice for its educational potential as well as for its promise in the growing day-care field.

NOTES

1. Mark Hatfield, "Shortage of Scientists, Engineers Has Become Crisis," *Eugene Register Guard*, February 19, 1990.

2. Gary S. Becker, "Why Don't We Value Schooling as Much as The Asians Do?" *Business Week*, December 12, 1990.

3. Regna Lee Wood, "Letters to the Editor," *The Wall Street Journal*, June 20, 1990.

4. "Future Bleak for Forgotten Half of U.S. Youth," *Eugene Register Guard*, November 18, 1988.

5. Gisela Bolte, "Will Americans Work for $5 a Day?" *Time*, July 23, 1990.

6. Becker, "Why Don't We Value Schooling."

7. Christopher Farrell, et al., "Why We Should Invest in Human Capital," *Business Week*, December 17, 1990.

8. Becker, "Why Don't We Value Schooling."

9. "Worker Training Gets High Priority," *The Wall Street Journal*, November 22, 1988.

10. Dana Wechsler, "Parkinson's Law 101," *Forbes*, June 25, 1990.

11. Ibid.

12. Ibid.

13. Steve Weiner and Charles Siler, "Trained to Order," *Forbes*, June 26, 1989.

14. Farrell, "Why We Should Invest in Human Capital."

15. John Hoerr, "Sharpening Minds for a Competitive Edge," *Business Week*, December 17, 1990.

16. Kenneth H. Bacon, "U.S. Says Students Often Lack Skills For College or Jobs," *The Wall Street Journal*, September 27, 1990.

17. Amanda Bennett, "Aetna Schooling New Hires In Basic Workplace Skills," *The Wall Street Journal*, November 10, 1987.

18. William M. Bulkeley, "Computers Failing as Teaching Aids," *The Wall Street Journal*, June 6, 1988.

19. Ibid.

20. Maria Shao, et al., "Computers in Schools: A Loser? Or Lost Opportunity?" *Business Week*, July 17, 1989.

CHAPTER 12

NATIONAL MEDICAL CRISIS
CREATES OPPORTUNITIES

It is not news to many thousands of Americans that our medical system is failing to meet the needs of our complex society. Health care costs are rising faster than inflation while personal incomes remain flat. At the same time government health programs are generally cutting back, while more and more people go without insurance. If nothing is done many of our citizens will receive little medical care at all in the coming decade.

The troubling state of health care in America is rapidly becoming an economic problem and a political issue at the same time. In response, the medical profession is making enormous efforts to cut costs and increase efficiency. For better or worse, Uncle Sam is also getting into the act. As the various remedies begin to take effect in the 1990s they will create tremendous opportunities for knowledgeable investors.

A LETHAL COMBINATION OF SOARING DEMANDS
AND SOARING COSTS

One of the biggest problems facing our health care industry is soaring demand for services by people who cannot pay for them. Growing ranks of the poor—including the working poor—are draining the finances of our health care providers. So are treatments to people with lingering diseases like AIDS. Long-term drug abuse, especially as it affects newborns, is also becoming critical. The Department of Health and Human Services Office of the Inspector General reports that at least 100,000 crack babies are born in the United States each year which is adding more than $125 million annually to local health care costs in major cities.[1]

Additional demands are placed on our health care system by an ironic twist of medical success. Modern medicine enables people to live longer than was true a generation ago. Of course, older people generally need more care than younger ones, and their ailments are usually more expensive.

Adding to these troubles is a proliferation of expensive high-tech equipment, complex treatments, and (sometimes) rising wages. As a result, charges to patients are increasing three times as fast as the national economy. According to data taken from several sources and reported in the June 11, 1990, *Barron's*, in 1965 Americans spent about $42 billion on medical bills which equaled 5.9 percent of the gross national product. In 1990 that figure rocketed to about $700 billion; 12 percent of the GNP. A projection of the current rate of increase shows that one-fifth of every dollar earned in the year 2000 will be spent on health care. By the year 2010 medical costs will consume 28.5 percent of the GNP.[2]

As health care costs escalate so do insurance premiums. Rising rates are forcing many people to drop coverage. The number of Americans without health insurance rose from 31 million in 1987 to 33.4 million in 1990, according to Census Bureau data.[3] Unfortunately, the trend toward higher insurance fees is unlikely to change. Aside from increasing medical costs, the insurance industry has huge and growing expenses for overhead. According to a November 1990 report by Citizen Fund, a research group that supports a national insurance plan, private insurers spend 33.5 cents of every claim dollar on advertising, sales commissions, research, and paper work.[4] As competition in the health insurance field becomes more intense those expenses are expected to rise proportionately.

Cuts in Medicare coverage will make matters worse even though working age people are not generally covered by that program. The cuts will reduce payments to health care providers who are expected to shift their costs to corporate programs. In response, already strapped employers are increasing the share of health care insurance costs which must be paid by their workers.

Small businesses are hit the hardest. Underwriting requirements for smaller firms often result in premiums that are 10 to 20 percent higher than for larger companies, for the same coverage. Two-thirds of all uninsured employees work for firms with less than 100 workers. Only 29 percent of companies with 25 or fewer employees carry health insurance, according to 1990 data from the Employee Benefit Research Institute.[5] Certain states have enacted legislation to force businesses to provide coverage to their workers no matter what it costs. That strategy is not working because many firms, especially smaller ones, are unable to afford the high rates for their entire workforce. Many are forced to close their doors or lay off less important workers to make up the difference. In the latter case, production is affected, revenues drop, and the businesses often fail.

AMERICANS ARE SPENDING MORE, BUT GETTING LESS

According to a September 1990 article in *The New England Journal of Medicine*, Americans spend 40 percent more than Canadians, and 90 percent more than Germans on medical bills.[6] But, Americans may not be better off medically than the citizens of those two countries. A Census Bureau report in the same year indicated that children born in the United States are healthier than in most Third World countries, but are not as well off as most European children.[7]

Of course, the previous studies are about Americans as a group rather than as individuals. America's medical care is still the best in the world to those who can afford it. But in a democracy that has 31 million people without health insurance, that isn't proving to be good enough. The people who are not being cared for are demanding to be included. It can be done, but at enormous cost and only with huge changes in the way we distribute and pay for medical treatment.

THE SOLUTIONS AND THE OPPORTUNITIES

For better or worse I believe the stage is set for a gradual move to national health insurance in the 1990s. Although national health plans may save money primarily by limiting services and are generally less efficient than private programs, I believe that both economic and political pressures make such a plan all but inevitable. However, for the first few years of the decade the emphasis is likely to be on lowering costs in our existing medical system, primarily by limiting services and reducing reimbursements. We can expect to see more generic pharmaceuticals and more efficient distribution of drugs. We will also see more outpatient clinics because they can often provide many services for lower costs than acute care hospitals. In addition, the health care industry will begin using many new medical technologies that relieve professionals from routine chores so that they can use their skills more productively.

Along with a nationwide trend toward limiting health care costs, I think that we will see the emergence of several statewide health plans. We already have such a program in Hawaii. Oregon is considering one as are several other states. The emergence of state sponsored health plans will almost certainly increase the pressure for a national plan. I think the first such plan will be enacted by the middle of the decade. It is likely to deal only with the indigent and those workers who are not already covered by some other health care program. However, a limited approach is unlikely to work very well. The government will end up paying for all the difficult and expensive cases while generally healthier more affluent patients remain—understandably—outside the system.

The cure will be a true national health insurance plan that covers everyone. I expect we will see it in place by the end of the decade. Although many of us may live to curse the day such a plan is enacted, as investors we must recognize that it will create many opportunities for investment profits.

INVESTMENT IMPLICATIONS

Many readers may question my optimism for any medical investments at a time when the health care industry is faced with various government sponsored insurance plans—and all the cost constraints that will go with them. The fact is, the United States is very unlikely to go to a completely socialized or centrally directed medical system such as the one in Great Britain. Such government dominated health care systems have produced appalling track records. They are famous for long waiting lists for critical surgery and poor quality care.

Instead we will almost certainly see the development of a plan that will look like a kind of super-Medicare. It will be government funded but it will be privately run. Because the services themselves will be delivered by the private sector, the health care industry should continue to offer investors many attractive opportunities. In fact, the turmoil in health care that we will see in the 1990s will create investment profits that would not emerge in more tranquil times.

STOCKS TO WATCH

Efficient Private Hospitals Point the Way

Thousands of America's hospitals are in serious trouble. They are in the midst of a vicious shakeout and have a difficult time getting reimbursed for their services. In the midst of this carnage one can find some hospitals that are doing quite well. Many of them are actually very profitable. This successful group is pointing the way to the future for the hospital industry. Because they are the leaders of that industry—and are likely to stay that way—they also represent very good opportunities for investors.

Successful hospitals have several characteristics in common. First, they are almost always chains rather than individual facilities. Because they are part of a larger group, they have the same economies of scale that are common to any large organization. Costs for advertising, staffing, buying supplies, and administration can be lower than any single facility can achieve. Billing is often done centrally using the most efficient practices and equipment. Personnel can be moved from place to place as needed. Drugs and supplies are purchased in huge quantities and distributed using just-in-time techniques pioneered by the factory automation industry. The list of advantages goes on and on.

Because of their efficiency, these private hospital chains should do well throughout the 1990s. When government sponsored insurance programs take effect these same companies should continue to be good performers because reimbursement schedules are likely to be based on their fees. Overall, many private hospital companies look very good for the long term.

Humana Inc. is a major hospital management chain running 83 facilities with a total of 17,439 beds in the United States and overseas. The company also provides group health insurance to about 1.3 million members, a practice that contributes 31 percent of revenues and is likely to be expanded. In addition, Humana has opened 29 specialty clinics that pursue continuing research and medical education. Humana's big advantage over its competition is the medical and administrative efficiency it can achieve as a result of its size and deep experience. The company is able to run top notch hospitals for less because it can make better use of its personnel, equipment, buildings, and money. I think the firm has an excellent future.

National Medical Enterprises is one of the top hospital management firms in the United States. It operates about 35 hospitals which served nearly 1,250,000 patients in 1990. Overall, the company is similar to Humana. However, National Medical is beginning to start specialty clinics which, as you will notice in a later part of this chapter, can be even more efficient than acute care hospitals. The move to specialty clinics appears to be wise because those facilities are ordinarily this firm's competition. As National Medical moves into its new markets it will make less and less difference to the bottom line where the public chooses to go for treatment. I think it is an excellent strategy for the 1990s.

HMOs Upgrade and Prosper

Health Maintenance Organizations (HMOs) also appear to have a bright future. Although the jury is still out regarding whether they deliver good care for less money or simply cost less money, the result is the same: they are attracting more business. As you may expect, HMOs—particularly the larger firms with contracts with several hospitals—use many of the practices that are common among hospital management companies. In addition, since HMOs are group care facilities they are able to manage their patients as well as their own personnel. Of course, that extra degree of control is a major reason they can limit costs.

Many HMOs had problems in the past due to overexpansion and excessive debt. Those problems were compounded when HMOs became overly cost conscious. They often employed large numbers of foreign-trained doctors who obtained U.S. licenses but were almost certainly not as skilled as their American counterparts. In many cases members were not able to choose their own doctors and this aggravated the problem. Lines for diagnosis and treatment were also long. All in all, many early HMOs treated their members as if they were products rather than people.

Not surprisingly, many members responded by dropping out. The people who remained in the program tended to be those with the greatest medical problems. Caring for that group sent costs through the roof. Consequently, many HMOs failed. However, HMOs that survived the shakeout are rapidly making changes to meet their patients' expectations within a cost-effective structure. Many plans now allow members to choose their own doctors, most of whom have been educated in the United States. Treatment is also more personal and stream-lined. As a result, several HMOs are on an upswing that should carry them through the 1990s.

U.S. Healthcare, Inc. is an HMO that serves more than a million clients on the East Coast. The company is also working with Blue Cross & Blue Shield in Missouri and Pennsylvania to develop additional group care facilities in those areas. U.S. Healthcare is successful because it manages to combine efficient medical practices with good customer services. For example, members are free to select their primary physician from a list of area doctors who have contracts with the plan. Members are also encouraged to see their doctors at the first sign of trouble. Of course, that enables the HMO to spot and treat most problems before they have a chance to become serious. The company also offers plans which provide prescription drugs plus eye and dental care. Through a special arrangement with the government, the company provides Medicare benefits to thousands of patients.

PacifiCare Health Systems is a successful HMO that operates on the West Coast and in Texas and Oklahoma. Through separate programs the company provides services to commercial groups, such as employees of a company, and to Medicare beneficiaries. PacifiCare is growing strongly not only in new markets but, more importantly, in areas where it is well established. New pharmacies and the decision to vertically integrate its operations should boost efficiency at the same time. The combination of good business practices and a growing population in its territory should continue to provide this HMO with good profits.

Growing Business for Outpatient Surgery Centers

Outpatient surgery centers often provide a cost effective alternative to hospitalization that is finding increasing favor with patients and insurers alike. Instead of going to a hospital for routine matters, patients may have problems attended to in an outpatient center, and they are released the same day. Everyone saves hundreds, sometimes thousands of dollars.

Of course, one of the main reasons outpatient surgery centers can offer lower costs than hospitals is because they don't generally treat the tough cases. Neither do they maintain 24-hour emergency rooms nor do they offer treatment to people who have no money or health insurance. Nevertheless, because the centers offer lower cost treatment for many medical problems, they are currently doing very well. I think they will continue to prosper in the future.

Medical Care International is the largest operator of outpatient surgical centers in the United States. Its nearly 300 clinics provide the facilities and necessary support staff for independent doctors to perform routine same-day procedures such as plastic surgery, oral surgery, eye, ear, nose, and throat procedures, orthopedics, and so on. Admissions are simpler than in hospitals and the atmosphere is more personal. Medical Care is a rapidly expanding company in a rapidly expanding field. Because it offers better efficiency and more attractive service to patients with minor medical problems it should have a bright future whether a national health insurance program is enacted or not.

A Solid Future for Outpatient Diagnostic Clinics

Outpatient diagnostic clinics are similar in many ways to outpatient surgery centers, particularly in terms of economics. With diagnostic centers, however, the savings come from the efficient use of high-tech scanners and other expensive medical equipment. In particular demand are outpatient centers that can offer Magnetic Resonance Imaging (MRI), a technology that in some procedures is often better than CAT scans but is ordinarily very costly.

Outpatient diagnostic clinics are able to offer lower fees because they don't provide the comprehensive services of an acute care hospital. In addition, they are able to make greater use of their capital and equipment than usually occurs in a hospital. Instead of having a million dollar machine sit idle for hours or even days, a diagnostic clinic may serve an entire city and use its equipment 12 hours or more a day. Of course, that brings the cost per use down considerably, which pleases patients and insurance companies alike. Those savings should ensure a bright future for this industry.

Health Images operates 26 outpatient clinics across the United States that offer MRI services. This important diagnostic service offers several superior features over CAT scans which it accomplishes without the use of X-rays. The technology is especially useful in the early detection of cancer, multiple sclerosis, and dozens of other ailments. The company has also recently entered the field of radiation treatment for cancer on an outpatient clinic basis, a field which offers considerable promise. Health Images experienced very fast growth during the end of the 1980s. It shows every sign of continuing that progress well into the current decade.

Specific Illness Centers Also Do Well

One way a medical facility can become more efficient, and more profitable, is to focus on patients who have one type of problem such as mental difficulties. Because of their specialization, such centers often offer the most cost effective treatment available.

There is also an insurance phenomenon occurring which is boosting the fortunes of specific illness centers. Many states are beginning to require all registered health insurance companies to provide coverage for problems that have growing social consequences such as drug and alcohol abuse. Those regulations are creating multimillion dollar incentives to create specialized medical centers to treat the problems. Insurance firms don't fight the trend because the clinics provide the required treatment within policy reimbursement limits.

The top centers offer effective treatment to people who usually need it very badly. The centers also provide treatment at lower costs than are available elsewhere. Overall, specific illness centers make sense and should find increasing business. Although the field is coming under increasing competition from hospitals that are discovering the available profits, for the present the sky appears to be the limit for this medical specialty.

Community Psychiatric Centers operates more acute care psychiatric hospitals than any other publicly-owned firm in the United States. The company now operates 50 centers with a total of about 5,000 beds. CPC also has centers in Puerto Rico and England. In addition to traditional mental health programs, the company provides drug and alcohol rehabilitation services.

Community Psychiatric appears to be well positioned for growth in the 1990s. Mental health treatment is on an upswing as is the whole drug and alcohol counseling field. It helps that the historical social stigma toward those who seek personal help has generally faded away. In addition, more mental health services are being covered by insurance programs. Finally, the stressful life of the 1990s is expected to create many more patients who need one form or another of counseling.

Vivra Inc. was spun off by Community Psychiatric Centers in 1989. The new firm specializes in kidney dialysis treatments to outpatients at independent clinics and in-home services. The number of people needing kidney dialysis treatment rose from 66,000 in 1982 to about 102,000 in 1988. Vivra addresses the need by operating more than 1,400 licensed dialysis stations from California to Pennsylvania. The company's move into the home health care field improves its outlook even further as it gives the firm greater access to the growing ranks of the elderly.

Rehabilitation Medicine to Expand Dramatically

One fast growing specialty that deserves separate mention is rehabilitation medicine. The field offers investors unusually attractive opportunities. Rehabilitation isn't a completely new idea. For years, people with recently removed casts have been given exercises with which to regain muscle strength and stretch shortened tendons. Appropriate help has also been given to people with other medical problems that left them impaired. In most cases the programs were demonstrated in the hospital and the patients were expected to carry them out at home.

In the 1980s doctors began to find that more structured and better supervised rehabilitation programs were needed. They also found that every dollar spent on rehabilitation could save two to three dollars in other medical costs. That is because rehabilitation programs speed recovery from surgery and reduce the incidence of complications. Proper rehabilitation also results in fewer relapses and longer stays away from the hospital, especially in older people.

Rehabilitation medicine is now becoming a hot field. There were 2,300 rehab clinics in America in 1982. By early 1990 there were nearly 4,000, according to the American Medical Association.[8] The area appears very attractive for the 1990s.

HealthSouth Rehabilitation is a pacesetting company that provides medical rehabilitation services in 21 states. The company operates through inpatient and outpatient facilities to serve patients with various disabling conditions including stroke, head injury, orthopedic problems, nervous system dysfunctions, and athletic injuries. HealthSouth is both medically effective and cost effective because it uses a coordinated interdisciplinary approach to treatment. It also offers well established performance goals to its patients, their doctors, and insurance companies. As a result, the company's outlook appears to be excellent.

Greenery Rehabilitation Group is an East Coast provider of specialized rehabilitation services for head injuries and other neurological problems. The company's Boston facility is the largest and possibly the most effective center of its kind in the nation. It has a reputation for returning its patients to society in less time and for less money than other facilities. Greenery also operates specialized nursing homes that accept medically demanding patients of all types including the elderly. Since the company is one of the few firms that will accept such patients, it is finding that its services are in increasing demand. Additional facilities are now planned to fill the need. This competent firm should continue to be successful.

Efficient Medical Labs Find Business Booming

One of the fastest growing medical fields is high-tech testing. CAT scanners and other impressive items are only the most visible part of that trend. The largest growth in testing is occurring at the test tube level where biotechnology and precise instrumentation are revolutionizing the business. Unfortunately, much of the new testing equipment is complicated and very expensive. Few clinics can afford the gear. As a result, independent medical labs are expanding rapidly to provide the needed services. The best of them are making very good profits that will almost certainly increase steadily in the future.

New diseases and growing drug problems are also giving independent labs a great deal of unexpected business. Drug tests alone are keeping many labs busy 24 hours a day. In addition, AIDS testing is increasing substantially. In both cases, treatment programs are long lasting and must be accompanied by repeated testing. Based upon numerous government and health care industry reports about our growing social problems, it appears that the need for all these tests will rise considerably during the 1990s. That can't help but increase the demand for laboratory services.

National Health Laboratories is one of the nation's leading clinical laboratories. The company provides services in more than 40 states. All labs test body fluids and tissues for various factors of importance to both general practitioners and specialists. In addition, the firm maintains 190 collecting stations in medical buildings around the country which send specimens to one of 16 laboratories for analysis. STAT labs provide immediate testing and fast reports on some critical tests.

National Health is also noteworthy for its marketing program and its full range of services to the health care industry. The company has a large sales force that regularly calls upon its clients to present information and collect suggestions. That practice should help keep National Health ahead of its competition as the medical testing business continues to expand.

More Demand for Medical Cost Containment Services

Except in emergencies, few expensive medical procedures are performed today without the approval of the health care reimburser. In many cases the guidelines for treatment are well established and approvals are all but automatic. In less common situations the health care provider contracts the review process to a medical cost containment company. Only with that firm's okay will the claim generally be honored on a 100 percent basis.

The cost containment industry also provides broader services to the medical industry. Often a health care provider will contract with a firm to oversee its operations. Sometimes the firm will recommend that the provider make cost-saving changes in its internal procedures. In other cases the cost containment firm will help a client obtain drugs and supplies less expensively. Finally, the company will often help providers do medical reviews on their own in order to ensure compliance with insurance and Medicare payment guidelines.

In the 1990s health insurance companies and hospitals will be seeking greater control over their operating expenses. The move will gain momentum as cost containment firms continue to prove that large savings are possible.

HealthCare COMPARE is a major provider of cost management services in the Unites States. The company focuses attention on three critical areas: unnecessary hospital admissions, time spent in the hospital, and the appropriateness of all medical procedures. The goal is to help its clients make better use of existing resources without lowering the quality of patient care.

Upon request, the company will also arrange a network of health care professionals who agree to furnish lower cost services for their clients. Such networks are offered to a wide range of clients and often result in great savings. New plans for dental and outpatient clinics are in the works.

United HealthCare Corporation is a nationwide leader in medical cost management. Many of the firm's services are similar to those offered by HealthCare COMPARE, but its clients are primarily HMOs and many group purchasers of health care. In addition, United HealthCare offers its clients an extensive network of physicians, pharmacies, and even hospitals. The company is now expanding its operations to include mental health and chemical dependency services, plus pharmacy cost management. All the markets serviced by United HealthCare are expected to expand significantly in the 1990s. That should keep this firm on the profits track.

MedStat Systems has a unique niche in the cost management industry. Instead of offering case by case decision services, the company provides statistical data—based on nearly 100 million claims—which makes it possible for its clients to create decision support systems for managing their own health care costs. Clients include insurance companies, independent cost containment firms, and large corporations such as Merck & Co, Ford, General Motors, and Blue Cross & Blue Shield of Missouri—to name only a few.

MedStat grew rapidly in the 1980s and should continue to do so in the 1990s. That is particularly true since the company is expanding its proprietary database and is developing new software products which use its information in new, profitable ways.

Pharmaceutical Cost Management Makes Its Debut

Cost management services for pharmaceuticals is a relatively new field. For years medical administrators avoided the area because no one seemed to know how to make the drug delivery process very efficient. After all, drugs are generally distributed in small doses on an individual basis. With the arrival of group health plans that included pharmacy benefits, opportunities for greater efficiencies in drug delivery presented themselves. Bulk purchases, centralized distribution and billing, and efficient cost review procedures all became possible. At that point the pharmacy cost containment industry was born. I think it will grow into a profitable new addition to the health care industry.

Pharmacy Management Services is a major nationwide provider of drug cost containment services. Its primary clients are workers' compensation insurers and groups that have comprehensive health plans for their members. Using a computerized system under the guidance of medical professionals, the firm manages drug dispensing for its customers along with related medical supplies and equipment. Pharmacy Management also offers next-day delivery services which avoid out-of-pocket purchases by patients. This young firm's client list is expanding rapidly which may continue for several years.

Low Cost Medical Supply Companies Take the Lead

In many industries the lowest cost suppliers are not always the leading suppliers. When budgets are flush, customers are often willing to pay a premium for convenience and for nonessential features. That situation has been true in the health care industry as well. However, as efficient hospital management becomes the dominant trend of the health care industry in the 1990s, low cost suppliers will dominate their industries. Indeed, the situation is already well underway. Aggressive cost containment procedures now all but guarantee that supply orders will go to companies that consistently provide quality goods at the lowest prices. Such firms offer today's investors excellent opportunities for long term profits.

The 1990s will also be a golden age for firms that supply devices which boost the productivity of health care professionals and increase hospital efficiency. Such devices include all types of specialized equipment which permit doctors to perform complex tasks quickly. Some of the new equipment qualifies as medical automation, a new field that is still in its infancy. Few people outside the health care profession even know it exists. By the mid-1990s, however, it is likely to be front page news. By that time many early bird investors will have made a great deal of money in its leading companies.

Baxter International is the world's largest provider of medical supplies and equipment to hospitals, with an emphasis on diagnostic, blood therapy, and related devices. Its new cost-saving diagnostic products give quick results from blood and urine tests.

A computerized "just-in-time" inventory management system is also noteworthy. The new system brings the efficiency of factory automation to hospitals and clinics which have always had an expensive problem managing their large stores of drugs and supplies. This badly needed inventory management equipment should be a big money maker for Baxter.

Baxter is also using automated systems in its own manufacturing facilities. In addition, the company is consolidating operations for greater efficiency. As a result, Baxter—with its recently acquired American Hospital Supply—will almost certainly remain a low cost supplier to the health care industry in the 1990s.

U.S. Surgical supplies several innovative instruments for use in operating rooms. One product eliminates the need for stitches after surgery. Using a staplegun approach, doctors are able to reduce operating room time as well as blood loss and further body trauma that would have occurred from time consuming manual suturing. Another product greatly speeds gall bladder surgery and improves a patient's chances for a swift recovery. In addition, the new device reduces costs for the procedure by approximately half.

U.S. Surgical's stock experienced meteoric growth in the first half of 1991. After an inevitable correction, the stock should again become attractive as the company continues to prosper by bringing greater productivity to the increasingly cost-conscious health care industry.

Stryker Corporation also provides specialized medical and surgical products that speed many hospital procedures. The company makes a complete line of medical drills, saws, and other powered tools that are most often used by orthopedic surgeons. It also makes prosthetic devices such as hip and knee replacement parts and various other products. Stryker's powered surgical tools, from which almost 80 percent of the company's revenues are derived, save operating time which makes surgery a more efficient procedure. The firm's strong position in the global health care market should keep profits flowing during the 1990s.

Medical Graphics is a leader in the emerging automated diagnostics industry. The company's products measure and evaluate heart and lung functions. A smaller and more portable version of the system can be used at a patient's bedside. Medical Graphics is now entering the field of nutritional and metabolic assessment which also have considerable promise.

Increasing Sales of Medical Computer Systems

The health care industry has been using computers for years. They do billing, keep track of patient's medical records, perform payroll functions, and so on. Smaller systems perform the same tasks for clinics and doctors in private practice. As is true in many industries, health care providers are beginning to find that their existing computer systems are out of date. Not only is their hardware below par but, much more importantly, so is their software. Consequently, during the first few years of the 1990s, sales of specialized medical computer systems should be very strong.

Demand for distributed computer information systems should also increase for the foreseeable future. Such systems employ nationwide networks to link members with medical databases used for cost containment, business office planning, scheduling, and so on. Shared systems are also available for centralized billing and other services.

Even though the number of hospital beds has not increased significantly in recent years, the demand for computer services is growing strong—thanks to increasing needs for efficiency and better health care information.

CyCare Systems is a leading supplier of medical computer systems. The company primarily serves small to medium health care groups, a rapidly growing part of the medical industry. CyCare's focus is on improving productivity and administrative effectiveness through managing patient appointments, streamlining billing and insurance, and maintaining medical records. In 1990, CyCare was recovering from what appeared to be a one-time charge from restructuring its operations to focus its activities on physician controlled clients. That action now appears to be complete which should clear the way for additional growth.

Shared Medical Systems is a major supplier of computerized medical information systems. It serves all sectors of the health care field, providing financial and patient management, decision support, and related cost containment functions. The company's systems make use of onsite computers, networks, and centralized databases. Clients include hospitals, clinics, and independent physicians.

Shared Medical presently serves clients in the United States, Canada, England, and Europe. As the demand for cost reduction continues to grow, this company should find increasing business for its comprehensive computer services.

A Growing Niche for Mail Order and Generic Drug Suppliers

Clearly, both the generic drug and the prescription-by-mail industries that were first mentioned in Chapter 6 will also profit from the trend toward greater health care efficiency. Consequently firms such as

Mylan Labs and **Medco Containment Services** deserve strong consideration as you plan your long-term portfolio for the 1990s.

NOTES

1. Deborah S. Pinkney, "Costs Increase with Numbers of 'Crack Babies,'" *AMN Journal*, June 1990.

2. Kathryn M. Welling, "The Sickening Spiral, Healthcare Costs Continue to Grow at an Alarming Rate," *Barron's*, June 11, 1990.

3. Aaron Bernstein, "Now, We Have No Insurance," *Business Week*, November 26, 1990.

4. Richard Koenig, "Insurer's Overhead Dwarfs Medicare's," *The Wall Street Journal*, November 15, 1990.

5. Bernstein, "Now, We Have No Insurance."

6. Victor R. Fuchs and James S. Hahn, "How Does Canada Do It?" *New England Journal of Medicine*, September 27, 1990.

7. Martha Farnsworth Riche, "Health, Well-Being of U.S. Children Lags," *The Wall Street Journal*, October 2, 1990.

8. Ellen Paris, "Straighten That Back! Bend Those Knees," *Forbes*, June 11, 1990.

CHAPTER 13

A WORLDWIDE BOOM FOR THE ENVIRONMENTAL INDUSTRY

The greening of America is becoming one of the strongest and most profitable trends of our age. It is altering virtually every industry and market from power generation to grocery store displays. During the 1990s the process will leave us with a mature and dynamic industry that will find an increasing supply of customers both at home and abroad.

It isn't difficult to see the need—and the potential—of our growing environmental industry. Each day we are presented with disturbing new information about overflowing landfills, oil spills, contaminated industrial sites, depletion of the ozone layer, infectious medical wastes, fouled air and water, and similar problems. Solving just the most pressing of those problems will cost billions of dollars and will take at least a decade. Of course, that situation is good for long-term investors who understand what is happening and what it will ultimately be worth.

PUBLIC AND POLITICAL PRESSURES FORCE THE ISSUE

Twenty years ago supporters of environmental issues were among the minority. Those who attended the first Earth Day in 1970 were primarily the same people who protested the Vietnam War and just about everything else connected with the establishment. However, in the years that followed the environmental movement rapidly expanded. By 1981, more than 45 percent of Americans supported more strict environmental protection laws.[1] More importantly, most of the new supporters were mainstream voters who often held conservative opinions on other issues.

During the 1980s environmental causes attracted even more strength. The Exxon oil spill in Alaska brought that rising tide to a peak. A nationwide poll taken by CBS News before the spill found that 66 percent of the public supported high environmental standards and continuing improvements regardless of cost. A month after the March 1989 spill, that figure rose to 74 percent.[2]

Following the sweeping grass roots support are many politicians who are wisely choosing the same course. The federal government is even making efforts to get its own back yard in order. Both the Department of Defense and the Department of Energy are now cleaning up their widespread pollution, some of which dates back to World War II.

The environment is becoming such a top priority that it is likely to receive attention during hard times. For example, the superfund taxes, earmarked for hazardous waste cleanup projects, were to have expired at the end of 1991, or when the fund reached $6.65 billion. However, congressional leaders agreed late in October 1990—during severe recession fears—to extend the deadline by four years and raise the ceiling to $11.97 billion. During the same time, Congress voted to approve the first Clean Air Bill in 13 years. It is a costly law aimed at reducing acid rain, car exhaust emissions, factory fumes, and damaging chlorofluorocarbons. Legislation at the state level is also making its mark. Typical is Pennsylvania's Mandatory Recycling Law which took effect in 1990. It requires municipalities with more than 10,000 people to recycle at least three common materials out of a list of seven. More than 30 states have recently established technical assistance programs to industry for waste reduction improvements. The list goes on and on.

THE OUTLOOK FOR INVESTORS

What does this mean to investors? The answer is as simple as it is profitable: demand continues to explode for sophisticated testing, treatment, and disposal technology, as well as outside certification of compliance for many environmental problems. Best of all from an investors standpoint, such services are almost always beyond the in-house abilities of most industrial companies and municipalities. The result is growing business for environmental firms, from those providing engineering and planning to the companies offering highly specific services. As in any emerging field, smaller companies predominate and enjoy a lion's share of the business. Gradually, however, the trend is moving toward consolidation. By the end of the decade larger companies that offer a full range of environmental services will almost certainly be the biggest money makers.

Of course, the environmental industry also has its problems. Because many green stocks appreciated strongly during the 1980s, they dropped sharply during the 1990–91 recession. As Dennis Schleider, an analyst at Ladenburg Thalmann noted in early 1990, "Earnings disappointments in environmental stocks generally have a lot more impact on the stock price, and it usually takes much longer to recover."[3] Early Gulf War fears also contributed to the slide. All those events proved, however, is that the industry is becoming firmly established in American life and commerce.

During the 1990s investors can expect more sudden dropoffs in environmental stocks, particularly for those with customers who are closely tied to the economic cycle. Nevertheless, solid long-term environmental investments promise to deliver some of the very best returns of the decade. In fact, I believe many turn-of-the-century investment millionaires are likely to be people who purchase high quality environmental stocks then sit back while they mature and prosper.

STOCKS TO WATCH

Demand Increases for Environmental Engineering and Consulting

Work of the magnitude and sophistication required by most environmental projects often begins with top notch engineering firms. The larger the project, the more essential competent planning becomes. Since engineering and design firms usually charge a percentage of a project's total cost, their profits are assured.

Not all environmental engineers show their customers how to clean up their businesses. Many consultants prosper by showing their customers how to avoid the production of hazardous wastes to begin with. For example, 3M's Columbia, Missouri, plant learned it could replace a toxic cleaning solvent with a specially designed abrasive machine. The result was a harmless sludge instead of 40,000 pounds of liquid poison. The immediate savings were substantial. The changeover could be worth as much as $400 million.[4]

The best engineering and consulting firms are good takeover targets. Even the leading companies are small by U.S. industrial standards. They can be—and often are—purchased by any large, established company that wishes to move quickly into the growing environmental area. For example, one small firm that I was planning to review in this section—ERC Environmental & Energy Services—was snapped up by Ogden Corporation in late 1990. ERC's stock went immediately from $9 to $16. Although the buyout locked the company's investors out of a long-term play, there is much to be said for accepting quick profits which can be reinvested elsewhere.

Roy F. Weston is a top environmental engineering firm that offers a comprehensive mix of planning services. The company's capabilities include solving complicated problems in the areas of air, water, and soil contamination, toxic materials handling, in-house industrial hazards, and energy conservation. The firm was involved in about 3,000 different projects in 1989 for more than 1,700 clients. Slightly less than two-thirds of its revenues came from major government projects that year, the rest from private industry. Weston's services begin with laboratory testing and end with fully planned and implemented environmental solutions. Its strong position in both the public and private sectors should keep the company at the forefront of the cleanup boom in the 1990s.

Harding Associates provides environmental engineering and consulting services through 17 western offices located from Hawaii to Colorado. The company also has an office in Washington, D.C. The firm had more than 1,500 clients in 1989-1990. Harding is best known for its expertise in the fields of hazardous waste site decontamination and the design of solid waste disposal facilities. The company is frequently selected for initial site investigations which usually lead to the design of remedial systems and construction management services. Harding should have a strong decade.

GZA GeoEnvironmental is an Northeastern environmental and remediation firm that provides many of the services Harding offers in the West. In addition, GZA provides geological evaluations to public and private agencies that are planning landfills, tunnels, dams, and other potentially damaging environmental projects. Compared to Weston and Harding, GZA is a small firm that first went public in July 1989. The firm closed out 1989–90 with nearly 1,500 customers, primarily in the private sector. I believe it is promising.

Comprehensive Environmental Firms Begin to Emerge

It was mentioned earlier that small, highly specialized firms are the first to emerge in any new industry. Then as the industry develops some of those firms expand their operations to related areas so that they can meet more of their customers' needs. That pattern is now occurring in the environmental industry and is quite significant for long-term investors.

In the field of hazardous waste cleanup, most specialty firms found there was an even bigger market for transporting and disposing toxic wastes than there was for decontaminating them. Now most hazardous waste firms provide such comprehensive services. The best of them are prospering because customers appreciate having one company completely deal with their environmental headaches. Comprehensive firms are also prospering because environmental regulations are becoming extremely complex. Understanding the constantly changing rules is moving beyond the ability of many companies. Those few firms who do understand them rarely have the necessary equipment and skills to provide their own remedies.

It isn't surprising that over half the industries with pollution problems now seek the help of full service environmental firms. I expect that percentage will go up steadily as the decade progresses and environmental demands increase.

Chemical Waste Management is the largest supplier of comprehensive waste services in America. The firm is proficient in problem evaluation, integrated site remediation, and a full range of waste management services. The company even provides transportation and storage for low-level radioactive materials that few other companies will handle. Chemical Waste's customers are typically private and industrial firms, government agencies, and even other waste management operations. This well positioned company should see strong, steady growth from the environmental cleanup trend in the 1990s.

Clean Harbors, as its name suggests, began as a specialized firm. Now it is one of the largest comprehensive environmental service providers in the Northeast. It offers a complete solution approach to environmental problems, including hazardous waste management, remediation, engineering, and analysis. Clients include chemical, petroleum, industrial firms, and government agencies.

Clean Harbors acquired a large aqueous waste company in 1989 which added additional capabilities to its diverse services. Unfortunately, an attempt to add a high temperature toxic waste incinerator was not successful, an event that had a negative impact on earnings in 1990. Nevertheless, this well respected firm should recover and continue to grow.

Browning–Ferris Industries is one of the world's biggest suppliers of comprehensive waste collection, processing, recovery, and disposal services. The company operates from 330 locations within North America and has 72 operations in foreign countries. It is also becoming involved in the development of waste resource recovery facilities, an area with top potential for growth. Because of its size and the hazardous nature of its business, Browning–Ferris is often involved in controversy. Accidental spills, problems with permits, and the like are favored targets of the media. Reporters rarely mention that Browning–Ferris solves environmental problems that are thousands of times more threatening to health and safety than the few they may produce. This company's size, international position, and diversity of services give it a distinct advantage for the 1990s.

Air Pollution Control Becomes a Billion Dollar Industry

One critical area in which the United States is making significant progress is the reduction of pollutants in the atmosphere. Nevertheless, many sections of the nation still have severe air quality problems which the government is being compelled to address. The most recent action occurred in 1990 when Congress passed additional air pollution legislation. The new rules may cost industry $25 billion per year in compliance measures.[5] Environmental firms that can help customers meet the tightened regulations will be among the biggest beneficiaries of the new legislation.

The longer term also looks good for air pollution control firms. Although the Clean Air Bill will help solve our growing problem with air quality, nearly every environmental expert predicts that we will see even tighter rules within a few years. Consequently, the fortunes of our top air pollution control firms seem assured. Although many of the leading stocks are no longer in Wall Street's bargain basement, they should perform very well over the long term.

Midwesco Filter Resources occupies a low-tech segment of the usually high-tech pollution control market. The company produces more than 5,000 different types and sizes of air filtering bags and related equipment used to remove airborne particulates that occur from industrial operations and power generation. This little-known firm produces almost all the seamless filter bags that are used in the United States. As the environmental boom continues through the 1990s,

Midwesco Filter should benefit from its niche in an unglamorous but essential business.

Advance Ross is a notch up the high-tech ladder from Midwesco Filter. The company manufactures and installs electrostatic precipitators that remove particulates from exhaust gases produced by utilities and industrial plants. The company also owns a minor part of NaTec (also reviewed in this section), a firm that performs acid rain pollutant reduction. As is the case with Midwesco Filter, Advance Ross offers relatively simple solutions to many environmental problems. Since those solutions are very cost effective they are used whenever possible.

Wahlco Environmental Systems is a top manufacturer of flue gas conditioning systems which control air pollution at electric utility plants. The firm's products increase the effectiveness of electrostatic participators—such as those made by Advance Ross—and are often able to allow that technology to meet modern air quality standards. Wahlco also makes a complete line of air, gas, and water system control devices in addition to equipment needed at electric utilities and industrial sites. San Diego Gas & Electric owns the majority of its stock. Approximately half of the revenues come from overseas—a market that holds considerable long-term promise.

NaTec Resources is a full service air quality firm that specializes in acid rain control. The company supplies its customers—primarily utilities and industrial power producers—with equipment and chemicals to reduce nitrogen oxide and sulfur dioxide emissions. Since acid rain presents an enormous environmental problem throughout much of the industrialized world, this small company may see an increasing supply of customers. I believe the company is speculative but worth investigating.

Water Purification, a Growing Industry

The mixed situation which exists with our nation's water supply is similar to that which is occurring with the air. More than $350 billion has already been spent cleaning up America's contaminated waters. Nevertheless, water quality remains a major problem in many areas. Without serious expansion of existing programs, most experts predict that our water quality problems will become much worse in the 1990s.

More than 50 percent of the nation relies upon groundwater for domestic use according to an April 1990 report by *The Conference*

Board.[6] The percentage tops 95 percent in rural areas. Since groundwater comes from natural drainage, it eventually receives disolved surface contamination such as pesticides, herbicides, fertilizers, and other toxins. The problem is aggravated by the loss of wetlands, nature's automatic water filters. According to *The Conference Board*, more than half of America's wetlands have already been destroyed. Although Congress recently acted to prevent any additional destruction of the essential areas there is no significant move to restore what has been already lost.

Clearly, there is only one practical solution to our growing water quality problem: more and better filtering and purification processes are needed, and soon. Some additional remedies will occur at the source to prevent hazardous substances from getting into the water in the first place. However, most of the decontamination will occur toward the end of the water chain. In both cases the costs will be huge. Of course, those costs will lead to impressive profits for many environmental firms.

Osmonics is a supplier of fluid filters and advanced purification devices that use high-tech membranes; a sophisticated field in which Osmonics is a clear leader. The firm also makes pumps and disposable filters needed for many fluid separation processes such as desalination, industrial processing, and the removal of contaminants. Primary customers include water purification plants, food and beverage producers, electronics firms, and chemical manufacturers. This innovative company was a strong performer during the 1980s. It should continue to be successful in the 1990s.

Chemfix Technologies offers a full range of water treatment services to both industrial and municipal customers. Services begin with engineering and extend through the installation of necessary equipment, securing permits, and even supplying trained operators for the finished facility. The company's proprietary technology converts hazardous materials in fluids to stable solid materials. Once the materials have been rendered immobile, they can often be disposed of conventionally. One end product has commercial value as construction fill. Another can be used in place of lime in agricultural applications.

A growing division of the firm is its mobile services, which I expect will find ready customers in the coming decade. The new service rounds out the firm's offerings and establishes Chemfix as a leader in the growing water treatment field.

Betz Laboratories supplies specialty chemicals that are used in treating water and wastewater in both municipal and industrial process systems. The firm also provides technical and laboratory assistance needed to maximize the effectiveness of its products and to help customers run their facilities efficiently. Betz's chemicals control the formation of deposits in large heating, cooling, and manufacturing systems. Its markets include a wide array of industries such as petrochemical, paper, chemical, steel, aircraft, automobile, electronics, and food. The company's strong emphasis on service has made it a steadily rising performer in recent years.

More Business for Solid Waste Firms

Americans produce more household garbage per person than is the case in any other country. Yet the United States is building fewer and fewer landfills. Consequently, one of the nation's largest environmental challenges in the 1990s will be how best to deal with our growing solid waste problem.

One solution is closed to us. We can't simply dig new pits wherever we need them and proceed as before. Public opposition to new landfill sites near population centers is very strong. In fact, one of the strongest grassroots reactions occurred in the Chicago area in 1984 when the city proposed using part of a forest preserve for a dump. The plan called for complete restoration of the area and contained many other safeguards. Nevertheless, it met with great opposition.

Tough new environmental rules also make new landfills difficult to open. Because buried wastes pose a major threat to groundwater supplies, solid waste sites must often be lined with impervious clay and be held to many other standards. Even when approval is finally given, most new waste dumps are strictly off limits for dozens of hazardous materials.

The size of the problem shows up in solid waste economics. Twenty years ago local communities spent about $5 per ton to dispose of solid waste. Today, the cost is about $100 per ton. Some experts predict that by the end of the 1990s disposal costs will reach $300 per ton.[7] Of course, those numbers provide a strong incentive to solid waste firms to find solutions for our disposal problems.

American Waste Services offers a complete solid waste management service, including site analysis, landfill operation, and waste transportation. The firm is also involved in handling and treating some hazardous materials. Clients include government agencies, as well as commercial and industrial facilities, primarily in the East and Midwest. American Waste is noteworthy for its aggressive expansion into other environmental areas. I think its goal is to become a comprehensive firm. If so, keeping an eye on its progress could be worthwhile.

Laidlaw Inc. is the third-largest solid waste management company in North America. Its position in the hazardous waste field makes it the second-largest of its kind. As of 1990, Laidlaw served more than 215,000 customers in the United States and Canada. A nonrelated division operates school buses, a business which generates approximately one-third of the company's revenues.

Laidlaw has over 40 solid waste dumps in operation which have considerable unused capacity. That means the company can continue to add customers without first developing new sites. That should keep profits expanding for at least the next few years.

Mid-American Waste Systems was formed in 1985 to conduct nontoxic solid waste operations from Ohio to South Carolina. The company's specialty is buying and consolidating smaller solid waste operations into its larger, more efficient, business. So far it has acquired several solid waste collection points and landfill sites. The company is also starting to provide recycling and composting programs. Mid-American plans to continue in its successful niche. More acquisitions are planned in the future as are more landfills and improved efficiency. Because the company has the potential to significantly expand its disposal business, it should do well in the 1990s.

Waste Management is America's largest full service solid waste management company. Clients come from every sector of the economy from residential to industrial. The company operates in 48 states, Puerto Rico, and Canada. Virtually every form of solid waste is handled—from household garbage to low-level nuclear materials. From 1980 to 1989 Waste Management's earnings rose steadily and so did its stock prices. In fact, investors made over 18 times their money in this firm between 1980 and 1990. The recession of 1990 had some impact on both numbers but its effects won't last. The future looks very good for this large, well established company.

Envirosafe Services specializes in off-site disposal of hazardous waste in special landfills. Its primary site locations are in Oregon, Idaho, and Ohio. The firm offers a full range of waste services, from initial analysis to materials stabilization and final disposal.

Envirosafe is in an enviable position for the 1990s because it owns 2 of only 23 hazardous waste sites that the federal government has licensed to accept our worst contaminants. Moreover, Envirosafe's sites still have considerable unused capacity. Permission has been granted to expand that capacity further if needed. As hazardous solid wastes are regulated more tightly, the demand for approved disposal sites will rise quickly. That situation should create additional profits for this firm.

Hazardous Waste Site Cleanup Goes into High Gear

America's 200-year-old throwaway mentality did more than create a giant solid waste problem. It also created many highly toxic industrial dumps that now threaten public health. The infamous Love Canal subdivision in Buffalo, New York, and Times Beach in Missouri are only representative portions of the problem. Toxic waste sites are to be found in every state. Even the relatively pristine state of Oregon has no less than 50 dangerous toxic waste sites. The situation in the industrialized Northeast is much worse.

Since only a handful of our toxic sites have been cleaned up, the future is very bright for the remediation industry. That is particularly true since a great deal of money has already been set aside for the job. At last count, the superfund had been increased to nearly $12 billion. Experts estimate that it will eventually take five times that amount to clean up even the worst areas. Clearly, the top hazardous waste cleanup firms have their work—and their profits—cut out for them.

Groundwater Technology supplies a wide range of remediation services to industries that have spilled, or have otherwise placed, toxic materials on the ground. In most cases where the company is called in, the toxins have contaminated the groundwater as well as the soil. The company's primary customers are oil firms, with other services to vehicle fleet operators, railroads, airports, and Department of Defense agencies. Groundwater Technology assesses the extent of the spill, plans remediation measures, and carries them out. Of equal importance to its customers, the company also works with the EPA and other federal agencies to certify compliance with all existing regulations.

Since new contaminated sites are being discovered every year and more classes of materials are being added to the toxic list, this firm is all but guaranteed a steady stream of customers in the 1990s.

International Technology is one of the oldest firms in the environmental emergency response business. The firm is often the first to be called in by the EPA to evaluate a toxic situation and plan for its remediation. In addition, the firm has an excellent reputation with private customers who have an unexpected environmental problem.

Several years ago International Technology began to expand its services into areas that were related to its core business and appeared to have promise. However, those ventures were generally unprofitable. Now, the company is refocusing on its strengths and shows very clear signs of making a strong recovery. If that process continues I think International Technology may recapture its former position in the industry.

Recovery and Recycling Services Will Prosper

One solution to our waste problems is to recover and reuse many discarded materials. We have done that for years with some products such as beverage containers. In the 1990s the list of valuable goods will be expanded much further—and so will the number of firms that make money from them.

Paper products will attract special attention by recyclers. Data released in February 1990 by Franklin Associates, Ltd., indicate that paper accounts for about 38 percent of the solid waste in American landfills.[8] In the past, recycling efforts have been limited to lower grade products such as newspapers. However, finer grades are now being recycled for use in photocopy machines and catalogs. Hopper Paper Company, a division of Georgia Pacific, has even produced a line of fine writing paper which contains 20 percent recycled material.

Plastic is also becoming a top product for recycling thanks to new technologies which finally make it both possible and profitable. The move is being accelerated by tough new legislation that encourages the practice with tax incentives for recyclers and stiff fines for those who ignore the law. Since, according to Franklin Associates, plastic products presently take up 18 percent of all landfill space, the potential for profitable recycling is enormous. Industry experts predict that by 1995 almost 2 billion plastic containers produced per year will contain recycled material.

A wide variety of toxic chemicals are also becoming too valuable to discard. For example, mercury is now almost completely recycled at paper mills not only because it is too toxic to release into the environment but also because it is too costly to waste. All in all, the combination of high environmental and material costs is leading to top profits for many specialty recyclers.

Chaparral Steel is a Texas mill that recycles scrap steel into structural components such as beams, reinforcing bars (rebars), and other medium-sized products. Unlike many steel mills Chaparral is equipped with advanced melting, shaping, and fabrication machinery that can be quickly modified according to customer orders. Customers are primarily the construction trades, automotive, defense, and railroad industries in both American and international markets. Although business is cyclical, the long-term outlook is quite good for this innovative company that also represents an attractive infrastructure play.

Proler International is a leader in the metal salvage and recovery business. It leaves resmelting and remanufacturing to companies like Chaparral Steel. Proler chops up and shreds scrap materials—mostly old cars—then separates the various metals which are cleaned, compacted, and sold. In addition to steel and aluminum, the company recovers lead, zinc, copper, brass, and tin from autos and various other sources.

Proler operates salvage and recovery operations in six states. Recovered scrap products are sold throughout the world. Exports contributed over 50 percent of revenues in 1989–90. The company recently formed an environmental subsidiary that is testing a process to be used in the treatment and disposal of certain waste materials.

Wellman Inc. is the largest recycler of plastic and film wastes in the United States. These materials are used in the firm's polyester and nylon fibers which appear in carpeting, furniture, and other applications. Now that Wellman has acquired Fiber Industries the firm is the only top fiber supplier using these waste materials as its primary source of materials. Some analysts are nervous that greater demand for recyclable plastic will increase costs for Wellman and thereby reduce profits. However, the enormous oversupply of used plastic available to recyclers will almost certainly keep prices on the floor for many years. It is much more likely that Wellman will profit handsomely from the public's growing demand for products that contain recycled materials.

TETRA Technologies is a ten-year-old company that first went public in April 1990. The firm recycles and sells chemicals extracted from environmentally sensitive industrial wastes. The recovered chemicals are then sold to customers primarily in the petroleum industry in

America, Canada, and Europe. TETRA is noteworthy because it solves environmental problems using technologies which pay for themselves. Investors should watch this promising young company for further signs of progress.

Safety-Kleen places parts cleaning machines in more than 420,000 service stations and industrial maintenance operations that use solvents to wash parts and equipment. The company then makes regular calls to service their machines and collect the used liquids which are recycled. Safety-Kleen has done well with its core business. Now it is extending its services to users and manufacturers of paints, chlorinated solvents, lubricating oils, and other fluids. Safety-Kleen should be in for a very prosperous decade.

Hazardous Waste Incineration to Burn Brightly

The only option for many toxic materials is destruction. One way to do this is by incineration in specially designed, high temperature furnaces. In some cases flue gases are recycled time and again through the combustion chamber to ensure that hazardous substances will be fully consumed. In other cases toxic wastes can be mixed with industrial fuel and destroyed during the normal combustion process. For example, in Chapter 10 I mentioned **Southdown,** a company that disposes of PCBs in its high temperature cement furnace. Several other organic compounds can also be destroyed as part of manufacturing or power generation.

As may be expected, finding locations for new toxic waste incinerators in inhabited areas can be difficult. Stiff opposition almost always occurs. However, the public clearly prefers the destruction of hazardous wastes to their burial. That preference for complete elimination almost always prevails when adequate safeguards are taken to ensure that the incineration process will be thorough.

Growth in the incineration industry has already been impressive. For example, **Clean Harbors**, an important East Coast environmental firm, bought its first waste transfer truck in 1980. Seven years later it began installing a $43 million hazardous waste rotary kiln. Now the company may need to expand again. Since American industry produces more than 250 million tons of toxic waste each year our leading incineration firms should be in for a prosperous decade.

Environmental Systems is one of the largest toxic waste burning companies in the United States. It also offers a full range of integrated waste management services from analysis to processing. Customers include private and commercial firms as well as government agencies.

The company uses one primary and one secondary incinerator in El Dorado, Arkansas, for almost every toxic waste it is licensed to destroy. Wastes are shipped in from all 50 states to the Arkansas facility which generally works around the clock, seven days a week. To handle new business the company is building an additional plant in Arizona which should be on-line in 1992.

Since many hazardous waste materials can no longer be dumped in landfills, Environmental Systems should soon find that its new Arizona operation will be fully utilized. That should lead to additional growth in the years ahead.

Rollins Environmental is America's largest toxic waste incineration firm. The company operates four facilities that operate at very high temperatures plus a low temperature unit for more easily destroyed substances. In addition, Rollins has a deep well injection system which is used to pump certain fluid wastes into stable geological structures. A federally licensed landfill rounds out the firm's toxic waste disposal capabilities.

Although incineration accounts for about three-fourths of Rollins' revenue, the company can be considered a full service toxic waste disposal firm. As such, it offers investors a diversified way to play this growing industry.

A Special Role for Specialty Environmental Companies

Some environmental problems demand attention by highly specialized firms that provide services many major companies are not equipped to handle. Several such firms should continue to do quite well in their niche markets. Of the group, I think that **Allwaste** and **Oil-Dri** have particularly good prospects for growth.

Allwaste, Inc. is primarily involved in industrial air powered and air moving technologies—including vacuum systems—that are used to transport various types of wastes and byproducts to filtration devices. The company provides the design and manufacture of equipment and systems to meet the specific needs of its customers. In addition, Allwaste offers certain resource recovery services to customers whose waste products have economic value.

Allwaste is also involved in the unglamorous but profitable tank cleaning business. Large containers of every type which are used to make a transport industrial materials need periodic cleaning, a service that few companies besides Allwaste are equipped to provide. A related asbestos abatement business is now being phased out. Allwaste appears to be secure in its unique markets which should continue to expand in the future.

Oil-Dri Corp. Of America is best known for its specialty clay materials used in cat litter boxes. The company's highly absorbent clay-based products can also be formulated to absorb and stabilize many hazardous substances. In addition, oil spills can readily be absorbed by using Oil-Dri's clays. In all cases the result is a granular substance that can easily be picked up and transported to an appropriate disposal site. Oil-Dri's products may lack glamour but they should find increasing demand in the future.

Note: One specialized cleanup field that I urge investors to avoid is asbestos abatement. Although the field is currently profitable it won't be long before most remediation work will be complete, which is why Allwaste is getting out of the business. Since there is no longer any asbestos being placed in buildings, the industry won't recover in the future.

NOTES

1. Kevin Phillips, "Oil Spill Fueling Environmental Revival in U.S.," *Eugene Register Guard*, May 28, 1989.

2. Ibid.

3. Manuel Schiffres, "A Cleaner Environment: Where to Invest," *Changing Times*, February 1990.

4. Eric Jay Dolin, "Industry Is Going on a Waste-Watcher's Diet," *Business Week*, August 22, 1988.

5. Rose Gutfeld and Barbara Rosewicz, "Clean Air Accord Is Reached in Congress That May Cost Industry $25 Billion A Year," *The Wall Street Journal*, October 23, 1990.

6. "U.S. Environmental Progress Since Earth Day, 1970," *The Conference Board*, April 20, 1990.

7. Ibid.

8. Randolph B. Smith, "Pressure for Plastic Recycling Prompts a Mix of Tough Laws and Cooperation," *The Wall Street Journal*, February 2, 1990.

SECTION 4

NEW TECHNOLOGY LIVES UP TO ITS PROMISE

CHAPTER 14

A NEW LIFE FOR ALTERNATIVE AND NUCLEAR ENERGY

Immediately beneath America's bustling economy lays a sleeping behemoth of energy troubles. Occasionally awakened over the last two decades by oil shortages and electrical brownouts, we have been scared a time or two. But each time the ominous giant disappeared beneath his covers, and we became complacent again.

The coming decade will see the convergence of several forces that will bring the monster of all energy problems back to life. Fortunately, many experts in the field already see this collision coming. As I mentioned in Chapter 10, plans are presently in place to expand our network of conventional electric plants. However, if recent reports of our growing needs are accurate, an even bigger push will be needed in the near future—a push that will involve nuclear power, alternative energy sources, and several new generating technologies.

THE PROBLEM IS ALREADY HERE

It is important to realize that our projected energy problems aren't the pipedreams of theorists. The first wave of troubles have already arrived for all to see. For example, during the winter of 1989 there wasn't enough electricity in Florida to go around. Utilities had to resort to rolling blackouts. Many communities were forced to take turns of two hours each without power. People living in the New England states had similar experiences during the summer of 1988 when brownouts were common throughout the region. According to industry consultants, many additional electricity shortages are expected to occur during the next 10 years.

Overall, America's long-term electrical power generating capacity needs to be expanded considerably beyond what is already planned. The United States will need to build about 200 more large electric power plants by the year 2010 based on a 1990 estimate from the U.S. Energy Information Administration.[1] That is about 40 years worth of utility installations plus transmission lines and related equipment that will need to be constructed in 10 years. Of course, the work will provide today's investors with many attractive opportunities to share in this profitable trend.

POLLUTION AND GLOBAL WARMING WILL SHAPE THE FUTURE

The need to protect the environment is also increasing the demand for new and better energy production than conventional plants can deliver. The problem with global warming is particularly important since controlling it will be very difficult and expensive. This is because carbon dioxide—the single largest contributor to global warming—is an unavoidable byproduct of burning fossil fuels. As carbon dioxide builds in the atmosphere, it holds in heat that would normally escape into space. The added heat may have serious effects on the world's climate.

Although global warming projections are controversial, political leaders around the world have chosen to stay on the side of safety. The general trend among regulators is to curtail carbon dioxide emissions and encourage the growth of more plant life. These developments will provide enormous economic impetus to modernize our vast energy industry. It is a significant trend of the 1990s, and will last well into the next century.

FOSSIL FUEL SHORTAGES AND HIGH PRICES ADD TO PROBLEMS

Another major reason for America to implement new and unconventional energy programs is that we are running out of fossil fuels. Ongoing research by major petroleum companies indicates that the present rate of consumption is running at 100,000 times what it took for fossil fuels to be formed by natural processes. What we have left is estimated to last 100 years or more, based on present demand. But projections that allow for continuing population growth based on current trends put the end of fossil fuel during the early part of the coming century.[2]

It gets worse. All the easy-to-find fossil fuel has already been located. Most of that has already been used. It is likely that the last 10 to 20 percent of this fuel will never actually be available because it will be too difficult and expensive to find and extract. The fossil fuel situation inside the United States is even more troubling. Present domestic oil reserves may last only eight years, gas for 12 years according to a September 1990 projection by energy analyst Charles Maxwell.[3] If we don't develop other energy sources soon, we will be forced to import a lot more oil in the near future. The corresponding increase in cost and its destructive effects on the nation's economy can be anticipated.

ENERGY CONSERVATION: NO LONGER A MAJOR SOLUTION

Many critics of an expanding energy program point to conservation as an alternative. Obviously the plan has some merit. The measures that were taken in the 1970s and 1980s resulted in significant energy savings in both homes and businesses. Unfortunately, most of the low cost, high payoff conservation measures have already been taken. Fuel-saving vehicles and furnaces are in widespread use and are beginning to reach the limit of efficiency. Likewise, most buildings have been insulated and weatherstripped as well as is practical. The least costly fuel for each situation has also been adopted. In short, the fat has already been cut from the worldwide energy hog.

As the world economy continues to expand, the energy saved by past conservation measures will soon be used up and the need for even greater amounts will resume its upward course. In August 1990 Frederick Seitz, former head of the National Academy of Sciences, stated that if we instituted every known conservation method, we could buy no more than a decade before consumption again overtakes supply.[4]

STOCKS TO WATCH

Clearly, we will need to develop new energy sources in the 1990s. It is also clear that the job will be of massive proportions. Investors who want to share in the profits created by that effort must understand where the best opportunities are most likely to be found and then take long-range positions in the most promising stocks. Here are the specific situations and investments which I feel appear to offer the greatest potential for the next several years.

Nuclear Power Makes a Comeback

America's current energy plan is to make cleaner and more efficient use of fossil fuels. No matter how efficient and carefully controlled they may be, however, fossil-fueled electric plants can't supply our needs long term. Not only do they create too much pollution, their fuel supplies are becoming harder to find, are of lower quality, and are more expensive. Lastly, according to Charles Maxwell, about 50 percent of America's fossil fuel must be imported, a situation that is almost literally breaking the bank.[5] All in all, we simply cannot continue to rely upon conventional technologies for many more years. And we won't.

Although controversial, many energy and environmental experts are now reconsidering the role of nuclear power as a solution to our energy needs. In a landmark September 1990 energy issue published by the *Scientific American* it is clear that many top scientists are coming to the conclusion that nuclear power may be less a threat to the environment than continued and escalating use of fossil fuels. That's particularly true since new reactor designs appear to solve the problem of accidents that could discharge radioactive materials. Further progress has also been made in the safe disposal of radioactive wastes produced by nuclear plants.

The supply of fuel for nuclear plants is also assured. America has natural uranium reserves, so its sources are not subject to control by outside interests. Uranium is also affordable. When measured on a cost-per-power basis, uranium fuel can be 30 percent less expensive than coal in many areas.

The movement to return to nuclear energy is being boosted by its impact on our balance of payments deficit. According to an October 1990 statement by the U.S. Council for Energy Awareness, since 1973 about 4.3 billion barrels of oil have been displaced by America's 112 nuclear plants. That equals about 740,000 barrels per day; which in turn translates to a trade deficit reduction of $125 billion.[6]

A major turning point for nuclear power recently occurred in July 1990 without much public fanfare. New plant licensing requirements adopted by the Nuclear Regulatory Commission were simplified and streamlined. By using an approved standardized design, a utility can now get a preliminary site license quite quickly.[7] Formerly, such licenses could take up to twelve years to obtain, if at all.

I am convinced that the long-term investment potential for nuclear power is very good. In addition to engineering and construction firms, there are nuclear services, uranium mining, nuclear cleanup companies, and nuclear equipment suppliers. The leading firms in each group are public companies. Best of all, these stocks have been depressed for a very long time which means that an upturn in the industry can be expected to produce very substantial profits. In fact, today's down-and-out nuclear power industry may provide bold investors with some of the best returns of the decade.

Nuclear Engineering and Construction to See a Rebound

The first beneficiary of a return to nuclear power will be the handful of companies that are able to build the facilities. As it turns out, the top firms also play a leading role in the design and construction of conventional electric plants. Consequently, investors who take positions in these firms for energy profits early in the decade may find themselves even bigger winners later on.

Morrison Knudsen has been mentioned for its leading role in public works construction projects including conventional electric power plants. The company is also experienced in the construction of nuclear facilities. Although Morrison had little chance to demonstrate its capabilities in the nuclear field for several years I expect that situation to change soon, perhaps dramatically. Morrison Knudsen's strong position in two major trends—rebuilding our infrastructure and energy—should prove to be very profitable in the 1990s.

Gilbert Associates is a leading electrical utility engineering and consulting firm. Its work includes electric generation stations, transmission networks, and distribution systems. The company is nearly a pure play in electric power. As is the case with Morrison Knudsen, Gilbert has nuclear capabilities that have not been used recently due to the decline in that field. However, an improvement in building more nuclear utilities should give this firm a big boost.

Stone & Webster is another all-service engineering and consulting firm to the energy field. Its primary experience is with nuclear, fossil fuel, and hydroelectric power plants. Stone & Webster is similar to Gilbert but it offers a broader scope of services, including serving clients in the petroleum, synthetic fuel, and chemical fields. It has also been involved in converting many coal-fired plants to oil burners. The company offers investors a diversified energy construction play.

Every Nuclear Plant Needs Equipment

Engineering and construction firms do not make the high-tech equipment which is used inside nuclear plants. Reactors, control systems, pumps, valves, generators, and so on are all produced by specialized suppliers. Of course, such firms will profit handsomely from an upturn in the nuclear power industry.

Some equipment suppliers will do well even if orders in new nuclear plants are slow in coming. That is because much of the existing nuclear equipment is nearing the end of its design life and will need to be replaced during the 1990s. That business should keep profits flowing—and production capabilities intact—while we wait for new construction to begin.

Westinghouse Electric is a top manufacturer of power plant equipment of all types. It isn't a pure play in the nuclear field because the company is very broadly diversified in many industries. However, its strong position as a major supplier of nuclear reactors and electrical equipment will enable it to benefit from any future expansion in nuclear energy, as well as conventional power needs both domestic and abroad.

Ragen Corporation is a manufacturer of precision mechanical equipment for the nuclear industry, as well as electronic products. As the nuclear industry slipped into the doldrums several years ago, Ragen switched its focus to smaller nuclear plants designed primarily for the military. Now the military program is also at a standstill. Of course, the double blow means that a turnaround in either of Ragen's markets should have a big positive effect on this stock.

Growing Business for Technical Support Services

After a nuclear energy plant is constructed, there remains an ongoing demand for trained plant operators and maintenance services. Hazardous waste disposal, independent testing and safety certifications, and so on are essential—and are almost always provided by outside suppliers. As is the case with the equipment industry our aging nuclear plants are creating additional business for support services. Because older equipment needs more maintenance this area should do well over the next few years.

Nuclear Support Services is an East Coast firm that specializes in meeting the needs of nuclear utilities, including repair, testing and waste management services. It also supplies trained staff members during nuclear plant construction and start-up operations.

The largest segment of this firm's business comes from repairing, analyzing, and testing the valves of nuclear reactors—the most vital components in any nuclear facility. The company's waste management operations are equally vital. They range from radiological monitoring to contamination control. Nuclear Support should continue to benefit from existing contracts while awaiting an increase in nuclear plant construction.

Older Nukes Are a Fertile Field for Cleanup

As existing nuclear plants age there will be a bright future for the nuclear waste disposal and decontamination industry. Many such plants are approaching the end of their useful lives and will need to be decommissioned. Other plants will need periodic cleanup services. The total cost of providing such services over the next two decades is estimated at $200 billion.[8] That will lead to top profits for specialized nuclear firms during this decade and the next whether new plants are built or not.

Quadrex Corporation is a provider of technical support services with an emphasis on resource recycling and radioactive decontamination. Its capabilities include the handling, removal, transportation, storage, and disposal of nuclear waste material. Quadrex should do very well in the 1990s by serving the growing needs of our aging base of nuclear plants. Government cleanup contracts also seem likely. A rebound in the nuclear utility would be frosting on the cake.

A Forgotten Fuel to Become Golden Again

Uranium is the principal fuel used in commercial nuclear power plants. At one time it was highly prized. However, with the demise of nuclear power, uranium was all but forgotten. Some mines haven't been worked in years. Wall Street has also forgotten the uranium mining industry. When I mentioned uranium stocks to a group of analysts recently they couldn't believe I was serious. Before long, however, I think investors will realize that they dismissed the uranium industry too quickly. Since many stocks are in the bargain basement right now, they stand to gain substantially from any recovery in the nuclear power industry.

Uranium Resources is an innovative company that uses a new leaching process, called solution mining, to extract uranium from the ground. The technology does not require the physical removal of ore to extract the metal. Instead, water is mixed with special substances then pumped through the ore site, dissolving the uranium. The metallic solution is then pumped back to the surface for collection. Solution mining offers the double benefits of low cost and minimum disturbance of the landscape. Of course, the chemicals that are forced into the ground pose a potential environmental problem but that seems to be under control. This company appears to be well positioned to supply low-cost uranium to the government and the nuclear power industry.

Denison Mines is one of the world's biggest suppliers of uranium. It is based in Canada and has operations around the globe. This firm began selling off its oil and gas properties in 1990—which had been the source of about one-third of its revenues—in order to focus on the nuclear industry. The company's size and position in the world market give it an advantage to meet the needs of an expanding nuclear power industry.

American Nuclear Corporation is a more traditional mining operation with vast ore properties in Wyoming. It is nearly shut down at present. However, a revival of the nuclear industry should bring this company out of hibernation. This investment is speculative but potentially very rewarding.

New Life for Alternative Energy

The multifaceted alternative energy industry should also stage a strong comeback in the 1990s. Here too, economics will be the driving force behind the recovery. As Nicholas Lenssen, a researcher at the Worldwatch Institute a Washington-based environmental study group, stated in July 1990, air pollution costs to industry are beginning to put "renewable energy on a level playing field" with conventional energy fuels.[9]

Although alternative energy technology is unlikely to be used to solve widespread problems, it is expected to find ready applications in specific areas. Alcohol fuels, solar heating, photovoltaics, and even geothermal power should be common within a few years. In addition, demand will increase for equipment that creates both heat and electricity from conventional fuels and turns waste products into useful energy. As is the case with nuclear power, it will be the early bird investors who will make the greatest gains by taking strategic positions in key companies.

Cogeneration Offers Big Payoffs

The production of electricity by burning fuel always produces heat as a byproduct. In most cases the heat is allowed to escape which, of course, is a waste of money. However, with cogeneration equipment both the electricity and the heat are put to use. The technology is the answer to a prayer for many energy-intensive industries.

Cogeneration is also very attractive for many industries that must produce large quantities of heat for their manufacturing operations. In such cases, leftover heat is directed through a special cogeneration system and used to create electricity. Heavy industrial companies of every type have found that cogeneration offers significant savings, which helps them regain their competitive position in the marketplace.

Although large cogeneration installations represent a multibillion dollar market, the biggest growth is occurring in small systems for hospitals, office buildings, light manufacturing facilities, schools, and similarly sized buildings that don't use enough electricity to qualify for the lowest commercial rates. These needs of smaller energy users are being met by new, prepackaged cogeneration units that are ready to run right off the truck, require little installation, and are almost fully automated.

The cogeneration market is expanding rapidly. In 1981, cogeneration supplied approximately 3 percent of the nation's energy. In 1983, the figure reached 5 percent. By 1986 the level reached 7 percent. I expect it to top 12 percent during the 1990s.[10]

York Research is a 30-year-old company that started out providing environmental consulting to public and private sectors. However, the company recently refocused its efforts on the cogeneration field. York now offers a full range of cogeneration services including the development, construction, and even the financing of its products. To date its customers have been primarily private industries and large residential complexes. Both markets have excellent potential.

Thermo Electron was first mentioned in an earlier chapter for its line of environmental instruments. The firm also makes cogeneration systems, process equipment, and other advanced technology systems. About one-third of its revenues are from cogeneration products. Although this company is not a pure play in the cogeneration industry it offers investors an opportunity to participate in two top trends at the same time: energy and the environment.

Bonneville Pacific operates throughout the broad energy industry. It is one of the top firms in the cogeneration and alternative energy fields. Bonneville also is involved in the processing of waste and the distribution of oil and natural gas. During 1990 Bonneville was involved in nearly 60 power projects that served a substantial list of customers in dozens of industries. Clearly, Bonneville is not a pure play in cogeneration. However, the company offers investors a broad way to participate in the modern energy and alternative energy fields.

Increasing Demand for Waste-to-Energy Systems
Sales of waste-to-energy systems should also soar in the 1990s. Such systems perform two functions which simultaneously solve two problems: they burn wastes that would otherwise require expensive disposal and they produce electricity. If waste-to-energy systems sound too good to be true, you are almost right. Some early plants ran into serious troubles, usually from burning unseparated trash that resulted in toxic emissions. Others, such as the one in Pinellas County, Florida, fell apart after one year due to the abrasive effects of glass and some plastics. Many plants also blew up when discarded spray cans and other pressurized flammables went into the boilers.

However, new waste-to-energy plants are able to control these problems and are finding ready markets. The obvious economics of turning trash into marketable power ensure their future.

Wheelabrator Technologies is one of the leading developers and operators of waste-to-energy plants. The company provides full services to its customers from design and construction to on-site managing and financing of its products. Wheelabrator is also involved in other alternative power development projects, including biomass, waste wood, waste coal, and natural gas systems. Water purification, wastewater treatment, and sludge handling services are also offered. This stock is possibly the broadest waste-to-energy and alternative energy play in America.

Ogden Projects is America's top waste-to-energy firm. It also provides on-site remediation of toxic contamination. The firm designs, builds, operates, and performs maintenance on its plants, which primarily burn municipal waste. Its operations account for one-fourth of the largest such plants in America. Ogden is a successful firm with a great deal of momentum in several innovative energy and environmental technologies. I think the company will continue to prosper in the 1990s.

Zurn Industries provides products and services to the waste-to-energy industry. The company also supplies products for water quality control systems. To a lesser extent, Zurn is involved in the construction of alternate energy power plants. Although Zurn operates mostly on the service and supply side of the waste-to-energy industry it is a very profitable niche that should grow as the technology expands.

Solar Power: New Strength But Can't Do It All

Solar power was once thought to be the solution to most of America's energy problems. Engineers calculated the total amount of solar energy that struck the United States each day and found that only a tiny fraction of that amount would supply all our power needs. Unfortunately, capturing that tiny fraction of energy proved to be difficult and expensive. Solar cells converted only a few percent of sunlight to electricity. In addition, they were only useful when they were linked with large and expensive banks of batteries. Even worse, early cells required more energy to make than they produced in their lifetime.

Solar systems to capture heat were equally inefficient. They were large and bulky, tended to leak, and also required large storage devices. The promise of solar power was not fulfilled. The promise of cost-effective solar power is likely to go unfulfilled in the 1990s as well, at least in terms of solving our general energy problems. However, many newly developed systems are now efficient enough that their use makes sense in special applications.

For example, solar cells and solar heating systems can be cost effective in many rural applications where sunlight is abundant. Solar energy can also be cost effective in urban applications when it is used to supplement rather than replace conventional energy. The Real Goods Trading Company—a leading mail order supplier of alternative energy equipment—in Ukiah, California reported in their 1991 catalog that solar energy systems for homes are becoming top-selling products.[11] Because solar power is finally finding its niche, I think it will begin to reward investors over the next few years. Those rewards could be substantial if, as I expect, tax credits for solar power installations are reinstated.

Energy Conversion Devices is rapidly developing many new energy products using its synthetic material technology. The firm is presently devoting a large portion of its efforts in the development of photovoltaic energy cells that produce electricity from sunlight. The company is also successfully working in another troubled area for solar power, high capacity battery storage.

Electricity from the sun still can't compete with electricity from conventional sources in most applications. However, rising costs from conventional power plus lower costs for solar cells is expanding the list of applications for photovoltaic technology. Energy Conversion Devices should profit from this trend.

Mor–Flo Industries is one of America's leading water heater manufacturers, using gas, electricity, and solar energy as fuel sources. Products are made for residential, commercial, and manufactured housing markets. Due to declining sales Mor–Flo suspended its line of solar water heaters in 1987. However, I expect the company to reintroduce its solar products in the event the outlook for that market improves. Since Mor–Flo's solar line was one of the most complete in the industry, the company should be able to make quick use of new solar energy opportunities as they develop.

Geothermal Power: Limited Use but Promising

Heat from molten rock beneath the earth is another source of cheap energy. Of course, it is limited to those places on the planet where the Earth's interior heat comes closest to the surface. Many such areas exist, especially in the rural West. Consequently, the potential for geothermal power is greater than is generally supposed.

Several geothermal power plants already exist, and many more are planned. Although they will never rival the output of conventional utilities, geothermal plants should create top profits for selected companies with expertise in the field.

Magma Power owns several geothermal sites in California and is developing more. Electricity is produced by pumping water into hot rock structures which turn it to steam. The steam is then used to run a turbine, producing electric power. Once a plant is constructed, its operational costs are minimal. No expensive fuels are burned. Neither does a geothermal plant produce any pollution. Magma Power is presently investigating many more geothermal sites throughout the West. As population centers grow near them, the future of this specialized company could be quite promising.

Natural Gas: The Fossil with a Future

As a group, fossil fuels are major sources of air pollution. Even when impurities are removed before the fuels are burned and the exhaust gasses are run through sophisticated filters, various toxins find their way into the air. And nothing can prevent the burning of fossil fuels from producing carbon dioxide, the main contributor to global warming. However, one fossil fuel, natural gas, is much cleaner than the others. Moreover, the United States and Canada have a great deal of it. As a result, we can expect to see the use of natural gas increase dramatically in the coming years until better alternatives are developed.

In addition to producing electricity, the biggest use of natural gas will be to heat buildings. In many areas of the country aggressive natural gas distributors are running new lines to customers as fast as they can dig the trenches. In those areas of increasing population such as the Pacific Northwest, natural gas profits should be especially strong.

Natural gas can also be used in motor vehicles where it will almost certainly receive widespread application over the next few years. About 700,000 cars around the world have already been converted to run on natural gas. The California market—where air standards are becoming the model for the rest of the nation—saw the installation of nine publicly accessible natural gas stations for vehicle use in 1990. British Columbia offers a network of 50 natural gas stations. General Motors is putting together a fleet of 1,000 company pickup trucks that will run on natural gas, while similar programs are underway by United Parcel Service and Federal Express.[12]

The cost of natural gas used as motor vehicle fuel is about two-thirds that of gasoline. Its burning produces 97 percent less carbon monoxide than gasoline. Natural gas is ideal for use in many areas where air pollution laws make the switch desirable. Overall, the outlook for natural gas is very good. Some of the better stocks should perform steadily throughout the decade.

Cascade Natural Gas is a medium-sized natural gas distributor that supplies about 85 communities in Oregon and Washington. After years of very modest expansion, Cascade suddenly found itself in one of the fastest growing areas of the country. In fact, relocations to the Pacific Northwest from other areas barely dropped during the 1990–91 recession. Now the company is scrambling to meet its orders, a pleasant situation which should persist for years.

Questar Corp. is one of America's most complete natural gas suppliers that operates principally in the mountain states. The company operates from the wellhead to the point where its natural gas is eventually burned. Some oil is also produced and distributed. Questar has several advantages which should keep profits high during the 1990s. It benefits from the cost-saving efficiencies which are available to vertically integrated companies. In addition, a great deal of its growth is in unregulated markets where rates can be increased without government permission. Lastly, the company's exploration efforts should pay off with additional supplies of low cost fuel.

Demand Increases for Alcohol Fuels

Alcohol-based fuels are another promising option for motor vehicles. Basically the same low-tech methods used to make liquor are used to produce ethanol from a long list of farm crops. Methanol, a related product, is obtained primarily from natural gas. About 90 percent of the passenger cars in Brazil run on an alcohol-based fuel made from sugar cane.

Alcohol fuels solve some major air pollution problems but they can create others. Ethanol reduces carbon monoxide emissions but it produces 50 percent more hydrocarbons and 8 percent more nitrogen oxides. Methanol emits formaldehyde, a respiratory irritant. Therefore, the use of alcohol, either straight or mixed with gasoline to make gasohol, is likely to be used primarily to reduce our dependence on foreign oil. That is reason enough to give this fuel much wider use in the future.

Archer–Daniels–Midland is a major U.S. firm involved in the processing of raw agricultural products. Its primary markets are in the consumer food and beverage fields, but the company also produces ethanol, one of the alcohol fuels readily used in automotive engines. ADM is America's principal supplier of ethanol. Recently the company announced plans to increase its production of ethanol which it makes from surplus corn products. Further increases are planned and can be implemented as demand for alcohol fuel increases. I think we will see those increases occur regularly in the 1990s.

Hydrogen Fuel: Great Promise but not for the 1990s

The automative fuel of the future may be what we now burn in space vehicles—hydrogen gas. Interestingly, it is made from water, and turns back into water vapor when burned. Of course, such exhaust is free of pollution although it might create fog when the weather is cold. To obtain hydrogen, electric power is used to separate it from ordinary water. From there, the technology becomes more complex and expensive. Because hydrogen is highly explosive and leaks through the tiniest gap, it requires heavy, thick-walled tanks for safe containment. In addition, the tanks don't hold very much fuel. A 700-pound tank in one test car only gave the vehicle a 100-mile driving range. The high-tech tank also cost over $20,000.[13]

All the major automobile makers are experimenting with hydrogen fuel. However, none of them expect to have a product ready for the market before the turn of the century, if then. Meanwhile, other alternatives are available which offer greater promise.

Electric Cars Will Clean Up Profits

In August 1990 the Environmental Protection Agency shocked the nation by stating that it is considering the idea of placing limits on the number of days that commuters may drive their cars in some cities. The Southern California area is being targeted first because air pollution is particularly dangerous in that area. The proposal intends to allow automobile use on alternating days according to an odd-even license plate plan.

In response to both existing and proposed air pollution laws by the EPA and other agencies, several alternative transportation systems are being readied for the market. As mentioned in the previous section, natural gas and sometimes alcohol will play bigger roles in many areas. However, the biggest play in many cities will be the electric car. In fact, measures taken by the California Air Resources Board in October 1990 require that 10 percent of all new cars sold by the year 2003 be electrically powered. That translates to about 200,000 such vehicles.[14] More importantly, other states are taking their cues from California and are considering similar laws for their most polluted cities.

Unfortunately, electric cars are not without their problems. The half ton of batteries they require must be replaced every 20,000 miles or so. Many batteries are not recycled, and battery components—lead and acid—are highly toxic materials, which add to the hazardous waste disposal problem.

Although electric cars by themselves are clean they can nevertheless cause air pollution. That's because they must be plugged in to be recharged. Of course, on the other end of the charging wire is an electric utility pumping merrily away. However, there is one bright spot regarding the charging cycle. Because it will occur mainly at night, during nonpeak hours, the use of electric cars may not substantially increase the need for additional electric plants. For better or worse, the electric car appears to be the leading alternative transportation play for both drivers and investors.

General Motors is the frontrunner in the electric vehicle market. The company already produces an electric delivery van with a top speed of 50 mph and a range between recharges of 60 miles. That is modest performance by any standards, but it is enough for many firms with limited needs.

By 1992 GM plans to introduce the Impact, a passenger car capable of freeway speeds and an expanded range of 120 miles on a six-hour charge. Although GM is not expecting many orders for the Impact outside the California market, I think they are mistaken. The little car is stylish, has impressive acceleration, goes over 100 miles per hour, moves with almost no noise, and contains many state-of-the-art amenities. If they perform as expected, I think GM will be swamped with orders.

General Motors, of course, is no pure play in alternative vehicles and probably won't be, at least in this decade. Nevertheless, I think the company will find that its decisive move into this market will create substantial profits. Since the company is also very innovative in other areas I think it represents a good long-term investment for the 1990s.

NOTES

1. Flemming Meeks and James Drummond, "The Greenest Form of Power," *Forbes,* June 11, 1990.

2. Ged R. Davis et al., "Energy for Planet Earth" (Special Issue), *Scientific American,* September 1990.

3. Charles Maxwell, "Interview with Charles Maxwell," *Investor's Hotline,* September 1990.

4. Frederick Seitz, "Must We Have Nuclear Power?" *Reader's Digest,* August 1990.

5. Maxwell, "Interview with Charles Maxwell."

6. U.S. Council for Energy Awareness, "Nuclear Energy Goes Prime Time," *The Wall Street Journal,* October 2, 1990.

7. Meeks, "The Greenest Form Of Power."

8. Shirley Hobbs Scheibla, "Nuclear Pollution, Cleaning It Up Is A $200 Billion Job," *Barron's,* December 5, 1988.

9. David Stipp, "Including Pollution in Utilities' Costs," *The Wall Street Journal,* July 23, 1990.

10. James B. Powell, *Dow Jones-Irwin Guide to High Tech Investing,* (Homewood, Ill.: Dow Jones-Irwin, 1986).

11. Real Goods Trading Company, 966 Mazzoni St., Ukiah, CA, 95482.

12. Jim Stiak, "Guilt-Free Driving (Almost), The Cleaner Cars of the Near Future," *What's Happening,* November 21, 1990.

13. Ibid.

14. Jim Herron Zamora, "EPA Threatens To Limit Driving in California," *The Wall Street Journal,* August 1, 1990.

CHAPTER 15

BIOTECHNOLOGY MATURES
AND DELIVERS

Every generation or so a revolutionary technology comes on the scene which offers investors returns that are unavailable anywhere else. Instead of the incremental gains common to established industries, investors in the new technologies have a chance to see their profits grow geometrically. In the 1950s we saw it happen in the aerospace industry. In the 1960s and 1970s computers appeared. Then in the 1980s biotechnology came along.

The path to riches is not without peril, however. Hope always precedes profits by many years which leaves most early bird investors with substantial losses. Only after the new technology has matured does it begin to fulfill its promise. It is at that point that investors should begin to take informed positions. Fortunately, during the transition period stock prices are so volatile that it is almost always possible to find an entry point that greatly increases the chance for long-term profits.

The biotechnology industry is now entering the important transition period from the development stage to an emerging industry that merits the attention of serious investors. In the first two years of the decade more biotech products should be approved than the industry produced in all its previous years. Moreover, the pace of new product development will accelerate as the decade progresses. Many firms are also turning the corner to profitability. By the end of the 1990s many of them will almost certainly be counted among America's most successful corporations.

STILL RISKY BUT IMPROVING

Although biotechnology is finally turning the corner from pure research to profitability, it still presents considerable risks for investors. In order to make successful selections we need to take an honest look at the risks we face. Investors' biggest problem is the lack of an objective way to measure the value of most biotech companies. Because most firms have no earnings at all, or they have very thin earnings, such commonly used fundamentals as price-earnings ratios and dividend yields cannot be applied. Even book value is of little use in the biotechnology industry because a company's assets are its people not its machinery or real estate as in most other industries.

Because traditional measures of value haven't been possible in the biotech industry, the market can put any price it wants on a stock. A company can just as easily be worth $10 or $100. Prices at any given time depend almost exclusively on hope and hype or fear and disappointment. Of course, that situation explains the huge price swings which are common in the industry.

Biotech's volatility is magnified by the type of investors that the big moves attract. These investors take positions in the expectation of quick riches and the emotional highs which go with large price changes. Those investors are simply not interested in a more tranquil industry no matter how profitable it may be long term.

Judging the potential of biotech products can also be very difficult. During my three years in the mid–1980s as editor of the newsletter *High Tech Investor* I learned that nobody—not even the people who develop the products—can say with much accuracy how a new development will turn out.[1] Even top firms like Genentech make big mistakes. Its wonderdrug, Activase (TPA), which costs about $2,000 a dose, was found by a major study to be no more effective than the older drug, Streptokinase, which costs about $100 a dose. When that news hit Wall Street, Genentech's stock hit the skids.

To make matters worse there is no guarantee that a new product will make it to the market at all. It takes between eight and twelve years for the average development to progress from the lab and then crawl through the FDA approval labyrinth. As John Kawaske, manager of Financial Strategic Health Sciences Portfolio, observed in April 1991 "The process is designed to weed out products."[2] It does that very well. Mr. Kawaske added that the chances of commercial success were no more than 20 percent to 25 percent in the first phase of testing.

Patent lawsuits add another level of uncertainty to biotech investing. As with any science, breakthrough ideas are pursued in many labs at the same time. That often creates disputes over ownership that threaten to send winner's stocks into the stratosphere and losers into the cellar. For example, Genetics Institute dropped by 50 percent recently when it lost a patent infringement suit with Amgen. On the same day Amgen jumped $12 and then doubled from January to June 1991. Another suit between XOMA and Centocor may be equally upsetting. What's particularly troublesome is that all four companies aren't second tier firms that are struggling to survive—they are industry leaders.

THE TRANSITION TO PROFITS BRINGS GREATER CLARITY

Fortunately, now that the biotech industry is beginning to meet with some financial success it is becoming easier to tell who the winners and the losers will be. Although fundamental measures of value are not entirely valid at low earnings levels, at least we are beginning to have something objective to examine. Stock prices will begin to approach rationality as the process continues. As a result, the biotech industry is becoming less of a gamble and more of an investment.

A second benefit to growing earnings should be decreasing price volatility. As mentioned earlier, with no fundamentals to go by stock prices respond primarily to changing emotions. Now that fundamentals are beginning to emerge those swings should begin to moderate, at least for the leading firms. That situation will be aided by the gradual loss of get-rich-quick investors who will improve the field by their absence.

Objective measures of evaluation will also trigger an industry-wide shakeout as biotech's backers flock to the top firms and abandon those which fall behind. Already the average lifespan for a biotech start-up has dropped from 49 months to 35 months.[3] Many older firms have also fallen by the wayside, including Biomerica, Genetic Engineering, and Quest BioTechnology. Others will surely follow in the 1990s. Although the weeding out process is not pleasant to watch, it will make it easier for investors to pick winning positions.

Major drug companies are already starting to pick winners. Hoffmann La Roche, the Swiss drug giant, purchased 60 percent of Genentech. Other firms including Merck, Johnson & Johnson, Sandoz, and Eli Lilly are making deals with leading firms for the right to market their products. In all such agreements, the infusion of outside money into emerging biotech companies can be expected to boost sales and raise stock prices.

Overall, the outlook for the biotech industry is changing dramatically—and for the better. Although considerable risks remain, those risks are shrinking and are becoming manageable. As a result, for the first time in their history, selected biotech stocks offer careful and dispassionate investors attractive long-term opportunities.

BREAKTHROUGHS ON THE WAY

Over a decade of intensive biotechnology research is now beginning to pay off. Many developments that were started in the early 1980s are emerging from the lengthy development and approval pipeline. Many others will make their debut later in the 1990s. Here is a quick, non-technical overview of what to expect.

Superdrugs have always been a primary focus of the biotech industry. In the past it was necessary to find a genetic code for what was needed and then transmit that code to an organism that would make the drug. That procedure works but it is enormously inefficient because it creates huge molecules of which only a tiny part is actually needed. By contrast the traditional pharmaceutical industry looks only for the tiny compounds it needs. That task requires the drug companies to evaluate thousands of likely chemicals to find just one that may be of value. Of course, that is also very inefficient.

Now biotech and chemistry are working together in "rational drug design" to create just what is needed. Drugs are identified by working backwards from what biologists know about a particular disease and how the body fights it. Once the active compounds are identified they can be made in quantity. Dr. Hans Mueller, president of Nova Pharmaceutical Corp. predicted in May 1991 that within a few years "all drug companies will use these tools."[4]

Drug delivery systems are also the object of intense focus. Such "magic bullets" are specially designed molecules that flow through the bloodstream and attach themselves to specific targets in the body such as cancer cells. Before they are injected, the highly specific molecules are linked with drugs which will be carried to the exact areas of the body where they are needed. Because the delivery systems bypass all tissues except those which are targeted, they can carry more powerful drugs—sometimes even poisons—that would otherwise be impossible to use.

During the 1990s many targeted drug delivery systems will emerge. A few of them, including a likely cure for AIDS, will make headlines. However, most developments will escape notice by everyone but the medical community that will use them as fast as they emerge. For investors that is much better news than the occasional creation of a blockbuster drug. As Michael Gianturco, president of Princeton Portfolios, observed in May 1989, ". . . the real strength of biotechnology lies in its power to create hundreds of products."[5] It will happen in the 1990s.

Diagnostic products are related to drug delivery systems except the molecular targeting takes place outside the body. Each test for a disease—or other condition such as illegal drug use—consists of mixing highly specific molecules with a blood or urine sample. If the telltale compounds are present the test molecules bond to them, causing the sample to change color. Results are often instantaneous.

A great deal of progress has been made in the field of diagnostic products, but hundreds of medical conditions remain for which no quick test has been developed. By the end of the decade most conditions will have diagnostic kits available. Many kits will be available for home use. In fact, within a few years thousands of people will use low-cost diagnostic test kits to closely monitor their health between annual physical exams. As is the case with drug delivery systems, most diagnostic tests won't make the headlines but they will generate millions of dollars in revenues for the biotech industry.

Gene therapy is the current cutting edge of biotech. As the name suggests, these new products will fix defective genes that cause diseases. Since hundreds of problems ranging from hypertension to cancer are thought to involve defective genes, the potential for gene therapy is enormous. The cure that is being pursued most actively at this point is "antisense" therapy, in which a highly specific molecule is used to find and attach itself to a defective gene. Once the molecular "key" has found the right "lock" it is left in place. Of course, that blocks the gene from causing further problems.

Actual gene replacement is also in the works. One test has already been done on a 4-year-old girl with a defective gene that prevented her immune system from fighting infection. Happily for the girl and the future of the technique, the infusion of corrected cells produced the desired result. Now researchers are looking at cystic fibrosis, melanoma, lung cancer, mental retardation, and several other problems that are known to have genetic origins. Thanks to their efforts, by the end of the decade many common genetic killers may no longer be major threats.

Agricultural biotechnology is also moving at top speed. As you may expect, nearly all the techniques which the biotech industry is using to create products for humans can also be applied to plants and animals. Doing so will be worth as much as $100 billion globally by the end of the decade.

Treating and improving plants is also beginning to progress. Advances have been slow because plants are much more resistant to genetic tampering than are animals. However, researchers have succeeded in making a handful of gene transplants into crops. In late 1990 one particularly important test at Rutgers University succeeded in placing genetically altered material into a plant's important photosynthesis code. The test plants' photosynthetic process—the way it makes food—was improved by the change.[6]

Other advances in crop genetics will follow until biotechnology rather than crossbreeding is used to create most new varieties of crops. Although the biggest gains in this area are unlikely to occur until after the turn of the century, we will see continued progress throughout the 1990s.

Biopesticides also show promise. By using techniques developed to create highly specific drugs the biotech industry expects to create equally specific poisons. The principal advantage to the new pesticides will be their selectivity—they will only kill their intended targets. Despite their potential, however, I expect a furious environmental fight over biopesticides that will retard their adoption for many years.

Environmental control products are also being actively pursued. High on the list are bacterial "superbugs" that eat oil spills. Researchers are starting with bacteria that are known to digest oil and are enhancing their capabilities. One open water test has already been done. The results indicated that the technique is worthy of further development which is presently underway.

Superbugs and blocking chemicals that consume or neutralize hazardous substances are also under development. The goal here is to sell the products to industrial companies that will use them to render toxic materials harmless. Then the toxins may be disposed of easily and safely. I expect the first products to become available by 1995. Because they will likely pay for themselves in greatly reduced disposal fees the new products should find ready markets.

WINNING INVESTMENT STRATEGIES

Because their prices are more the product of emotion than they are of reason, biotechnology stocks are among the most cyclical on Wall Street. **Amgen,** the current industry leader, came out at $9 (split adjusted) then fell promptly to $3. **Immunex,** another top firm, made its debut at $11 and almost immediately fell to $6.[7] More importantly, those price swings continue even after a company has been out for several years. Down moves of 50 percent and explosive rates of 100 percent are common.

Not only does each stock soar and swoon on its own changing fortunes but so does the industry as a whole. Improving prospects for one company can make biotechnology a darling on Wall Street, as happened when the Hoffmann La Roche/Genentech deal touched off a rally. The opposite is also true. **Genentech's** 1988 problems with Activase (TPA) touched off a rout that took biotech stocks down 39 percent.

Although the lemming-like behavior of biotech investors may be repelling, the huge price swings it creates give more reasoned investors top opportunities to make attractive buys. The strategy is simple: wait until there is "wailing and gnashing of teeth" among biotech investors then buy the leading firms which should be held for the long term.

Currently, [early summer 1991] biotech stocks are favorites again. From January to June 1991 they climbed a breathtaking 80 percent while the Standard & Poor 500 rose only 20 percent.[8] If history is a guide we can expect the biotech rally to be replaced by an equally sharp retreat, perhaps as soon as late 1991 or early 1992. Whenever it occurs, investors must be ready to ignore the doom and gloom that triggers the drop and take decisive positions.

I would also urge investors to make diversified plays. That is a much better strategy than trying to identify the most promising companies on the basis of their upcoming products. As I mentioned earlier, not even their own developers can predict how individual biotech developments will turn out. The chances of an individual investor doing so are even lower. In fact, being drawn into the technical morass of product evaluations can be counterproductive. Instead, investors should buy several top firms in the almost certain knowledge that they will be tomorrow's leaders as well.

I can't overstress the necessity of sticking with top firms. Investing in second tier biotech stocks is a gamble. Fortunately, there are only about a dozen top companies. Among them should be found some of the greatest success stories of the 1990s. Those odds should be good enough for anyone.

INVESTMENTS TO WATCH

There are three principal ways to invest in the biotech industry, each of which offers investors a different blend of risks and rewards.

Biotech Supply Companies: The Best Blend of Risks and Rewards

For most investors, the best way to take positions—and one I recommend very strongly—is to ignore the front line firms and invest instead in the biotech industry's leading suppliers. As I pointed out in Chapter 9 an industry's suppliers share in its profits without sharing in its risks. Suppliers make money no matter which front line firms are the most successful. They also continue to make money when some of their customers fail because another company always picks up the business. "Win, lose, or draw, the suppliers serve them all," is a well known phrase among professional investors. It's well worth remembering.

Suppliers are also at an advantage because they make money continuously even if their customers must wait years to show a profit. That's a big advantage in the biotech industry where years of red ink always preceed success, if it comes at all. The biotech supply business is particularly attractive because its research oriented customers use large quantities of expensive equipment and chemicals. Unlike other industries where research and development is often given a backseat to other needs, it is the very core of biotechnology. Research and development is so important that its appropriations are virtually recession-proof.

Biotech suppliers are also nearly immune to competition. There are only a handful of firms in the industry. Although they have overlapping product lines they tend to emphasize separate niches. Neither is competition from outside the industry a problem due to the highly specialized nature of the products.

The long-term outlook for biotech supply companies is becoming more attractive with each passing year. As more front line firms make the transition to profitability they will spend additional sums on new product development. Of course, a good portion of that money will flow to the suppliers.

The supply companies will also profit handsomely by selling products for the actual production of biotech developments. That will be true whether the biotech companies make the products themselves or, as in the usual case, they license drug companies to do so. Each newly approved biotech development from superbug to superdrug will require highly specialized production equipment and an ongoing source of biochemicals.

All in all, the suppliers occupy a very comfortable niche. They deserve the serious consideration of investors who desire a relatively safe way to share in biotech's growing profits.

Applied Biosystems is the world's leading supplier of specialized laboratory equipment for the biotech industry. To a lesser extent the company also supplies chemicals to the industry, primarily those which are needed to operate Applied Bio's laboratory products. Applied Bio is best known for having automated many biotech R&D procedures. "Gene machines," protein synthesizers, and various other devices allow biotech researchers to accurately determine genetic codes and then duplicate them. The company's equipment is highly sophisticated and is generally considered to be the best in the world.

Applied Bio continues to expand its capabilities. In addition to launching several new products of its own, the company recently acquired Bio-Ion Nordic, Brownlee Labs, and the Kratos Division of Spectros International. The three acquisitions helped the company round out its product line in areas it didn't wish to develop itself. Foreign operations contribute approximately 58 percent of revenues. Applied Biosystems appears to be extremely well positioned to profit from the maturation of the biotechnology industry.

Life Technologies is to specialized biochemicals and related supplies what Applied Biosystems is to laboratory equipment and instrumentation. The company offers a full range of products from basic chemicals to products that have been prepared for specific biotech and life science procedures. Life Tech is particularly noteworthy for its products which are designed for the commercial production of biotech developments. Serums, growth media for microorganisms, and other products for the production of drugs are offered. This line should do very well in the 1990s as increasing numbers of biotech products come to market.

Life Tech is on the prowl for acquisitions. To do so the company accumulated a great deal of cash. The firm's goal is to increase sales from $151 million in 1990 to $500 million by the middle of the decade. Although that may be overly ambitious, a doubling of sales is a reasonable expectation.

Bio-Rad Laboratories offers a product line that combines both instrumentation and supplies for biotech and other life science markets. Although neither line is as extensive as those offered by Applied Biosystems and Life Technologies the company has done quite well by targeting specific medical subsectors such as AIDS and cancer research.

Perhaps more important for future growth is Bio-Rad's growing line of diagnostic kits. The company is best known for its products which detect AIDS, illegal drug use, and sickle cell anemia—all of which are becoming common problems throughout the world. All in all, the Diagnostic Products division should do very well. Bio-Rad Labs offers investors an opportunity to combine the relative safety of the biotech supply business with the growth potential of a front line firm.

New Brunswick Scientific manufactures equipment that is used to grow the microorganisms used extensively in the biotech industry. The firm's most important product is fermentation equipment. Fermenters are used throughout the biotech industry to sustain genetically altered microorganisms so they may produce pharmaceuticals, enzymes, and other products. New Brunswick is of particular interest because fermentation and related gear will be needed in large quantities for the commercial production of biotech developments. Because of the company's focus on the production side of the industry, it lagged other suppliers during the long years when biotech products were few and far between. However, with many new developments now on the way New Brunswick Scientific may finally see its business prosper. I believe the company is speculative but promising.

Front Line Biotech Firms: The Rewards often Outweigh the Risks

For all its glamour the biotech industry is currently quite small. According to the U.S. Office of Technology Assessment, the value of its products in 1990 totaled a mere $1.2 billion, about the price of a medium-sized battleship or a couple of stealth bombers.[9] More importantly, $8 to $10 billion would buy the entire U.S. biotech industry. That's not very much money considering how fast the value of biotech products is growing. In fact, there are few industries where a share of stock offers so much potential return. When purchased intelligently for the long term, leading biotech stocks should be worth the extra risks they present.

Depending upon how one classifies them, there are between 200 and 300 biotechnology companies in the United States. Less than a dozen are currently emerging from the development stage to profitability. Four have already made the transition and are of particular interest at this time.

Profitable Biotech Companies

Amgen is the current leader in the biotech industry. The company firmly crossed the line into the black in 1990 with a $0.56 per share profit. The firm's leading products treat human anemia (Epogen) and stimulate the immune system to right disease (Neupogen). They have been successful beyond the expectations of most analysts. Various license agreements exist with Johnson & Johnson, Kirin Brewery, and Hoffmann LaRoche. The company also distributes its own products in noncompeting markets.

In addition to its current earnings Amgen is attractive because it has several additional products in the pipeline. Seven developments are now in clinical testing and should be approved soon. More are in earlier stages of the process. Although any single product could fail at any step of the way, the company will almost certainly emerge with enough winners to continue growing strongly. All in all, Amgen appears to be well positioned for the 1990s and should be a rewarding stock once a correction returns the price to attractive levels.

Biogen first broke the profit line in 1989 when it earned $0.1 per share. That jumped to $0.7 per share in 1990. Continued success is expected for this company that emphasizes products with large markets. Biogen's drugs and/or vaccines presently exist for AIDS, cardiovascular problems, inflammation, and even the common cold.

Biogen has also been quick to use licensing agreements to boost revenues. Royalties from Merck, Schering–Plough, SmithKline Beecham, Abbott Labs, and others currently contribute over half of the company's income. Several new products on the way promise to keep Biogen firmly on the growth track.

Chiron became profitable in 1990 with earnings of $0.24 per share. The company has several successful products for diagnosing various infectious diseases. Several vaccinations have also been developed. In addition, Chiron offers specialty drugs for various markets including the eye care industry. Eight additional products are in clinical testing, which bodes well for Chiron's future.

Chiron is also noteworthy for its blend of biotech and more conventional products, an approach which is unusual in the industry. The company's strategy appears to be to have a range of complementary products which fit each particular niche that Chiron targets. The company has several R&D, licensing, and marketing deals with outside firms including CIBA–GEIGY, Novo Nordisk, Warner–Lambert, and Johnson & Johnson.

In a surprise move in July 1991 Chiron agreed to buy out Cetus for $650 million in stock. If the offer is accepted by shareholders, Chiron will acquire several new products, excellent new facilities, and many top people from Cetus. I think the move will greatly improve Chiron's prospects in the 1990s.

Genentech became well known as the world's first successful biotechnology company and experienced meteoric growth on Wall Street. Despite its early track record the company had a deficit of $1.05 in 1990 primarily due to lower than expected sales of Activase and high costs connected with its 60 percent buyout by Hoffmann–LaRoche. However, those problems appear to be behind the company. Earnings of $0.60 per share or better are expected in 1991.

Genentech should do even better beginning in 1992. The FDA is expected to approve Activase for use in new cardiac procedures where it may be superior to competing drugs. In addition, the company has nine new products in clinical testing for AIDS, cancer, childbirth, bronchitis, and other applications. All in all, Genentech appears likely to live up to its potential in the 1990s.

Soon To Be Profitable Biotech Companies
In addition to the profitable front runners there are other leading biotech companies that are expected to break into the black within a year or two. Some will be profitable for the first time, others will return to profitability after experiencing problems or making heavy outlays for future developments. Because several members of this group also have considerable promise, their progress should be monitored.

Cetus is worthy of mention in the chance that its stockholders do not approve its merger with Chiron. The company was an early biotechnology pioneer along with Genentech. As occured with its rival, Cetus also stumbled after first turning profitable on early successes. Fortunately, the outlook for Cetus is improving rapidly due to several new products which should be on the market soon. Most promising is a drug (Proleukin) which treats kidney cancer and may be effective with other cancers as well. Factor VIII for hemophiliacs could also be very profitable. A line of forensic tests has met early favor by the FBI which should trigger growing sales by police agencies around the world. 1992 should either by a turnaround for Cetus—or the company will benefit Chiron as the case may be.

Centocor presently develops and produces several diagnostic test kits which are intended to detect damaged heart tissue, restricted cardiac arteries, blood clots, breast cancer, ovarian cancer, and certain other maladies. In addition, the company is developing treatments for various diseases.

Centocor was profitable from 1987 to 1989 but incurred a substantial loss in 1990 resulting from the buyout of two R&D partnerships plus the purchase of certain capabilities of Invitron Corp. Over the long term those expenses may well prove to have been good investments. A clearer problem exists with Centocor's patent infringement suit with XOMA (see the following item) over its septic shock product. If Centocor wins the suit it may be back on the profits track quite soon.

XOMA has two products that are nearing the end of the FDA approval pipeline. One of them (CD5) helps ensure the success of bone marrow transplants, a small but growing market. The product is also being tested for treating rheumatoid arthritis, a much larger market. The second promising product (E5) which treats septic shock is being developed jointly with Pfizer. However, XOMA's patent infringement suit with Centocor over E5 is a cloud over earnings that should be resolved soon. A loss could hurt XOMA short term but not derail the company's chances for longer term success.

Genetics Institute has an excellent reputation for innovative biotechnology developments. Most of the firm's products are for treating various blood disorders including anemia, abnormal clotting, and insufficient white blood cells. In addition, the company produces various cancer and bone growth compounds. Genetics Institute should become profitable in the next year or so as more of its products enter the marketplace.

Immunex Corp. focuses on developments which regulate the function of the body's immune system. The company's products restore or improve the immune system's ability to fight certain cancers and infections. One product now has FDA approval. Five more are currently in the final stages of testing. Eastman Kodak, Sterling Drug, and Hoechst AG have recently signed various agreements with Immunex which should prove to be mutually beneficial. This niche company has considerable potential.

Genzyme offers several products which are used in diagnostic test kits. The company also supplies specialized chemicals that have application in both the biotech and pharmaceutical industries. Genzyme recently entered the therapeutic market directly with an enzyme (Ceradase) that is used in the treatment of Gaucher's disease, an inherited disorder. Two additional therapeutic products should gain FDA approval by 1995. If Ceradase is successful, Genzyme should be in the black before that time.

Mutual Funds Offer Diversification

A mutual fund should not be needed by investors who intend to take positions in the top biotech supply companies. Such indirect biotech plays offer reasonable safety by themselves. However, investors who wish to take positions in the front line biotechnology firms—and who don't wish to buy more than one or two—should consider using a mutual fund instead. Two of them look particularly attractive.

Fidelity Select Biotechnology Portfolio is a low-load (2 percent) fund that is as aggressive as any normal investor might want, yet it offers needed diversity. Unlike many other med-tech funds, Fidelity Biotechnology generally keeps a tight focus on its target industry and does not stray very far into related areas. That allows the fund to share fully in the biotech industry's wins and losses. If investors feel certain that the biotech industry will rise, this is the fund to be in.

Financial Strategic Health Sciences Portfolio (no-load) takes a broader view toward the med-tech and health care industry. The fund often holds leading biotech companies including Amgen, Chiron, and Genentech. In addition, the fund includes more stable health care firms such as Johnson & Johnson and Bristol–Myers Squibb. The mix changes as conditions warrant. This Financial fund should be well suited to more conservative investors who would rather not ride the front line biotech roller coaster no matter how profitable that strategy may be long term.

NOTES

1. Alexander P. Paris, ed., *High Tech Investor,* Barrington Research Associates, P.O. Box 860, Barrington, Ill., 60010.

2. Anne Newman, "Caution Urged in Choosing Biotech Stocks," *The Wall Street Journal,* April 29, 1991.

3. John Barbour, "Biotech Valley Wants to Wipe Out Disease," *Eugene Register Guard,* May 12, 1991.

4. Joan O. Hamilton, "The Search for Superdrugs," *Business Week,* May 13, 1991.

5. Michael Gianturco, "Bullish on Biotech," *Forbes,* September 17, 1990.

6. Associated Press, "Strides Reported in Plant Genetics," *Eugene Register Guard,* November, 1990.

7. Flemming Meeks and Mary Beth Grover, "Recombinant Stock Prices," *Forbes,* Jun. 24, 1991.

8. Ibid.

9. Lee Edson, "Greed Was in the Genes," *Across The Board,* January/February 1990.

CHAPTER 16

A SECOND WIND FOR INDUSTRIAL AUTOMATION

Sometimes a trend will make a strong appearance which attracts great attention then it will seem to fade away. That occurred in the 1980s with the industrial automation revolution. After nearly three years of almost daily coverage by the media, Americans began to notice that the revolution in manufacturing was largely limited to a handful of showcase experiments. Almost overnight, industrial automation was forgotten both by the public and by Wall Street.

The technological revitalization of America's manufacturing and process industries didn't go away. It simply ran into problems that needed a few additional years to solve. Now that those solutions are arriving, the industrial automation trend will resume strongly. As is always true with investments that have great potential, the people who understand what is happening and then act on that knowledge will be the biggest winners.

THAT WAS THEN, THIS IS NOW

By far the biggest problem to befall the industrial automation trend of the 1980s was that newly developed high-tech machines often didn't live up to their promises. Many of them would not perform their tasks at all. Others did so only with constant tinkering by high-priced experts. It didn't take long for the disappointing news to get out and for orders to evaporate.

Fortunately, the reliability problem has now turned around. The marriage of computers and machinery has advanced to the point where no human can compete with modern systems in terms of quality, endurance, and cost. In addition, the new machines are able to work with each other as coordinated systems. Of course, that increases the machine's effectiveness even more.

Also high on the list of stumbling blocks was inexpensive Asian labor. Armies of first generation robots and automated machines could not compete with armies of humans who were willing to work for less than the cost of installing and operating high-tech machines. A robot engineer at GM noted the problem and admitted that when human capability was needed it was cheaper to hire a human. As American manufacturers learned that lesson most jobs that needed greater efficiency simply moved overseas. Now, many of those jobs are moving back to the United States. Not only are new production machines capable of doing better work than humans can do—no matter how motivated they may be—they can do so less expensively. That trend is continuing as new equipment becomes cheaper at the same time costs rise dramatically for overseas labor.

American labor and cultural problems also stalled the emerging industrial automation trend. In a misguided attempt to save jobs, many unions fought the introduction of efficient machinery. In many cases white-collar workers also took stands against new technology which they didn't understand and found threatening. In recent years there has been a dramatic turnaround by both workers and managers regarding highly efficient production equipment. Almost everyone now agrees that greater productivity is the only way to save any jobs at all. For example, in GM's trendsetting Saginaw Vanguard plant in Saginaw, Michigan, the United Autoworkers Union was instrumental in getting new technology installed and working properly. That situation is now common throughout American industry.[1]

The booming U.S. economy of the 1980s put another damper on factory modernization by giving the nation a false sense of security about our ability to compete internationally. The heady years of the last decade appeared to make a mockery of warnings that growing problems in our manufacturing sector would have disastrous consequences. In addition, Americans were given the illusion that we could prosper as a service economy while leaving the production of goods to others.

Now, ten years later and billions of dollars in debt we know better. There is a new realism in America and a new national will to turn our production sector around and bail ourselves out. As several innovative U.S. companies have clearly demonstrated, the only way to do that is to become more efficient than our competition. That, in turn, will require spending billions of dollars for modern industrial equipment.

Many critics of our ability to modernize our industrial base point to a lack of money to get the job done. It is true that tight money during the 1980s made modernization quite costly. While many Japanese companies borrowed funds for new equipment at 4 percent interest rates, Americans often needed to pay twice and sometimes three times that amount. But America is rapidly moving away from the madcap consumption that kept money in short supply and interest rates high during the last decade. As I stressed in earlier chapters, a nation of older and wiser Americans now favor the accumulation of capital rather than goods. This renewed emphasis on savings will provide the needed funds for industry. In fact, it is already having a positive effect. By late 1990, Robert Unger, chief stockpicker at the Columbia Growth Fund noted, "The consumption side of the economy is exhausted, while the production side is starting to ripen."[2]

NO TIME TO WASTE

Of course, simply removing impediments to a trend doesn't mean it will develop. It is also necessary to have compelling reasons for it to get underway. In the case of industrial modernization the motivating reasons are not only compelling, they are becoming critical. High on the list of motivators is our loss of competitiveness in global markets. That loss is greater than is generally supposed. Each year another American industry slips into second place to foreign competition. Some have fallen to third place and lower.

For example, in the 1970s we lost our edge in steel, aluminum, and several other basic industrial items. In the 1980s we lost televisions, video cassette recorders, small, high-performance automobiles, and dozens of other consumer items. Now we face losing our edge with big ticket items such as commercial aircraft, advanced semiconductors, and computers of all sizes. The bottom line is clear: either we act now to stem the tide or we slip further into an economic abyss.

Automated production facilities are also needed to make up for a shortage of skilled labor that is crippling many industries. The baby busters featured in an earlier chapter can't begin to meet the needs of traditional labor intensive factories. In addition, many of today's workers are too poorly educated to perform the critical tasks that were child's play for earlier generations. As long ago as October 1988, factory expert Robert Pritzker reported, "What do you do when you have a fully grown adult who is uneducated not only in reading, writing, arithmetic, but also doesn't know how to sit still, to pay attention or listen to instructions?"[3] One solution is to employ high-tech machines that can produce top quality work in a variety of industries.

Modern production equipment is also necessary to help shorten product design and manufacturing cycles. American firms can no longer spend months planning new products and more months tooling up to produce them. Any company that tries that today will be trounced by competitors that can do the job in a few weeks. Many U.S. product cycles are now so long that goods are obsolete before they appear in stores. That situation must be changed.

We also need top notch factories to make small runs of products efficiently. Today's demanding consumers want goods that fit their needs. That is why items as simple as electric coffee makers are available in so many variations from top suppliers such as Krups and Braun. It is equally important that each variation be kept affordable even when only a few thousand are made. The secret is programmable production lines where products can be altered almost instantly by slipping a new disk in the master computer. Without such equipment, there is no way we can keep up to date with fast-changing markets.

Finally, we desperately need to turn around our nation's balance of payments. The deficit is a monetary hemorrhage that is lowering the standard of living for millions of Americans. I think the situation could reach a critical point in the 1990s which would be very damaging to our country both economically and socially. It must be avoided at all costs. The only way to do it is to regain our role as a major exporter of goods. We can do that if we modernize our industrial sector.

THE OUTLOOK FOR INVESTORS

Fortunately, the turnaround of America's industrial problems is underway. The United States is upgrading its production capabilities in nearly every industry and it is doing so in a big way. The job won't happen overnight but it will be worth billions of dollars during the 1990s. Longer term we can also expect rising orders for factory equipment of all types from Eastern Europe where production facilities are as much as a half century out of date. As Peter F. Drucker wrote in a July 1990 article for *The Wall Street Journal,* "For Central Europe to regain a modicum of prosperity, let alone social and political stability, its industries must become productive and competitive in no time at all."[4] It doesn't matter that such countries are broke—they will get the money from the United States, Germany, and Japan.

One caution is in order. Industrial automation stocks are often cyclical. They rise and fall with the fortunes of their customers who are tied closely to the economy. However, an October 1990 credit report from Moody's demonstrated that some top companies like Ford will now risk having their debt downgraded a notch in order to keep capital spending levels high.[5] As Robert A. Gale, president of the American Machine Tool Distributor's Association noted in September 1990, even when times are tough many U.S. manufacturers now feel there is less risk in borrowing for new machinery than there is trying to compete with obsolete equipment.[6] The reports indicate that the order cycle is likely to smooth out for the industrial automation sector.

Finally, don't expect conformation of the industrial automation trend to be found in the investment press until long after the biggest moves—and the biggest profits—have occurred. Industrial automation's false start in the 1980s embarrassed the financial media because they featured it heavily. The trend is rarely mentioned now. Consequently, for the next year or so this area will be most suitable for investors who are in the habit of making up their minds independently of others, and then sticking to their decisions.

STOCKS TO WATCH

Automated Machine Tools Take the Lead

Automated machine tools were invented over a century ago. A few years after Eli Whitney introduced the concept of standardized parts, Joseph Jacquard developed an automatic loom which was controlled by a set of punch cards. The technology progressed from there to rolls of punched paper—as in a Player Piano—and then on to magnetic tapes. In the late 1960s computers were added. By that point American firms were the world leaders in automated machine tool technology.

In the 1960s, however, the Japanese started a crash program to produce automated tools of their own to help them rebuild their war-torn industrial base. Twenty years later they were exporting their machines to America. Japanese products found ready markets because they were cheap and effective. Japanese companies continue to maintain dominant positions in many industrial markets. Now, however, many machine tool orders are swinging back to American firms. Not only have our products been upgraded but so have our services. Although U.S. products can still cost more than those from Japan, the difference often isn't enough to outweigh the advantage of doing business with a local firm.

Leading American machine tool makers are also prospering by learning where *not* to compete with the Japanese. Instead of going head to head in areas where we can't win, many U.S. machine tool makers now offer Japanese lines themselves. Most often the imported machines are smaller, single function units that are difficult to produce efficiently in America.

One area where U.S. firms are beginning to dominate is the production of larger systems that are designed to perform dozens of different operations in one place. Such systems are much more cost effective and less troublesome than running products through a series of individual machine tools however advanced they may be. Since we developed such large-scale manufacturing centers we are getting the lion's share of the business. Of course, profits are substantial for the big ticket items.

The U.S. machine tool industry isn't out of the woods as yet. However, according to The Association for Manufacturing Technology it appears to be on the right path.[7] Orders will still be cyclical and foreign competition will continue to be stiff. Nevertheless, the outlook for the industry is very good long term as demand for automation increases at the same time U.S. suppliers become more competitive.

Cincinnati Milacron is one of the world's leading producers of machine tools. Although the company has a full range of products it is best known for its larger, more advanced units. In particular, the company's fully computerized manufacturing systems are highly regarded because they make it possible for U.S. customers to compete successfully in world markets.

In addition to machine tools, Cincinnati Milacron supplies plastics processing equipment that is used to make many popular products. Since new recycling technologies are boosting the appeal of plastics in many applications (see Chapter 13) this firm should profit from that trend as well.

Monarch Machine Tool also supplies a full range of production equipment from manually operated machine tools to computer operated systems. In addition, Monarch produces advanced fabrication equipment for various sheet and strip metal operations. Monarch's sheet systems form the basis for complete production lines in modern steel and aluminum mills. This diversified company should see rising orders in the 1990s.

Giddings & Lewis is America's leading supplier of the very largest automated machine tools which are designed for factory-wide systems. In addition to individual products and complete manufacturing centers, the company makes automated assembly equipment. One such installation will assemble large body sections for GM's new Saturn automobile.

Potential investors should not be fooled by Gidding's apparent lack of a track record. The company is over a century old but it has operated under other names. In addition, the firm was purchased by AMCA International in 1988 and disappeared from the investment pages altogether. The company again became public in mid–1989. In a surprise move in mid–1991, Giddings & Lewis acquired its closest rival, Cross & Trecker. The move establishes Giddings & Lewis as an even more powerful company in the automated machine tool industry. I think the company will have a very profitable decade.

Met–Coil Systems produces automated equipment that turns sheet and strip metals into finished products such as heating ducts, metal cabinets, shelving, and auto parts. The company is particularly well known for successfully integrating its machines into complete production systems that turn out finished products with a minimum of labor. Met–Coil recently entered into a joint venture with the Japanese and now have an operation in that country. Exports from all operations are growing.

A Growing Role for Material Handling Systems

Outside DeKalb, Illinois, the Minnesota Mining and Manufacturing Company (3M) erected a huge building in the midst of the corn fields. The local people know it is a warehouse but it is actually more than that—the building is a machine. When an order comes into the 3M warehouse, a worker taps a few buttons on a keyboard then sits back to wait. Inside the building computers spring to life and motors begin to hum. A few minutes later the desired packages show up at the loading dock. The whole system functions much like a giant vending machine.

Within many U.S. factories similar systems are now being installed to handle incoming materials and outgoing products. They are bringing efficiency to operations which formerly defied attempts to boost productivity. In fact, automated material handling systems often pay for themselves more quickly than any other part of a modern factory. It's little wonder that they are among the biggest sellers in the industrial automation industry.

As is the case with large machine tools and factory-wide systems, American firms are leaders in automated material handling equipment. Because the new systems offer significant cost savings, sales tend to hold up better during uncertain times than is the case with other expensive industrial automation products.

Raymond Corp. is an important supplier of innovative material handling equipment including both manually controlled and fully automated systems. Products include driverless carts that locate items in specially constructed warehouses then either retrieve or store them as needed. Another of the company's systems resembles a giant carousel. It rotates shelves and their contents to warehouse workers in response to coded commands. Raymond incurred a small deficit in 1989 when it made a very large investment in automated production equipment for its own use. Profits returned almost immediately in early 1990.

Harnischfeger is not a pure play in the materials handling industry but it is an important supplier. The company makes automated systems for warehouses and manufacturing applications. However, Harnischfeger is best known for its very large installations that move heavy industrial products including generators, engines, and coils of wire. As America's industrial base continues to recover, this company should see rising orders.

Robots May Rise from the Grave

No part of the industrial automation movement has been a bigger disappointment than robotics. In the early 1980s a dozen small U.S. robotic companies were struggling for shares of a market that analysts promised would be worth billions of dollars by 1985. When larger industrial firms learned of the potential profits in robotics they also got into the frenzy. Westinghouse Electric snapped up Unimation, the inventors of industrial robots. General Electric quickly responded by starting its own robotics firm. IBM and Cincinnati Milacron also got into the business.

Now, most of these companies are out of the robotics business. Those that remain have only token involvements. They didn't bail out because they overestimated the potential market. They got out because their machines didn't perform as expected. In many cases problems that could have been corrected were ignored in order to boost short-term profits. It was a classic case of greed and shortsightedness upsetting what would have been a profitable long-term business. Now the Japanese all but own the industrial robot market which was handed to them on a silver platter.[8]

A decade later, there are hopeful signs that we may take that platter back. This time, U.S. robot makers are starting small and working up, as the Japanese did a decade ago. Since we have some advantages in advanced semiconductor and software technologies, U.S. makers have a fighting chance for long-term success.

First up are several U.S. robots that are designed for service applications. Many are now being employed to clean up nuclear wastes, put out fires, dispose of bombs, inspect undersea cables, and even patrol buildings. Typical of the new breed of robots is Rosa, a machine designed by Westinghouse. Rosa moves easily through radioactive tunnels in nuclear plants to inspect miles of steam pipes. When necessary Rosa makes welding repairs on the spot. At the other end of the spectrum is "pizzabot" developed at Carnegie Mellon's Center for Human Service Robotics. It may first appear that the pizza making robot is little more than an expensive stunt put together by fun-loving engineers in training. This is not so. Pizzabot was designed to allow just a few people—including disabled workers—to run businesses by themselves.

In both Japan and America the companies that have the most promising robots fit into two groups. Either they are large firms for whom robotics is a very small business or they are small private companies. The former offer little opportunity to investors as robotic plays. The latter do not currently have stock for sale to the public.

Although presently unavailable, the private firms may eventually offer considerable promise to investors. That's because the best of them are likely to go public within a few years. I urge you to watch for initial public offerings by **Intelledex Corp., Adept Technology, Ben-**

thos, and **Cybermotion.** Three firms that are already traded on the stock market are also of interest.

Graco, Inc. is not a pure play in robotics. However, the company is a leader in the one robotics success story of the 1980s—automated paint sprayers. Systems are now in use in many industrial applications painting automobiles, cabinets, and dozens of other products. Graco's robots are in demand because they are cost effective and because they do jobs that are unhealthy for humans to perform. Wider applications for such systems are in the works which should benefit the company.

Prab Robots makes conventional and automated conveyor systems, scrap metal recycling equipment, and robots. These robots are designed primarily to lift and move heavy objects in factory and warehouse applications. Prab recently created and produced a robot that was designed to serve the handicapped. It responded to voice commands and could do many common but necessary chores such as pick up objects, turn equipment on and off, get food and drinks and so on. Nevertheless, for all its utility the robot wasn't successful commercially. Prab posted a loss of $1.61 per share in 1989 but bounced back with a $0.24 per share gain in 1990 which is very encouraging. I suggest that you investigate the company as a potential winner in the recovering U.S. robotics industry.

Denning Mobile Robotics is a small and thinly traded firm that has been in the robotics business since 1983. The company sells robots for security and floor cleaning applications plus robotic platforms for television cameras. Customers include many top companies including United Parcel Service. Denning is also struggling to find profits in its troubled industry. Because success has been elusive, and robotics are out of favor on Wall Street, Denning has been forgotten. Of course, that means that success—if it comes—should have a dramatic impact on the stock. I feel it is speculative but worth investigating.

Artificial Vision Makes a Turnaround

As was the case with the fledgling U.S. robotics industry, artificial vision systems were also overrated in the 1980s. Systems that were designed to guide robots were the biggest failures. Inspection systems for assembly lines were more successful but could only be made to work under ideal conditions. The principal stumbling block for artificial vision was a lack of raw computing power. That is because to a machine an image is a vast array of individual dots, each of which is represented by a number. To analyze an image each dot must be scanned individually. Both the numbers and the patterns they form must then be compared with information stored in memory. Then if any differences exist, those differences must be evaluated.

For example, a system that looks for flaws in newly made gears must scan each gear and compare it with an image of a perfect gear that is stored in its memory. If the new gear has a chip in one of its teeth, the system will detect a difference in the two images. Then the system must decide if the difference is big enough to warrant rejection. A human could make such an inspection almost instantly, but early computers took as long as a minute. Consequently, even when early artificial vision systems worked, they were usually too slow to be useful.

As you may expect, the recent development of massively powerful yet affordable computers is breathing new life into the artificial vision industry; and the industry is making full use of its new potential. According to the Automated Imaging Association sales were estimated to be well over $400 million in 1990.[9] I think they could top a billion dollars by the end of the decade. Best of all for investors, one public company may reap the lion's share of the business.

Cognex Corp. is a small company when measured by usual Wall Street standards but it is a giant in the artificial vision industry. The company produces most of the top systems that are in use around the world including many in Japan, where industries account for approximately 40 percent of the company's revenues. In late 1990 Cognex was thought to control about two-thirds of the market for artificial vision systems.

Cognex has not been content to focus its efforts totally on new and better systems. To the great relief of most customers the company also made its vision equipment easier to program. A new version of a popular Cognex system can be controlled with a Macintosh computer using a set of visual commands. Cognex is still struggling in an industry that is far from secure. However, the firm's clear lead looks good for the future.

Process Controls Prosper

There is a frequently overlooked side to industrial automation that also holds considerable promise for investors. That industry is process control. Unlike the situation with factory automation, where products are made one at a time, industrial process controls regulate batch or continuous production as found in a paper mill or a chemical factory. In such a plant sensors continuously monitor and adjust production variables such as temperature, thickness, pressure, and so on. Only when everything is in balance can the plant operate efficiently.

As is true with artificial vision, process control systems also need considerable quantities of computer power. Equally important are high speed computer networks that tie everything together. That is particularly true for the largest and most efficient systems that oversee an entire plant. They must make thousands of interrelated split-second decisions and must be coordinated perfectly.

Top-notch software is also critical to process control. Many of the best programs took years to write and more years to debug. In most cases the software is leased not sold to customers. That makes the leading process control firms very difficult for would-be competitors to dislodge. Because the process control industry is dominated by a handful of companies, investors can concentrate most of their efforts on timing rather than selection. I suggest taking positions when the stocks appear to be at cyclical lows then simply holding on to them until they perform as expected.

Measurex is one of the world's leading process control suppliers. The company is particularly advanced in sensor technology with which it can monitor critical production variables common to several industries including paper, plastics, rubber, chemicals, and pharmaceuticals. Measurex also excels in mill-wide computer systems including proprietary software products which control the operation of an entire process plant. Foreign sales account for over half of revenues.

Measurex is now moving cautiously into the factory automation area with systems designed for aerospace, automotive, and electronic markets. The firm is developing such systems through alliances with IBM, Mitsubishi, and Beloit. At present, Measurex is closely tied to the fortunes of the pulp and paper industry, their biggest customer. Because that industry is cyclical so is Measurex. Consequently, good timing is very important when taking positions in this stock.

Marcam Corp. produces software designed for various process industries. In the fall of 1990 the company had 12 programs available that increase the efficiency of food, pharmaceutical, and chemical production. A new product was recently introduced to increase warehouse productivity. The company licenses rather than sells its software. Marcam was formed in 1980 and first went public in August 1990. Its early success indicates that the company may have a promising future.

Computer Aided Design and Engineering: Mature but Strong

One big success story of the early factory automation industry was computer aided design (CAD) and computer aided engineering (CAE). That success continues today. In fact, powerful CAD and CAE systems are now available to individuals for use on personal computers. New industrial CAD and CAE systems do more than speed the creation of designs. The best systems go on to optimize the designs for efficient production by automated equipment. A few systems actually translate the designs into instructions that can be fed directly into manufacturing systems.

Sometime in the 1990s a revolutionary new technology will be added to CAD and CAE. "Virtual reality" translates computerized designs into realistic 3-D images which are viewed through special helmets. The effect places the operator *inside* the system. With the addition of electronic gloves which are linked to the computer, the operator can reach out and rearrange things as desired. It is all very lifelike.

Matsushita is working on a virtual reality CAD system that consumers can use to select appliances to best fit their homes. Customers can type in their kitchen's dimensions then "drop in" Matsushita stoves and refrigerators. The user can even "walk" through the kitchen opening doors, reaching for items, placing pots on the stove and so on to see how well everything works together. All in all, the potential is nearly endless for systems that combine virtual reality with CAD and CAE. This exciting new technology will be covered more in the next chapter.

The CAD and CAE industry is also becoming quite specialized. Some highly successful firms make systems that design computer chips. Others are tailor-made for the design of aircraft. The list goes on and on. Here are the CAD and CAE firms that look the most promising.

Intergraph Corp. is a CAD pioneer. After helping invent the field a decade ago, the company is still one of its leading players. The company offers complete systems with both hardware—computer workstations—and software. Most products are compatible with popular computers, peripherals, and software from third-party vendors which increases their appeal. Over 900 individual design, engineering, and data base programs are available.

Intergraph appears to be in a particularly good position for the 1990s due to its strong lead in the industry. In addition, increasing emphasis on software is making it possible to keep margins high in an environment where severe hardware price cutting is hurting other makers. Foreign sales accounted for nearly half of revenues in 1989. The outlook appears to be quite good for Intergraph.

Gerber Scientific supplies specialized CAD systems that are used principally in the design of printed circuit boards and in graphic arts applications. Other systems are used to design parts and machines used in a variety of industries. Gerber takes its CAD systems beyond the drawing board to the shop floor where special machines translate the designs into finished products. Gerber's devices—which resemble giant computer plotters—quickly slice out parts using lasers, torches, or cutters. The systems are popular in the apparel, automotive, aerospace, and similar industries that must cut parts from sheets of material.

MacNeal–Schwendler produces computer software for engineering applications. The company's CAE programs make it possible not only to design products but also to analyze them before they are put into production. Customers include industrial companies, universities, and government research facilities.

MacNeal–Schwendler is noteworthy because it leases rather than sells its CAE software. Not only does that practice keep revenues flowing but it attracts customers who appreciate having a top-notch CAE system for a low initial cost. An extensive research and development program should keep this firm on the profits track.

Autodesk Inc. is the leading maker of powerful CAD and CAE software designed to run on personal computers. The company has growing sales throughout the world and is expanding rapidly to meet the demand. Low debt and substantial cash reserves [mid-1991] should allow that expansion to proceed with minimal risk.

As is the case with MacNeal–Schwendler, Autodesk spends heavily on R&D to keep abreast of the market, and ahead of the competition. A promising virtual reality CAD program is particularly noteworthy. However, this young firm is highly dependent upon a small number of products. If any one of them should begin losing market share, this stock could drop sharply. Although I am impressed with Autodesk's potential, it should only be considered by investors who will monitor it regularly.

Not To Be Overlooked: Companies That *Use* Industrial Automation

Sometimes the best way to invest in a promising technology is to take positions in the companies that use it rather than the companies that make it. For example, several firms including **Caterpillar, John Deere, Motorola, Nabisco,** and **General Motors** have been heavy buyers of the most efficient industrial automation equipment. Those purchases have enabled the firms to compete in markets that were becoming dominated by foreign companies.

John Deere is a good example. This century-old tractor company was nearly plowed under by Japanese firms that not only made cheaper machines but also made higher quality machines. Rather than throw in the towel, Deere went to Cross & Trecker for a state-of-the-art factory that would put them on an equal footing with the competition. It was a big gamble, and it was tough going for a couple of years; but it worked. Deere is now a top competitor in its industry again, and it has the profits to prove it. Now the company is moving aggressively into consumer markets. Deere looks very good for the 1990s.

General Motors is also worthy of notice. As mentioned before, the firm's new Saturn manufacturing plant is a model of modern industrial automation. Even the Japanese are impressed. More than that, the Japanese are worried. The Germans are petrified. Although the GM facility has several problems to overcome the same was true at Deere. I believe GM will overcome them. When it does so, the company's new automobiles are likely to be the best transportation values in the world. I think it will happen.

As the decade progresses you can expect to see many additional examples of U.S. firms updating and turning around. I suggest that you follow such news closely as it will point the way to top profit opportunities.

NOTES

1. William J. Hampton, "GM Bets an Arm and a Leg on a People-Free Plant," *Business Week,* September 12, 1988.

2. Michael Fritz, "Hunch Player," *Forbes,* November 12, 1990.

3. Jonathan R. Laing, "Producing Joy: After 40 Years, Bob Pritzker's Still in Love with Factories," *Barron's,* September 5, 1988.

4. Peter F. Drucker, "Junk Central Europe's Factories and Start Over," *The Wall Street Journal,* July 19, 1990.

5. "Ford's Long-Term Debt Was Downgraded by Moody's," *The Wall Street Journal,* October 25, 1990.

6. Ralph E. Winter, "Machine Tool Orders Climbed During August," *The Wall Street Journal,* September 24, 1990.

7. Ibid.

8. Amal Kumar Naj, "How U.S. Robots Lost the Market to Japan in Factory Automation," *The Wall Street Journal,* November 6, 1990.

9. Ruth Simon, "The Vision Thing," *Forbes,* December 10, 1990.

CHAPTER 17

ELECTRONIC TECHNOLOGIES FINALLY COME TOGETHER

In the chapter about biotechnology investments, we were warned about Wall Street's costly tendency to abandon a disappointing new technology just before it delivers on its promises. In most cases, if investors had waited a little longer for the young industry to mature they would have seen the handsome gains which they expected.

Of course, investors can also get out too early with a wildly successful technology that they feel has reached its potential. Investors look at the impressive gains that have been delivered and conclude that the play must be over. The comment one usually hears is, "Nothing goes up forever." All too often the successful technology then enters its second stage of development and shoots up once again. It has happened many times.

A case in point that is underway now is the broadly based office electronic revolution that began in the 1970s and appeared to reach a peak in the 1980s. We saw record gains from personal computers, software, networks, modern office equipment, and consumer electronics. Then about five years ago growth slowed down. Investors assumed that the show was over and promptly turned their attention elsewhere. In my opinion, they should have been buying not selling.

THE SECOND ACT

As impressive as modern electronics may be, it represents little more than the groundwork for what is about to emerge—the union of separate technologies into powerful integrated systems. Those systems will be so useful and efficient that they will be adopted throughout the world. The result will be another powerful surge for the electronics revolution. Best of all for today's investors, the curtain on the second act is about to go up; and the play should last for nearly a decade.

In order to see the potential of the electronic revolution of the 1990s it is necessary to take a critical view of our present technology and notice how it falls short of what is needed—and was promised. For example:

- Most offices have desks covered with electronic boxes including a fax machine, a laser copier, a laser printer, an optical scanner, and a computer. Those boxes all share similar technologies. However, many of them don't work together at all or they do so very poorly. The result is wasted time and money.

Very soon, office electronics will be fully integrated which will greatly increase efficiency and lower costs at the same time.

- A decade ago we were promised a "paperless office." Instead we have more paper to wade through than ever before. We sit in our modern offices with our state-of-the-art electronics and still spend hours thumbing our way through file cabinets whenever we need a document.

Fortunately, most paper files will be on computer within a few years.

- Our state-of-the-art computers fall way below their potential because they don't work very well together. To be sure, good networks exist for sharing files and programs. But what is really needed are networks that make individual computers into systems that are powerful computers themselves.

They're on the way.

- Our software is also below par. Most programs that work efficiently by themselves don't work well together. That greatly reduces their utility and the potential of the system. Although new software programs such as Windows allow some individual programs to share information, the result falls short of full integration.

The 1990s will see the emergence of "everything software"—and not too soon.

- Nowhere is there more room for improvement than in the union of computers and telecommunications. Even technical illiterates know intuitively that when we call people on the telephone we should be able to see them. We should be able to have effective electronic meetings, complete with visual aids. And, as we talk we should be able to send along appropriate data with just a few key strokes.

Much of that technology is now available but is currently very expensive. Within just a few years it will be within the means of most Americans.

• The lack of integration between computers and electronic media is equally obvious to most people. To be sure, most televisions can serve as mediocre computer monitors but that is little to cheer about. What is needed is the ability to merge video, audio, and text. We should be able to bring images and sounds into our computer programs and vice versa.

We will see most of those capabilities within three years.

• Finally, for all their power computers are still unbelievably stupid which greatly limits their utility. For example, even with the newest models if one searches a database for titles about "elephants" the computer will skip over anything about "pachyderms." Because even the most elementary discrimination is beyond the ability of current systems their users must compensate by learning an enormous amount of specialized information. Many people are beginning to wonder if the latest programs are worth their time and trouble.

By 1994 or 1995 computers should be a lot brighter and a lot easier to use than they are today.

Overall, the electronic products we currently have available offer little more than a hint of what we are about to see. And yet, most investors either have not noticed the advances which are just around the corner or they don't recognize what they will be worth. As a result, few investors are taking positions in the electronic integration trend that is just now getting underway. Those few investors are likely to be among the biggest winners of the 1990s.

OUTLOOK FOR INVESTORS

The timing appears to be right for investors who wish to catch the beginning of the most promising new trends in electronics. In fact, some developments are already here. The best of them are still high-end products that the mass market can't afford. However, we can expect prices to drop dramatically over the next few years. As that occurs we will see sales climb rapidly. Other products will come on-stream later in the decade. Since their developers are often the same companies that are introducing current advances, today's investors can use many of the same stocks for both short-term and long-term profits.

In many electronic industries investors will also be able to choose the size and risk levels which suit them best. One can select from the bluest of the blue chips to the tiniest of companies. I strongly suggest that investors choose the middle course when choosing electronic stocks. The giants are not pure plays in any niche and are unlikely to turn in stellar performances. On the other hand, the smallest firms often present extraordinary risks—so much so that Charles Allmon editor of the popular investment newsletter *Growth Stock Outlook* frequently refers to high tech as "high wreck."[1] Only mid-level electronic companies offer an attractive blend of risk and reward. Such firms made many investors into millionaires during the 1970s and 1980s. I think they will do so again in the 1990s.

Because most electronic products are expensive and are sold primarily to businesses, their sales are tied to the economy. Of course, that makes their stock prices cyclical. Savvy investors should use those cycles to their advantage.

There are exceptions to the general rule about price cycles that are difficult to see in advance. For example, during the tough recession of 1981–82 many microcomputer and telecommunication stocks bucked the downtrend to make strong advances. They did so because their products were so badly needed that customers made whatever budgetary adjustments were necessary in order to buy them. We are likely to see that phenomenon occur again as electronic integration creates products which cannot be ignored—no matter what the economy might be doing at the time.

STOCKS TO WATCH

There are two basic strategies that may be taken by investors who wish to participate in the strong trend toward electronic integration. The first is to take positions in several major computer, network, and software companies. Because they are at the heart of the trend, they will have a role in all the new developments. The core stocks represent the most conservative and longest lasting plays which are available.

The second strategy is to focus on specific advances and take *individual* positions in leading developers. Making the right choice in a winning technology can yield blockbuster results. Of course, such plays can also be expected to be volatile and may be short-lived as market leadership changes.

Powerful New PCs Make the Trend Possible

After experiencing explosive growth in the first half of the 1980s sales of microcomputers began to slow down. Speaking in February 1990, Tim Bajarin from the market research firm Creative Strategies in Santa Clara, California, observed, "In the early days we had a compound annual growth rate of 30 to 35 percent. By 1988 that had slowed dramatically to 20 percent. This year the U.S. market will grow at 8 to 9 percent."[2] Not only was his projection almost perfect for 1990 but sales may prove to be no better in 1991.

The slowdown should be no surprise to readers who are familiar with microcomputers. After 1986–87, advances in the technology were incremental rather than revolutionary. Power and memory increased significantly but they were simply more of the same. Millions of owners found that they didn't really need the added power. As one of my associates observed when we were considering a switch, "We already have the Porsche of microcomputers—do we really need to trade up to a Ferrari?"

Now, after a five year breather, the microcomputer industry is introducing new generation machines that are definitely not more of the same. The new PC workstations are so powerful that they threaten to decimate sales of minicomputers and small mainframes. More importantly, because they share common standards and are designed to work as teams, the new machines will make it possible for true electronic integration to occur. Perhaps best of all, the products are already here and prices are rapidly falling into the microcomputer range.

Fortunately for today's investors, microcomputer customers " . . . are just now beginning to appreciate the value of what the industry is producing," said Esther Dyson, one of the industries most respected observers, in February 1990.[3] That small lag will make it possible to take inexpensive positions for what should be very attractive long-term gains. All the major computer makers are offering new generation machines. **IBM, Hewlett-Packard,** and even **Digital Equipment** have products for this market. However, investors will almost certainly do better with more focused firms. Their powerful new products will have a far bigger effect on their stocks over the next few years.

Intel, the worldclass chip maker, is at the very heart of the trend. The company's powerful microprocessors—including the latest 486 products—provide the power and the related features which make electronic integration possible. In addition, the company supplies many additional types of semiconductors which are also used in computers and in many other electronic devices.

Because Intel's chips are used by dozens of leading manufacturers the company represents a very broad play in the multifaceted electronics industry. When purchased at attractive prices Intel should perform very well for long-term investors.

Apple Computer is world famous for its powerful and user-friendly computer systems. This pioneering company led the way into the computer era and continues to introduce state-of-the-art systems. Although Apple now has many rivals, most analysts believe that its commanding lead will ensure the company a bright future. That is particularly true now that Apple and IBM—its biggest rival—have joined forces to make their software, and ultimately their hardware, compatible. It is a smart move for both companies, but Apple stands to gain the most.

COMPAQ Computer was first introduced in Chapter 5 for its growing exports. The company merits additional coverage for its leading role with powerful new microcomputers. The firm's popular and affordable DESKPRO 486/25 is selling very well. The more versatile SYSTEMPRO series is even more promising. COMPAQ started out as a maker of IBM-compatible clones. The company went on to become a leading innovator in the microcomputer industry. Although COMPAQ's stock is often volatile, when it is purchased at attractive levels it should prove to be very rewarding.

Dell Computer is doing to COMPAQ what COMPAQ once did to IBM: it's offering stiff competition to its larger rival in terms of both price and performance. The company offers several 486 microcomputers and has more advanced products on the drawing board. Dell is also coming on strong in customer satisfaction—it has one of the highest ratings in the industry. Products are sold through a national sales force and through mail order. The company appears to have considerable promise.

Sun Microsystems is entering the PC workstation market from a different direction than the one taken by COMPAQ and its rivals. Instead of moving up from less powerful computers, the company is moving down from the engineering workstation industry where it is a leading supplier. Sun is selling its new SPARC workstations itself and is also licensing its technology to others. Since the SPARC line is compatible with the company's high-end systems, it will be able to run many advanced engineering, scientific, and technical programs that were previously unavailable to small businesses. That should create considerable interest in the new PC workstations both for new customers and as add-on units for existing clients.

There is one cloud on Sun's horizon. Several hardware and software firms have proposed a new standard for PC workstations that is not compatible with Sun's system. There is no word yet whether the proposal will be adopted. If it is adopted it could limit Sun's ability to capture a large share of the PC workstation market. The situation should be updated before taking positions.

New Software: The Key to Electronic Integration

Powerful new computers are of little value without software advances that can make full use of their capabilities. Although software tools generally lag hardware developments, and they are doing so again, many new programs are now on the way.

To see the potential for the new application software it is necessary to understand that it will not simply offer more speed. Few users would spend a great deal of money for new computer systems just to perform tasks a few times faster. What users need are greater capabilities and a higher degree of simplicity. For example, new generation software will not require people to memorize pages of arcane commands that must be repeated precisely. Instead, plain text commands will suffice. New software will also make it easier for teams of people to work on projects together, and to work faster.

The result will be that more people will be able to use top-level application programs than ever before. A software engineer at a major supplier told me recently, "For the first time, all a user will need to know is their field such as accounting or engineering—they won't need to know much of anything about computers or specialized programs."

Equally promising are more universal software products which will allow the new machines to offer capabilities that are not available today. Fully integrated programs are at the head of that list. Experts predict that such packages will plug into each other directly without the need for a master program.

All the leading suppliers of application software will benefit from the move to new generation computers and electronic integration including **Lotus Development, Ashton–Tate, Adobe Systems,** and **Autodesk.** Those companies would see revenues climb sharply in the 1990s as people buy new machines and find it worthwhile to upgrade their old programs. However, the main beneficiary of current trends in office electronics may be **Microsoft,** the leading supplier of operating systems and other management programs which are used throughout the world.

Microsoft needs little introduction to microcomputer users. The company supplies MS DOS and OS/2 operation systems that are used on millions of IBM and IBM compatible computers throughout the world. Everytime such a system is sold, Microsoft receives a portion of the proceeds.

Microsoft is also a major player in the move to integrate different types of application software from separate vendors. The company's popular Windows program is its most visible effort. Other programs allow PCs to share data and resources with each other. Additional products for new PC workstations are in the works.

Microsoft's application programs for word processing, spread sheets, and database management are also popular. They promise to be even more so in the future because the company is putting a premium on ease of use and program integration.

Two clouds obscure Microsoft's otherwise bright future. The first is a lawsuit by Apple Computer. Apple claims that some aspects of Windows infringe on the company's copyrights. If Microsoft should lose the suit it could be very damaging. Hopefully, a decision in the case will be made in late 1991. Secondly, the surprise July 1991 technology sharing agreement between Apple Computer and IBM threatens to break Microsoft's domination of the software industry. I think that Apple and IBM will find it very difficult to dislodge Microsoft from its well established niche. However, investors must bring themselves up to date on this development before taking positions.

Super Networks Complete the Picture

Along with new PCs are new generation networks which permit individual computers to function together as integrated systems. That integration is so complete that the system itself becomes a computer. At the heart of the new links are specialized high speed servers and super-servers that hold and distribute information to the system. When combined with new generation PCs and the appropriate software, the new servers often make minicomputers and mainframes unnecessary. In fact, in many situations having a large computer in the loop will slow the system down.

It is important to understand the degree to which the new networks differ from their predecessors. Local area networks (LANs) of the 1980s made it possible for computers to share data and use common peripheral equipment such as printers and modems. But for all their benefits, first generation microcomputer networks were incomplete links. To get needed power, one had to tie everything to an expensive large computer. By contrast, new client server networks meld each element into a coordinated system. Those systems are much more powerful than the sum of their parts. In addition, users need do nothing to direct or coordinate the work which appears to happen right in their desktop PCs.

The new networks are much more efficient than hooking individual PCs to minicomputers or mainframes. When the power of a large computer is broken up and distributed throughout a system, it becomes more versatile and more readily available to users. In addition, a distributed system can be easily and economically upgraded by simply adding more components.

Overall, powerful new PCs and their networks are ideal for many applications. As Charles E. Exley, Jr., chairman and CEO of NCR Corp. said in November 1990, "The microprocessor revolution is becoming an irresistible force. Ultimately, every business will want to move from their mainframes to microprocessor-based systems."[4] That changeover should become a multibillion dollar trend by 1995.

The leading computer and software companies including **Apple, COMPAQ, IBM,** and **Microsoft** are also leading makers and suppliers of new generation networks, servers, and programs. For example, COMPAQ's SYSTEMPRO functions as a general purpose PC server. Microsoft is an important supplier of networking software including SQL Server which it developed jointly with Ashton–Tate and Sybase Corp. Of course, the top LAN companies such as **Novel** and **3Com** are also making essential contributions by providing both hard links and software for the new systems.

Finally, several privately held firms are on the scene with servers including Auspex Systems, Parallan, NetFRAME, Torque Computer, and Tricord Systems. Investors may get a chance at them later if they go public to raise funds for expansion. Meanwhile two public firms, Sequent Computer and Teradata are doing well with powerful new servers for the new markets.

Sequent Computer Systems is a leading supplier of servers that deliver the power of mainframe with much greater speeds to large microcomputer systems. The company's products employ as many as 30 microprocessors which perform tasks in parallel to serve the needs of as many as 1,000 PC workstations. Products are sold directly to end users and to computer companies that supply them under their own labels. Sequent's outlook appears to be very good for at least the next several years.

Teradata Corp. is best known for its specialized relational database computers which are connected to mainframes. The company's specialized systems greatly increase the speed at which a mainframe can process information. A new system that is being developed will contain 1,000 parallel processors.

Now Teradata is moving into the microcomputer market with powerful servers which process and feed data into PC networks. Initial customers such as Kmart and NCR report that they can now process data quickly enough for it to be useful in the daily administration of a large company. Teradata's well-timed move into the growing microcomputer market should prove to be very profitable long term.

Novel is the world's leading supplier of network products for microcomputers. The firm's NetWare operating system currently holds over 50 percent of the PC market. Versions exist for both IBM and Apple configurations. All major multi-user application software products are compatible with Novel's products which are sold through retail chains, directly to end users, and to computer manufacturers. Novel has competition, primarily from **3Com,** but it appears likely to retain its leading position in the PC network market.

Image Processing: Top Technology of the 1990s

The first and perhaps the most promising computer technology to appear is image processing. That is, storing and manipulating photographs, drawings, and former paper files with a computer. Scott McCready of IDC/Avante Technology, a market research firm in Framingham, Massachusetts, predicted in November 1990 that the market for imaging systems would reach $35 billion by the end of the decade.[5] Judging from sales of the new systems so far, the final figure may turn out to be much greater.

Large corporations are just now switching from paper files to image processing technology. They are attracted to the efficiencies of computerized filing which includes great savings in space, easy searches, instant resorting, fast cross-referencing, multiple access, and reliable long-term storage. (All of which hold dire implications for the microfilm industry.) It is no wonder that image processing is catching on fast. By 1993–94 image processing will also become affordable to the enormous PC market. At that point the move to the new technology will become a stampede. Already, one excellent system from Canon costs as little as $15,000. When it falls to $5,000, the race will be on.

Every major computer company is making an effort to capture part of the promising market for image processing systems. According to Mr. McCready IBM could get as much as 30 percent of its income from such systems by the end of the decade. **Hewlett–Packard, Digital Equipment, Fujitsu, Wang,** and about a dozen others are also working on image processing systems, particularly for high-end markets. Leading PC workstation firms such as **COMPAQ** will also find a role as they add image processing to their list of capabilities.

However, the biggest profits may come from outside the computer industry. Kodak, Canon, and other firms that are already in the imaging business are frontrunners in the new technology. Not only does that give them an early shot at corporate sales, but it also makes them leading contenders for the vast PC market.

Canon, a large Japanese office equipment and camera company, looks particularly promising. The company's Canofile 250 image processing system is already on the market and is doing very well. The unit resembles a personal computer but underneath the monitor is a stack loader for papers, a scanner, and an optical memory system with removable disks. Image retrieval is done quickly by a built-in microprocessor. At $15,000 the Canofile is within the reach of many small businesses.

Canon is also noteworthy for its effort to combine electronic equipment that contains the same technologies. The company's Navigator desktop office system combines a fax, a telephone, an answering machine, a printer, a scanner, and a personal computer—all in one box. Of course, all the systems are integrated. In addition, the company's line of full feature fax machines and laser copiers provide links to personal computers. The list of innovations goes on for this global company that is strongly positioned for the 1990s. Although the firm is based in Japan its shares are actively traded in the United States via ADRs.

Eastman Kodak, the large photography, office copier, chemical, and pharmaceutical company, is also moving strongly into image processing. In addition to high-end systems for the corporate market, the company is developing consumer products that take and display pictures electronically. Instead of film, the new cameras and projectors use either magnetic or optical disks. Another system for use by photoprocessors converts existing photographs to CD disks. Of course, Kodak is far from a pure play in the image processing industry. Nevertheless, the technology is being emphasized by the firm which should translate into growing profits. Since its other businesses also look good for the 1990s, Kodak should be of interest to conservative investors.

Wang Laboratories was a pioneer in the computer industry. After many years of success the company fell out of the mainstream when it held onto its proprietary technology instead of adopting industry-wide standards. Now, after years in the doldrums Wang is making a bid to recover, to a large extent by moving strongly into image processing. The company is already far along with affordable systems for mid-level markets.

If Wang is able to establish a leading position in the growing image processing industry, the firm could become one of the biggest turnaround plays of the decade. The company is well worth watching, particularly since it announced its decision to switch from its proprietary systems to standardized IBM hardware.

Videoconferencing: From Boardrooms to Living Rooms

Sending images over telephone lines is not a new development. The technology was first demonstrated in the late 1940s. The market has been clamoring for it ever since. Unfortunately, the problems associated with the large data requirements of image transmission kept videophones and videoconferencing in check. Standard telephone lines lack the capacity to transmit full-featured images in real time. Even sending a still photograph can take over a minute, as any fax owner has probably discovered.

Now, two technologies are making videoconferencing both possible and affordable. The first allows a video image to be compressed sufficiently that it may be sent over many business telephone links. In essence, a computerized processor examines each picture for areas that do not require great detail, such as a background scene that doesn't change. Those portions of the picture are given less attention than more critical areas such as faces. The result requires much less transmission capacity than an unprocessed image. High capacity telephone lines are also becoming available almost everywhere. Most important are Fiberoptic links that have thousands of times the capacity of older copper wire systems. A strand of glass smaller than a human hair can easily handle many videoconferences simultaneously.

As is the case with image processing, videoconferencing is now primarily a corporate market. According to a March 1991 prediction by Albert Lill, an analyst with the Gartner Group, sales to big companies for the year should double for the primary suppliers.[6] That growth should accelerate as videoconferencing systems begin to become more cost effective than sending people to meetings.

Compression Labs is the leading supplier of videoconferencing systems. The company's products transmit two-way, full-motion images in color using commonly available business telephone lines. Prices for complete systems start from $25,000 which is well within the range of many corporate customers. A videophone for homes and small businesses should be available in 1992 for just under $1,500.

Compression Labs received an unexpected boost from the war in the Persian Gulf. Due to fears about terrorist attacks on airlines, many businesses substituted videoconferencing for travel. Most of the firms that tried it found that it worked quite well. Now videoconferencing is beginning to gather momentum.

Compression Labs may also cash in on its technology in the direct broadcast, pay-per-view television industry. Subscribers will be able to receive broadcasts from satellites without using a dish. Although the company's involvement with this emerging technology is very small at present, it may increase significantly in the future.

Voice Processing Holds Even Greater Promise

Although less dramatic than video systems, voice processing technology may reach a much bigger market. After all, our primary means of communication is speech. When we want something it is much more natural to ask for it than to type a message, press buttons, or manipulate a mouse. Nearly all the advances in computer and telecommunication technologies are needed for the new voice processing systems. Fiberoptic links, fast processors, high capacity data storage, and smart software are all brought into play. The result will be integrated computer and telephone services that will have customers standing in line.

Voice recognition systems are the most sophisticated products in the group. These devices which convert speech into text are already on the scene for limited markets, and they are popular. Sight impaired people find that the new systems are an answer to a prayer. Emergency room personnel also rely on voice recognition systems to dictate case files while they keep their hands busy saving lives. Before long, affordable systems will be available for PCs as well. We will literally talk to our computers. Since we can talk faster than we can type—and we can be much more expressive at the same time—voice recognition promises to give a big boost to productivity.

Longer term, voice recognition will be added to telephone systems. Instead of using touch tone keys we will place telephone orders and make other requests by simply giving instructions. Rudimentary programs that understand simple commands such as "yes," "no," and "list" are already here. As their capabilities expand so will their applications.

Voice mail systems for large corporations are already growing rapidly. Speech is digitized then stored in a firm's computer for later retrieval. The systems can be easily accessed with touch-tone telephones.

As prices continue to fall, voice mail will be offered to the mass market by local telephone companies. The service is already available in some areas. That is good news for everyone but the makers of home answering machines.

Voice response systems are also selling well. Callers access a computer's database with touch-tone keys. The systems are popular with banks, mutual funds, and other businesses that have many customers who need specific information regularly.

Call distributing systems are also becoming popular. Callers are given a list of recorded options which they can access by touch-tone commands. Although first-time callers often dislike getting a machine instead of a person, repeat callers who have learned the codes like the speed with which they can get through the switchboard. The systems are sold primarily to companies with large numbers of employees who receive many calls.

Audiotex is the hottest product at present. This simple system makes it possible for callers to access prerecorded information—such as a theatre schedule—with Touch-Tone™ phones. Sometimes voice response features are also available.

According to a Spring 1991 report by Hambrecht & Quist, an important high-tech research and brokerage firm, voice mail and voice response systems alone should be worth $1.3 billion in 1991.[7] Audiotext will add another billion according to Link Resources, Inc., a market research firm.[8] Those numbers should continue to grow steadily throughout the 1990s.

Octel Communications is a leading supplier of voice mail and related systems, primarily to large customers. The firm's systems allow callers to record voice messages for specific people or for groups. A bulletin board feature allows anyone on the system to stay abreast of company news. Of course, messages may be accessed from anywhere in the world.

Hewlett–Packard has an exclusive agreement to market Octel's products in Europe under the HP label. The company also recently purchased 10 percent of Octel and has the right to buy up to 20 percent of the company through August 1991. Insiders own approximately 10 percent of the company which speaks well for their view of the future.

Syntellect is a major supplier of voice response equipment which permit users to access a computer with a telephone. By using touch-tone keys callers may conduct a wide variety of transactions and request specific data stored in the computer. The computer may reply with synthetic speech—as in giving a bank balance—or prerecorded messages for more general information. Most products are marketed under the "Infobot" trademark.

A major contract with IBM provides Syntellect with both a benefit and a problem. The profits from the contract are attractive but if IBM develops its own system Syntellect will lose about 25 percent of its business. Since that is unlikely to hurt the company long term, bad news from Big Blue should present investors with an attractive buying opportunity.

Aspect Telecommunications is an important supplier of automatic call distributing systems. The company's products are sold primarily to firms that have a high volume of calls which are expensive to answer and direct manually. Aspect is now moving beyond automatic call distributing and is adding other features to its systems including voice and data processing. If Aspect is successful in integrating a full range of teleprocessing features in an affordable system the company should be very successful.

Multimedia Makes Its Debut

The union of sound and images with high-capacity computer and telecommunication technology comes to its zenith with multimedia systems. Such systems permit the creation of complete instructional and entertainment programs that are more powerful than anything presently in existence. The few systems that are already on the market are having a big impact. As John Sculley, president of Apple Computer stated in October 1989, "Multimedia will change the world in the 1990s as personal computing did in the 1980s."[9]

Multimedia systems are proving to be highly effective for two reasons. First, they make full use of our primary senses and our minds. As educators have known for centuries, people learn best when they hear, see, and do. The interactive nature of multimedia programs is especially important. Unlike conventional video and audio programs that move along at their own pace, and in fixed sequences, multimedia programs adapt to their users. An entertainment program may allow people to vary the plot and the ending to suit their preferences. A more complex instructional program will teach, test, reteach, reinforce, and reward—all according to how the user reacts along the way.

Telecommunication technology comes into play when multimedia programs are centrally located and are sent to users by cable television. Interactive TV, a very simple version of multimedia entertainment, is already being tested. Typical is the report that with an interactive system, one has the feeling that the programs were created just for you. More complex multimedia presentations are now on the way.

Multimedia systems currently face two obstacles which place a limit on profits: they are expensive and few programs currently exist. However, the leading multimedia players are working overtime to overcome those limitations. By 1995 multimedia will no longer be a novelty. By the end of the decade millions of people will be using it. By that time, multimedia is likely to be a multibillion dollar business.

Dozens of companies are active in multimedia developments. Of the group, three firms stand head and shoulders above the competition.

Microsoft is moving strongly to become a major developer of multimedia operating systems. The company's efforts are particularly welcome because it may have enough influence to impose standards on the new industry that might otherwise develop incompatible technologies. That situation would benefit no one. So far, IBM, AT&T, Tandy, Fujitsu, and several other computer companies have pledged to support Microsoft's approach to multimedia. As a result, Microsoft has a good chance to occupy a central role in the new technology.

Intel is also taking a key role in multimedia. The company recently introduced two inexpensive computer chips which permit microcomputers to combine music, video, photographs, drawings, and computer text in one program. To date, over 200 companies are developing products which use the new chips. As is true with Microsoft, Intel's strong following by the leading players should ensure long-term profits.

Apple Computer is clearly the leading hardware company in the multimedia field. The firm saw the development coming years ago and moved decisively to make full use of its potential. As a result, most of the company's products are already capable of providing many multimedia functions. The Macintosh line in particular is heavily oriented toward high-quality graphics and have expanded audio capabilities as well. Apple is sufficiently far ahead with multimedia, and it will almost certainly retain its lead for years no matter what the competition may develop.

Virtual Reality Completes the Picture

In the previous chapter virtual reality was introduced. It is a technology which promises to revolutionize the field of computer graphics and computer aided design (CAD). With a virtual reality system a user wears a projection hood and special gloves to become part of a program, not just as an observer, but as an active participant. Aircraft can be flown, homes can be lived in, faraway places can be visited, surgeons can perform operations, and so on. Of course, products can also be designed using virtual reality systems. The list of applications is nearly endless.

At present there are no specialized virtual reality companies with available stocks. Top visual reality pioneers such as VPL Research and Sense8 Corp are privately held. They may have public stock offerings before very long. The few public virtual reality players such as **Mattel** (games), **Autodesk** (CAD systems), and **Silicon Graphics** (VR computers) are far from pure plays. Nevertheless, they should be monitored for additional involvement in the growing visual reality industry that promises to generate a great deal of money in the future. In particular, I would keep a sharp eye on Mattel.

NOTES

1. Charles Allmon, Ed., *Growth Stock Outlook,* 4405 E. West Hwy, Bethesda, MD, 20814.

2. Jeff Shear, "Personal Computers Battling for a Niche in a Tight Market," *Insight,* February 26, 1990.

3. Ibid.

4. John W. Verity, "Rethinking the Computer: With Superships, the Network Is the Computer," *Business Week,* November 26, 1990.

5. David Churbuck, "Computers' New Frontier," *Forbes,* November 26, 1990.

6. David Churbuck, "Wait and Save," *Forbes,* March 4, 1991.

7. Peter Coy, "Your New Computer: The Telephone," *Business Week,* June 3, 1991.

8. Ibid.

9. Maria Shao, et al., "It's a PC, It's a TV—It's Multimedia," *Business Week,* October 9, 1989.

APPENDIX

DIRECTORY OF FEATURED INVESTMENTS

NAME	SYMBOL	EXCHANGE	PHONE
Acuson Corporation	ACN	NYSE	(415)969-9112
ADT Ltd.(ADR)	ADTLY	NASDAQ	(201)316-1000
Advance Ross Corp.	AROS	NASDAQ	(312)346-9126
AEGON N.V.(ADR)	AEGNY	NASDAQ	Note 3
Allwaste, Inc.	ALWS	NASDAQ	(713)632-8777
American Express Company	AXP	NYSE	(212)640-2000
American Health Properties	AHE	NYSE	(213)477-9399
American Integrity Corp.	AIIC	NASDAQ	(215)561-1400
American Nuclear Corp.	ANUC	ASDAQ	(307)265-7912
American Tel & Telegraph Co	T	NYSE	(212)605-5500
American Waste Services, Inc.	AW	NYSE	(216)759-7476
Amgen, Inc.	AMGN	NASDAQ	(805)499-5725
Angelica Corporation	AGL	NYSE	(314)991-4150
Apple Computer, Inc.	AAPL	NASDAQ	(408)996-1010
Applied Biosystems, Inc.	ABIO	NASDAQ	(415)570-6667
Applied Solar Energy Corp.	SOLR	NASDAQ	(213)968-6581
Archer-Daniels-Midland Co.	ADM	NYSE	(217)424-5200
ASEA, AB(ADR)	ASEAY	NASDAQ	Note 2
Asia-Pacific Fund, Inc.	APB	NYSE	(212)214-3334
Aspect Telecommunications Corp.	ASPT	NASDAQ	(408)441-2200
Astec Industries, Inc.	ASTE	NASDAQ	(615)867-4210
Atkinson (Guy F.) Company	ATKN	NASDAQ	(415)876-1000
Autodesk, Inc.	ACAD	NASDAQ	(415)332-2344
Baker, Michael Corp.	BKR	ASE	(412)495-7711
Baxter International, Inc.	BAX	NYSE	(312)948-2000
Ben & Jerry's Homemade, Inc.	BJICA	NASDAQ	(802)244-5641
Betz Laboratories, Inc.	BETZ	NASDAQ	(215)355-3300
Beverly Enterprises	BEV	NYSE	(818)577-6111
Biogen, Inc.	BGEN	NASDAQ	(617)864-8900
Biomet, Inc.	BIOP	NASDAQ	(219)267-6639
Bio-Rad Laboratories, Inc.	BIO.B	ASE	(415)234-4130
Black & Decker Corp.	BDK	NYSE	(301)583-3900
Boeing Company	BA	NYSE	(206)655-2121
Bonneville Pacific Corp.	BPCO	NASDAQ	(801)363-2520
BRE Properties, Inc.	BRE	NYSE	(415)445-6530
Browning-Ferris Industries, Inc.	BFI	NYSE	(713)870-8100
Calgene, Inc.	CGNE	NASDAQ	(916)753-6313
Calgon Carbon Corp.	CRBN	NASDAQ	(412)787-6700
California Energy Company	CE	ASE	(415)391-7700
CalMat Company	CZM	NYSE	(213)258-2777
Canon, Inc.(ADR)	CANNY	NASDAQ	(516)488-6700
CareerCom Corp.	PTA	NYSE	(717)774-1477
Carnival Cruise Lines, Inc.	CCL	ASE	(305)573-6030
Cascade Natural Gas Corp.	CGC	NYSE	(206)624-3900
Caterpillar, Inc.	CAT	NYSE	(309)675-1000

NAME	SYMBOL	EXCHANGE	PHONE
Centex Corporation	CTX	NYSE	(214)559-6500
Centocor, Inc.	CNTO	NASDAQ	(215)296-4488
Cetus Corporation	CTUS	NASDAQ	(415)420-3300
Champion Parts, Inc.	CREB	NASDAQ	(312)573-6600
Chaparral Steel Co.	CSM	NYSE	(214)775-8241
Chase Manhattan Corp.	CMB	NYSE	(212)552-2222
Checkpoint Systems, Inc.	CHEK	NASDAQ	(609)848-1800
Chemfix Technologies, Inc.	CFIX	NASDAQ	(504)831-3600
Chemical Waste Management, Inc.	CHW	NYSE	(312)218-1500
Chili's/Brinker Inter'l, Inc.	EAT	NYSE	(214)980-9917
Chiron Corporation	CHIR	NASDAQ	(415)655-8730
Cincinnati Milacron, Inc.	CMZ	NYSE	(513)841-8100
Citicorp	CCI	NYSE	(212)559-1000
Clayton Homes, Inc.	CMH	NYSE	(615)970-7200
Clean Harbors, Inc.	CLHB	NASDAQ	(617)849-1800
Club Med, Inc.	CMI	NYSE	(212)977-2100
Coca-Cola Company	KO	NYSE	(404)676-2121
Cognex Corporation	CGNX	NASDAQ	(617)449-6030
Colgate-Palmolive Company	CL	NYSE	(212)310-2000
Community Psychiatric Centers	CMY	NYSE	(415)831-1166
COMPAQ Computer Corp.	CPQ	NYSE	(713)370-0670
Compression Labs, Inc.	CLIX	NASDAQ	(408)435-3000
Concorde Career Colleges, Inc.	CNCD	NASDAQ	(816)474-4750
CyCare Systems, Inc.	CYS	NYSE	(602)952-5300
Davis Water & Waste Ind. Inc.	DWW	NYSE	(912)226-5733
Deere & Company	DE	NYSE	(309)765-8000
Dell Computer Corp.	DELL	NASDAQ	(512)338-4400
Denison Mines, Ltd.	DEN.A	NASDAQ	(416)865-1991
Denning Mobile Robotics, Inc.	GARD	NASDAQ	(508)658-7800
Deutsche Bank AB(ADR)	—	OTC	Note 1
Digital Equipment Corp.	DEC	NYSE	(508)493-5111
Disney, Walt Company	DIS	NYSE	(818)840-1000
Dreyer's Grand Ice Cream, Inc.	DRYR	NASDAQ	(415)652-8187
Dreyfus Corporation	DRY	NYSE	(212)715-6000
Eastman Kodak Company	EK	NYSE	(716)724-4684
ECC International Corp.	ECC	NYSE	(215)687-2600
Echlin, Inc.	ECH	NYSE	(203)481-5751
Electrolux AB(ADR)	ELUXY	NASDAQ	Note 3
Electronic Associates, Inc.	EA	NYSE	(201)229-1100
Empresa Nacional de Elec.(ADR)	ELE	NYSE	Note 3
Energy Conversion Devices, Inc.	ENERC	NASDAQ	(313)280-1900
Environmental Systems Company	ESC	NYSE	(501)223-4100
Envirosafe Services, Inc.	ENVI	NASDAQ	(215)962-0800
Ericsson Telephone Co.(ADR)	ERICY	NASDAQ	Note 2
Europe Fund, Inc.	EF	NYSE	(212)751-8340
Fabri-Centers of America	FCA	NYSE	(216)464-2500
Fabricland, Inc.	FBRC	NASDAQ	(503)666-4511
Federal Realty Investment Trust	FRT	NYSE	(301)652-3360
Fidelity Distributors Corp.			(800)544-6666
Financial Strategic Portfolios			(800)525-8085
First Iberian Fund, Inc.	IBF	ASE	(212)214-3334
First Philippine Fund, Inc.	FPF	NYSE	(212)759-3339
FlightSafety Inter'l, Inc.	FSI	NYSE	(718)565-4100
Florida Rock Industries, Inc.	FRK	ASE	(904)355-1781
FlowMole Corporation	MOLE	NASDAQ	(206)395-0200
Ford Motor Company	F	NYSE	(313)322-3000

NAME	SYMBOL	EXCHANGE	PHONE
Foster Wheeler Corp.	FWC	NYSE	(201)730-4000
France Fund, Inc.	FRN	NYSE	(212)701-2875
France Growth Fund, Inc.	FRF	NYSE	(212)713-2000
Franklin Resources, Inc.	BEN	NYSE	(415)570-3000
Future Germany Fund	FGF	NYSE	(212)474-7000
Genentech, Inc.	GNE	NYSE	(415)266-1000
General Electric Company	GE	NYSE	(203)373-2111
General Motors Corp.	GM	NYSE	(313)556-5000
Genetics Institute	GENI	NASDAQ	(617)876-1170
Genuine Parts Company	GPC	NYSE	(404)953-1700
Genzyme Corporation	GENZ	NASDAQ	(617)451-1923
Geothermal Resources Inter'l	GEO	ASE	(415)349-3232
Geraghty & Miller, Inc.	GMGW	NASDAQ	(516)249-7600
Gerber Products Company	GEB	NYSE	(616)928-2000
Gerber Scientific, Inc.	GRB	NYSE	(203)644-1551
Geriatric & Medical Centers	GEMC	NASDAQ	(215)476-2250
Germany Fund, Inc.	GER	NYSE	(212)612-0676
Giddings & Lewis, Inc.	GIDL	NASDAQ	(414)921-4100
Gilbert Associates, Inc.	GILBA	NASDAQ	(215)775-5900
Graco, Inc.	GGG	NYSE	(612)623-6000
Grand Metropolitan PLC(ADR)	GRM	NYSE	Note 3
Granite Construction, Inc.	GCCO	NASDAQ	(408)724-1011
Greenery Rehabilitation Group	GRGI	NASDAQ	(617)824-7200
Grenier Engineering, Inc.	GII	ASE	(214)358-6208
Groundwater Technology, Inc.	GWTI	NASDAQ	(617)769-7600
GZA GeoEnvironmental Tech. Inc.	GZEA	NASDAQ	(617)969-0700
Handleman Company	HDL	NYSE	(313)362-4400
Harding Associates, Inc.	HRDG	NASDAQ	(415)892-0821
Harnischfeger Industries, Inc.	HPH	NYSE	(414)671-4400
HealthCare COMPARE Corp.	HCCC	NASDAQ	(708)719-9000
Health Care Property Investors	HCP	NYSE	(213)473-1990
Healthcare International	HII	ASE	(512)346-4300
Healthdyne, Inc.	HDYN	NASDAQ	(404)423-4500
Health Images, Inc.	HIMG	NASDAQ	(404)587-5084
HEALTHSOUTH Rehabilitation Corp.	HSRC	NASDAQ	(205)967-7116
Hechinger Company	HECHB	NASDAQ	(301)341-1000
Heinz, H J Company	HNZ	NYSE	(412)237-5757
Helvetia Fund, Inc.	SWZ	NYSE	(212)867-7660
Hewlett-Packard Company, Inc.	HWP	NYSE	(415)857-1501
Home Depot, Inc.	HD	NYSE	(404)433-8211
Home Nutritional Services, Inc.	HNSI	NASDAQ	(201)515-4900
Honda Motor Company Ltd(ADR)	HMC	NYSE	Note 3
HON Industries, Inc.	HONI	NASDAQ	(319)264-7400
Hong Kong Telecomm. LTD.(ADR)	HKT	NYSE	Note 1
Houghton Mifflin Company	HTN	NYSE	(617)725-5000
House of Fabrics	HF	NYSE	(818)995-7000
Huffy Corporation	HUF	NYSE	(513)866-6251
Humana, Inc.	HUM	NYSE	(502)580-1000
Hunt Manufacturing Company	HUN	NYSE	(215)732-7700
Imatron, Inc.	IMAT	NASDAQ	(415)583-9964
Immunex Corporation	IMNX	NASDAQ	(206)587-0430
Indonesia Fund, Inc.	IF	NYSE	(212)832-2626
Ingersoll-Rand Company	IR	NYSE	(201)573-0123
Insituform of North America	INSUA	NASDAQ	(901)363-2105
Intel Corporation	INTC	NASDAQ	(408)987-8080
Intergraph Corporation	INGR	NASDAQ	(205)772-2000

NAME	SYMBOL	EXCHANGE	PHONE
Inter'l Business Machines Corp.	IBM	NYSE	(914)765-1900
International Recovery Corp.	INT	ASE	(305)884-2001
International Technology Corp.	ITX	NYSE	(213)378-9933
Ionics, Inc.	ION	ASE	(617)926-2500
Jakarta Growth Fund, Inc.	JBF	NYSE	(800)833-0018
Jostens, Inc.	JOS	NYSE	(612)830-3300
Justin Industries, Inc.	JSTN	NASDAQ	(817)336-5125
Kasler Corporation	KASL	NASDAQ	(714)884-4811
Kaufman & Broad Home Corp.	KBH	NYSE	(213)312-1200
Kewaunee Scientific Corp.	KEQU	NASDAQ	(312)251-7100
Kinder-Care Learning Cntrs, Inc.	KIND	NASDAQ	(205)277-5090
K Mart Corporation	KM	NYSE	(313)643-1000
Knape & Vogt Manufacturing Co.	KNAP	NASDAQ	(616)459-3311
Knogo Corporation	KNO	NYSE	(516)232-2100
Koger Equity, Inc.	KE	ASE	(904)398-3403
Korea Fund, Inc.	KF	NYSE	(212)326-6200
Lafarge Corporation	LAF	NYSE	(703)264-3600
Laidlaw Transportation, Ltd.	LDMFB	NASDAQ	(416)336-1800
La Petite Academy, Inc.	LPAI	NASDAQ	(816)474-4750
Latin America Investment Fund	LAM	NYSE	(212)832-2626
Lenner Corporation	LEN	NYSE	(305)559-4000
Lifeline Systems, Inc.	LIFE	NASDAQ	(617)923-4141
Life Technologies, Inc.	LTEK	NASDAQ	(301)840-8000
Lifetime Corporation	LFT	ASE	(617)330-5080
LVMH(ADR)	LVMHY	NASDAQ	(212)529-9190
MacNeal-Schwendler Corp.	MNS	ASE	(213)258-9111
Magma Power Company	MGMA	NASDAQ	(619)487-9412
Malaysia Fund, Inc.	MF	NYSE	(800)332-5577
Manor Care, Inc.	MNR	NYSE	(301)681-9400
Marcam Corporation	MCAM	NASDAQ	(617)965-0220
Marion Laboratories, Inc.	MKC	NYSE	(816)966-5000
Marriott Corporation	MHS	NYSE	(301)380-9000
McDonald's Corporation	MCD	NYSE	(312)575-3000
McGraw-Hill, Inc.	MHP	NYSE	(212)512-2000
Measurex Corporation	MX	NYSE	(408)255-1500
Medco Containment Services, Inc.	MCCS	NASDAQ	(201)794-9010
Medical Care Inter'l, Inc.	MEDC	NASDAQ	(214)490-3190
Medical Graphics Corp.	MGCC	NASDAQ	(612)484-4874
Medicine Shoppe Inter'l, Inc.	MSII	NASDAQ	(314)993-6000
MEDSTAT Systems, Inc.	MDST	NASDAQ	(313)996-1180
Medtronic, Inc.	MDT	NYSE	(612)574-4000
Merry-Go-Round Enterprises, Inc.	MGRE	NASDAQ	(301)828-1000
Met-Coil Systems Corp.	METS	NASDAQ	(319)363-6566
Met-Pro Corporation	MPR	ASE	(215)723-6751
Mexico Equity and Income Fund	MXE	NYSE	(212)667-5000
Mexico Fund, Inc.	MXF	NYSE	(212)326-3500
Microsoft Corporation	MSFT	NASDAQ	(206)882-8080
Mid-American Waste Systems, Inc.	MAW	NYSE	(614)833-9155
Midwesco Filter Resources, Inc.	MFRI	NASDAQ	(703)667-8500
Monarch Machine Tool Company	MMO	NYSE	(513)492-4111
Mor-Flo Industries, Inc.	MORF	NASDAQ	(216)663-7300
Morrison Knudsen Corp.	MRN	NYSE	(208)386-8000
Motorola, Inc.	MOT	NYSE	(312)397-5000
Myers, L.E. Company Group	MYR	NYSE	(312)990-4666
Mylan Laboratories, Inc.	MYL	NYSE	(412)232-0100

NAME	SYMBOL	EXCHANGE	PHONE
Napco Security Systems, Inc.	NSSC	NASDAQ	(516)842-9400
Natec Resources, Inc.	NATC	NASDAQ	(713)552-2552
National Computer Systems, Inc.	NLCS	NASDAQ	(612)829-3000
National Education Corp.	NEC	NYSE	(714)474-9400
National Environmental Controls	NECT	NASDAQ	(504)831-3600
National Health Laboratories	NHLI	NASDAQ	(619)454-3314
National Medical Enterprises	NME	NYSE	(213)479-5526
Nestle S.A.(ADR)	—	OTC	(203)322-0456
New Brunswick Scientific Co.	NBSC	NASDAQ	(201)287-1200
New Germany Fund	GF	NYSE	(212)474-7000
Nordstrom, Inc.	NOBE	NASDAQ	(206)628-2111
Novel, Inc.	NOVL	NASDAQ	(801)429-7000
Nuclear Support Services, Inc.	NSSI	NASDAQ	(717)838-8125
Oakwood Homes Corp.	OH	NYSE	(919)855-2400
Octel Communications Corp.	OCTL	NASDAQ	(408)942-6500
Odetics, Inc.	O.A	ASE	(714)774-5000
Ogden Corporation	OG	NYSE	(212)868-6100
Ogden Projects, Inc.	OPI	NYSE	(201)882-9000
Oil-Dri Corp. of America	OILC	NASDAQ	(312)321-1515
Osmonics, Inc.	OSMO	NASDAQ	(612)933-2277
Owens-Corning Fiberglass Corp.	OCF	NYSE	(419)248-8000
PacifiCare Health Systems, Inc.	PHSY	NASDAQ	(714)952-1121
Pacific Gas & Electric Company	PCG	NYSE	(415)972-7000
PDA Engineering	PDAS	NASDAQ	(714)540-8900
Perceptronics, Inc.	PERC	NASDAQ	(818)884-7470
Pharmacy Management Systems	PMSV	NASDAQ	(813)626-7788
Pioneer Financial Services, Inc.	PFSI	NASDAQ	(815)987-5000
Polygram N.V.(ADR)	PLG	NYSE	(212)333-8050
Powell Industries, Inc.	POWL	NASDAQ	(713)944-6900
Prab Robots, Inc.	PRAB	NASDAQ	(616)329-0835
Proctor & Gamble Company	PG	NYSE	(513)983-1100
Proler International Corp.	PS	NYSE	(713)675-2281
Quadrex Corporation	QUAD	NASDAQ	(408)866-4510
Questar Corporation	STR	NYSE	(801)534-5000
Ragen Corporation	RAGN	NASDAQ	(201)997-1000
Raymond Corporation (The)	RAYM	NASDAQ	(607)656-2311
Republic Gypsum Corportion	RGC	NYSE	(214)272-0441
Reuters Holdings PLC(ADR)	RTRSY	NASDAQ	(212)603-3500
Rollins Environmental Services	REN	NYSE	(302)492-2757
Ryland Group, Inc.	RYL	NYSE	(301)730-7222
Safety-Kleen Corp.	SK	NYSE	(312)697-8460
Scudder New Asia Fund	SAF	NYSE	(212)326-6200
Scudder New Europe Fund	NEF	NYSE	(617)330-5602
Senior Service Corp.	SENR	NASDAQ	(203)834-1644
Sensormatic Electronics Corp.	SNSR	NASDAQ	(305)427-9700
Sequent Computer Systems, Inc.	SQNT	NASDAQ	(503)626-5700
Service Corp. International	SRV	NYSE	(713)522-5141
Shared Medical Systems Corp.	SMED	NASDAQ	(215)296-6300
Siemens AG(ADR)	—	OTC	(212)258-4346
Sigma-Aldrich Corporation	SIAL	NASDAQ	(314)771-5765
SI Handlings Systems, Inc.	SIHS	NASDAQ	(215)252-7321
Singapore Fund, Inc.	SGF	NYSE	(800)933-3440
Southdown, Inc.	SDW	NYSE	(713)658-8921
Spain Fund, Inc.	SNF	NYSE	(212)964-0700
Stanley Works	SWK	NYSE	(203)225-5111

NAME	SYMBOL	EXCHANGE	PHONE
Stone & Webster, Inc.	SW	NYSE	(212)290-7500
Stride Rite Corp.	SRR	NYSE	(617)491-8800
Stryker Corporation	STRY	NASDAQ	(616)385-2600
Sun Electric Corp.	SE	NYSE	(815)459-7700
Sun Microsystems, Inc.	SUNW	NASDAQ	(415)960-1300
Syntellect, Inc.	SYNL	NASDAQ	(602)789-2800
T. Rowe Price Investment Funds			(800)638-5660
Taiwan Fund, Inc.	TWN	NYSE	(617)570-6327
Telefonica de Espana, S.A.(ADR)	TEF	NYSE	Note 3
Telefonos de Mexico SA(ADR)	TFONY	NASDAQ	(905)518-8220
Teradata Corporation	TDAT	NASDAQ	(213)524-5000
TETRA Technologies, Inc.	TTRA	NASDAQ	(713)367-1983
Texas Industries, Inc.	TXI	NYSE	(214)637-3100
Thai Capital Fund, Inc.	TC	NYSE	(609)282-4600
Thai Fund, Inc.	TTF	NYSE	(800)332-5577
Thermo Electron Corp.	TMO	NYSE	(617)622-1111
Tiffany & Company	TIF	NYSE	(212)755-8000
Time-Warner, Inc.	TL	NYSE	(212)522-1212
Toll Brothers, Inc.	TOL	NYSE	(215)938-8000
United Dominion Realty Trust	UDR	NYSE	(804)780-2691
United HealthCare Corp.	UNIH	NASDAQ	(612)936-1300
United Kingdom Fund, Inc.	UKM	NYSE	(212)530-8446
United Services Real Estate Fund			(800)873-8637
United States Surgical Corp.	USS	NYSE	(203)866-5050
Uranium Resources, Inc.	URIX	NASDAQ	(214)934-7777
U.S. Healthcare, Inc.	USHC	NASDAQ	(215)628-4800
Vanguard Inter'l Index Funds			(800)662-7447
Vivra, Inc.	V	NYSE	(415)397-6151
Volkswagen AG(ADR)	—	OTC	Note 3
Vulcan Materials Company	VMC	NYSE	(205)877-3000
Wahlco Environmental Systems	WAL	NYSE	(619)268-9982
Wal-Mart Stores, Inc.	WMT	NYSE	(501)273-4000
Wang Laboratories, Inc.	WAN.B	ASE	(508)459-5000
Washington R.E. Investment Trust	WRE	ASE	(301)652-4300
Waste Management, Inc.	WMX	NYSE	(312)572-8800
Waxman Industries, Inc.	WAXM	NASDAQ	(216)439-1830
Webb (Del E.) Corp	WBB	NYSE	(602)468-6800
Weingarten Realty Investors	WRI	NYSE	(713)866-6000
Wellman, Inc.	WLM	NYSE	(201)388-0120
Western Investment R.E. Trust	WIR	ASE	(415)929-0211
Westinghouse Electric Corp.	WX	NYSE	(412)244-2000
Weston (Roy F.), Inc.	WSTNA	NASDAQ	(215)692-3030
Wheelabrator Technologies, Inc.	WHTI	NASDAQ	(617)777-2207
WICAT Systems, Inc.	WCAT	NASDAQ	(801)224-6400
XOMA Corporation	XOMA	NASDAQ	(415)644-1170
York Research Corporation	YORK	NASDAQ	(212)557-6200
Zurn Industries, Inc.	ZRN	NYSE	(814)452-2111

For financial information regarding this ADR contact:

1) The Bank of New York, ADR Division, (212)815-2009
2) Chase Manhattan Corp. ADR Office (212)552-2222
3) Morgan Guaranty Trust Company, ADR Office (212)648-3485

INDEX

A

Adept Technology, 255
Adobe Systems, 270
ADT Limited, 101, 126
Adult day care industry, investing in, 98, 115-16
Advance Ross, 202
AEGON N.V., 29
Agricultural biotechnology, 237
Ahlburg, Dennis, 93
Air pollution control industry, investing in, 201
Alcohol fuels industry, investing in, 228-29
Allen, Barbara K., 132
Alliance Capital Management L.P., 26
Allmon, Charles, 266
Allwaste, Inc., 210-11
Alternative and nuclear energy industry investing in, 222-30
needs in, 215-17
promises offered by, 8
stocks to watch in, 217-30
Altmann, Rosalind, 19
AMCA International, 253
American Depository Receipts (ADRs), 18, 274
American Express Company, 81-82
American Health Properties (REIT), 145-46
American Integrity Corp., 98
American Nuclear Corporation, 222
American Waste Services, 204-5
Amgen, 234, 238, 242
Angelica Corp., 96
Apartment building industry, investing in, 139-40

Apple Computer, 173-74, 268, 270, 272, 279
Applied Biosystems, 240
Archer-Daniels-Midland, 228-29
Armstrong, C. Michael, 76
Artificial vision systems industry, investing in, 256-57
ASEA AB, 28-29
Ashton-Tate, 270, 272
Asia Pacific Fund, 69
Aspect Telecommunications, 278
Assisted living industry, investing in, 97-98
Astec Industries, 155
AT&T, 16, 35, 86
Audiotex, 277
Auspex Systems, 272
Autodesk Inc., 260, 270, 280
Automated machine tools industry, investing in, 251-53
Automated Testing Systems, 176-77
Automobile market
conservation in, 112-13
impact of middle class squeeze in, 124-25
investing in U.S., 84-85

B

Baby boomers, 5, 104-6
Baby busters, 5, 106-7
Baby industry, investing in, 113-14
Bajarin, Tim, 267
Bartley, Robert L., 66
BASF, 41
Baskin-Robbins, 42

287

ABOUT THE AUTHOR

James B. Powell resides in Eugene, Oregon, where he is president of James B. Powell and Associates, an investment advisory and research firm. He has been advising individual and institutional investors on important and lucrative investment trends for over 20 years. Mr. Powell is frequently featured on VALuTRAC, a monthly audio-cassette advisory service. Mr. Powell is the author of THE DOW JONES-IRWIN GUIDE TO HIGH TECH INVESTING and several popular CONSUMER GUIDES, including THE BEST-RATED INVESTMENTS FOR $1,000 TO $10,000.

A NOTE TO READERS

Readers wishing to contribute information or discuss this book with the author may write to him at the following address:

James B. Powell
James B. Powell and Associates
P. O. Box 11500
Eugene, OR 97440

OTHER BUSINESS ONE IRWIN BOOKS OF INTEREST:

Investing for a lifetime
Paul Merriman's Guide to Mutual Fund Strategies
Paul Merriman

Shows you how to make successful investment decisions in healthy or weak financial markets. Includes strategies and tactics for beating the market using Merriman's own successful timing techniques. (250 pages)
1-55623-485-6

Sooner Than You Think
Mapping a Course for a Comfortable Retirement
Gordon K. Williamson

Now is the time to determine a financial plan that will meet your retirement goals! Chock-full of charts, checklists, warnings, pro and con checklists, fill-in timelines, information sources, and a unique tickler system that alerts you to important decisions, Williamson's book removes the mystique of retirement planning. (275 pages)
1-55623-541-0

Raging Bull
How to Invest in the Growth Stocks of the '90s
David Alger

Raging Bull is your guide to making the move from stable, slow-growing blue chips to smaller stocks with potentially higher growth. Alger shows you how to discover the next Apple Computer, Amigen (Cellular One), or Nike. (200 pages)
1-55623-462-7

Stan Weinstein's Secrets for Profiting in Bull and Bear Markets
Stan Weinstein

Finalist, 1989 Benjamin Franklin Award, Business Books.
Weinstein reveals his successful methods for timing investments to produce consistently profitable results. (348 pages)
1-55623-079-6